Sanctuary, Sovereignty, Sacrifice

Law and Society Series
W. Wesley Pue, General Editor

The Law and Society Series explores law as a socially embedded phenomenon. It is premised on the understanding that the conventional division
of law from society creates false dichotomies in thinking, scholarship,
educational practice, and social life. Books in the series treat law and
society as mutually constitutive and seek to bridge scholarship emerging
from interdisciplinary engagement of law with disciplines such as politics,
social theory, history, political economy, and gender studies.

Of interest and also in the series:

Anna Pratt
Securing Borders: Detention and Deportation in Canada (2005)

Catherine Dauvergne
*Humanitarianism, Identity, and Nation: Migration Laws of Australia
and Canada* (2005)

A complete list of volumes in this series appears at the end of the book.

Randy K. Lippert

Sanctuary, Sovereignty, Sacrifice: Canadian Sanctuary Incidents, Power, and Law

UBCPress · Vancouver · Toronto

15 14 13 12 11 10 09 08 07 06 05   5 4 3 2 1

Printed in Canada on ancient-forest-free paper (100% post-consumer recycled)
that is processed chlorine- and acid-free, with vegetable-based inks.

Library and Archives Canada Cataloguing in Publication

Lippert, Randy K., 1966-
    Sanctuary, sovereignty, sacrifice : Canadian sanctuary incidents, power, and law /
Randy K. Lippert.

(Law and society)
Includes bibliographical references and index.
ISBN 13: 978-0-7748-1249-4 (bound); 978-0-7748-1250-4 (pbk.)
ISBN 10: 0-7748-1249-8 (bound); 0-7748-1250-8 (pbk.)

    1. Asylum, Right of – Canada. 2. Refugees – Legal status, laws, etc. – Canada.
3. Church work with refugees – Canada. 4. Refugees – Government policy – Canada.
5. Canada – Emigration and immigration – Government policy. 6. Refugees –
Canada. I. Title. II. Series: Law and society series (Vancouver, B.C.)

BV4466.L56 2005   305.9'06914'0971   C2005-905368-2

Canadä

UBC Press gratefully acknowledges the financial support for our publishing
program of the Government of Canada through the Book Publishing Industry
Development Program (BPIDP), and of the Canada Council for the Arts, and
the British Columbia Arts Council.

This book has been published with the help of a grant from the Canadian
Federation for the Humanities and Social Sciences, through the Aid to Scholarly
Publications Programme, using funds provided by the Social Sciences and
Humanities Research Council of Canada.

Printed and bound in Canada by Friesens
Set in Stone by Artegraphica Design Co. Ltd.
Copy editor: Robert Lewis
Proofreader: Dianne Tiefensee
Indexer: David Luljak

UBC Press
The University of British Columbia
2029 West Mall
Vancouver, BC V6T 1Z2
604-822-5959 / Fax: 604-822-6083
www.ubcpress.ca

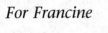

For Francine

Contents

Tables

Acknowledgments

This book has taken four years to research and write and has benefited from the help of several individuals along the way. Anonymous sanctuary providers from across Canada who took time to speak with me at length about sanctuary incidents, and especially those who made their files available, deserve special thanks. Sean Miller supplied research assistance of a superb quality for the project. Thanks to my contemporaries Anna Pratt, who is always willing to listen and respond to my musings, Jesse Seary for sharing his contagious passion for social theory during and since our time in the PhD program at the University of British Columbia, and James W. Williams for graciously agreeing to comment on the manuscript at a crucial juncture. I am grateful as well to the anonymous reviewers of the manuscript for their insightful and helpful comments. I also wish to thank Alan Hunt, Mariana Valverde, Richard V. Ericson, and Mitchell Dean. Their always brilliant, theoretically informed empirical work has inspired a new generation of socio-legal scholars, a cohort that includes myself. These four scholars influenced my thinking in this book in vital ways. Thanks are also due to Paul Henman, Gary Sigley, Deborah Bray, Dany Lacombe, Heidi Erismann, and Heather Leslie for their help or encouragement. I am also grateful to Randy Schmidt, acquisitions editor at UBC Press, and W. Wesley Pue, the series editor, for their patience and encouragement. While I acknowledge this help, any errors are of course my own. I also acknowledge a three-year Social Sciences and Humanities Research Council of Canada standard research grant, without which this kind of study would have been impossible. As always, heartfelt thanks to Francine Lippert for her love, patience, and wonderful optimism.

Most of Chapter 2 was first published as "Rethinking Sanctuary: The Canadian Context, 1983-2003," which appeared in the *International Migration Review* 39, 2 (2005), and is reprinted with permission from the Center for Migration Studies. Much of Chapter 3 is a revised and condensed version of

"Canadian Refugee Determination and Advanced Liberal Government," which appeared in the *Canadian Journal of Law and Society* 13, 2 (1998): 177-207, reprinted with permission of the Canadian Law and Society Association, and "Rationalities and Refugee Resettlement," from *Economy and Society* 27, 4 (1998): 380-406, reprinted with permission of Taylor and Francis. A portion of Chapter 4 and a very small part of Chapter 5 are revised versions of "Sanctuary Practices, Rationalities, and Sovereignties," which appeared in *Alternatives* 29, 5 (2004): 535-55, reprinted with permission from Lynne Reinner Publishers. Finally, most of Chapter 6 appeared as "Sanctuary Discourse, Powers, and Legal Narratives" in *Studies in Law, Politics and Society* 35 (2005), which is reprinted with permission from Elsevier. The comments of the editors or anonymous referees associated with these articles were particularly helpful.

Sanctuary, Sovereignty, Sacrifice

1
Introduction

All human behavior is scheduled and programmed through
rationality. There is a logic of institutions and in behavior and
in political relations.
– Michel Foucault, "Truth Is in the Future," *Foucault Live*

Placing on display a masked and hooded Guatemalan migrant facing certain deportation by immigration officials at a televised press conference on
20 January 1984,[1] an ecumenical group of church officials and community
supporters pronounced St. Andrew's United Church on the outskirts of
Montreal a sanctuary. Referred to only as "Raphael," the twenty-two-year-
old migrant living concealed in a converted minister's study in a church
building for five weeks beginning in December 1983 remained silent during
the entire spectacle.[2] That sanctuary was granted to Raphael was exceptional. It was, in fact, the first incident of its kind in Canada.[3] Twenty years
later, although similar acts are now more prevalent, they remain rare. Yet
this incident was exceptional in another sense. Granting sanctuary to Raphael
was about making an exception to a rule. Instead of becoming one of the
thousands of mostly invisible migrants removed annually from communities and the nation to face bleak fates and possible death, here there was
sudden, visible intervention, and Raphael's life was spared. Strategically situated next to church officials and community supporters in the church amidst
the gaze of television cameras and photographers, Raphael had become the
object of a sovereign power. Such a power, with its capacity to make exceptions and its affinity for spectacle, is typically thought in current scholarship, when reflected upon at all, to flow from the modern nation-state. But
this was an instance, as Raphael's protectors put it, of "God's law coming
before the government's."[4] Authorized by this and other "higher" laws, here
a sovereign power began to flow from a much older wellspring of local
church and community and then to surge through channels of mass media

to become a torrent of spectacle sufficient to attract onlookers, including political authorities in high places.

Less mediated and more mundane, the provision of sanctuary, which entailed the daily care for Raphael's needs while he remained hidden and confined to church property for those five weeks, was shaped by a different power, but one of no less importance. These caring practices were an instance of pastoral power, a less celebrated logic that Michel Foucault likened to that of a shepherd overseeing a flock.[5] Pastoral power entails care for "the lives of individuals."[6] During the weeks preceding the press conference, and afterward, Raphael became the object of this power and transformed into a needful, silenced "sheep" cared for and watched over by sacrificing "shepherds."

Within hours of the spectacle generated at the church, Canada's federal immigration minister publicly announced a temporary halt to all deportations to Guatemala and declared that these sanctuary providers, despite violating immigration law, were to be spared legal prosecution. Another exception was made. Since 1983, in churches and communities across Canada, sanctuary has been similarly provided to migrants exhausted of legal appeals and threatened with deportation. This book is about these incidents and the diverse powers and legal narratives that have shaped and made them possible. It is based on a comprehensive and detailed empirical study of all thirty-six sanctuary incidents that occurred in Canada during a twenty-year period commencing with the "Raphael" incident in 1983. This four-year research endeavour entailed forty-six personal interviews with sanctuary providers along with the collection and analysis of some 1,600 documents pertaining to these incidents.

This book has two main purposes, through which it seeks a broader relevance than a study of contemporary sanctuary incidents might otherwise possess. The first purpose is to serve as a corrective to the voluminous research intimating that contemporary sanctuary is an exclusively US-based religious social movement that commenced in the early 1980s and that had expired by the early 1990s. By documenting sanctuary incidents in a different national context – that of Canada – over the same period and in the ensuing decade, this book attempts to free sanctuary from this idiosyncratic scholarly treatment thereby revealing it as more widespread and prevalent than the almost exclusively US-based research has implied and therefore as more significant. Although sanctuary's form may vary across national contexts, this book seeks to show that in the matter of contemporary sanctuary, there is little justification for US exceptionalism. Consistent with this purpose, common features of Canadian sanctuary incidents have been researched and where possible compared with sanctuary activities in the US.

The second (but not secondary) purpose of this book is to cast light on theoretical issues in relation to the innovative and expanding body of scholarship known as "governmentality studies." This varied literature, which was developed by British, Canadian, and Australian scholars primarily through the 1990s and early 2000s, is inspired by the later writings and lectures of Michel Foucault. With their postmodern affinity for historical contingency, specificity, and discourse, governmentality studies have had a profound influence on the trajectories of several disciplines, including law, sociology, criminology, geography, political science, and anthropology. It is not an exaggeration to suggest that a new generation of scholars has embraced governmentality studies and their accompanying assumptions in order to explore a wide range of historical and contemporary domains. Yet, despite their remarkable growth and demonstrated capacity to both unsettle and shed new light on what are often thought to be self-evident realms and practices, governmentality studies have not developed free of contentious issues and lingering questions, including those centred on neglected forms of power and their relations with law. Consistent with this second purpose, special attention has been paid to sanctuary discourses and practices and to the diverse powers and legal narratives that constitute sanctuary. In the chapters that follow, it is assumed that sanctuary – while relatively rare, ostensibly anachronistic, and based primarily on tradition – can ironically reveal much about governance, law, and resistance in the present.

Sanctuary

Sanctuary has an extensive history.[7] The Old Testament refers to cities of refuge.[8] There are detailed historical accounts of sanctuary in ancient Greece, Rome, and Byzantium as well as throughout Medieval Europe.[9] Among ancient Hebrews, sanctuary was a way to manage revenge for a slaying by providing time and space for negotiations between the murderer and the offended party. In the fourth and fifth centuries, secular authorities recognized ecclesiastical sanctuary as distinct territory under church control.[10] The state first recognized church sanctuary in the Theodosian Code in AD 392 and sought to limit those to whom it could be applied based on the nature of their crimes.[11] Although at the outset sanctuary was limited to the church altar, its territory gradually expanded to include bishops' residences and even cemeteries. By the Middle Ages in Europe, sanctuary as a space and as a set of discourses and practices gradually receded in the face of the growing power of states.[12] In Britain, where sanctuary had been intensively regulated for centuries, it was formally abolished under James I by statute in 1624.[13]

Despite the existence of assorted historical accounts, a long-term genealogy of sanctuary has still to be researched and written. Whether sanctuary retained its link with the church, moved to other sites in civil society, or ever completely vanished from Western societies thus remain empirical questions (see Chapter 7). What is clear is that contemporary sanctuary has taken the form of groups of churches and communities harbouring individual migrants or migrant families threatened by imminent arrest and deportation by federal immigration authorities. Beginning in the 1970s, sanctuary returned to Britain,[14] and through the 1980s, 1990s, and 2000s, it also appeared in Germany, France, Belgium, the Netherlands, Norway, Switzerland, Australia, and Canada, among other nations.[15] In the US, sanctuary underwent something of a revival beginning in 1982.[16] This resurgence occurred amid US-backed war and oppression in Central America and a resultant increase in the number of migrants desperately fleeing this region by illegally entering the US.[17] But sanctuary plainly has not been limited to these US sanctuary activities, which had ceased by the early 1990s. Nor has sanctuary elsewhere and since that time necessarily shared features revealed by studies of US sanctuary. To date, no research has yielded a portrait of sanctuary incidents arising in other national contexts. By investigating sanctuary in Canada, this book responds to this omission.

Governmentality Studies and Theoretical Issues

This book adopts a conceptual approach inspired by the later works of Michel Foucault. Since his death more than twenty years ago, the governmentality perspective developed from his concepts has been elaborated upon and refined. Nevertheless, this approach continues to deploy three major concepts – programs, rationalities, and technologies of government – each of which requires brief description before the enduring issues evident in this literature can be discussed. First, programs are imagined projects, designs, or schemes for organizing and administering social conduct. Programs claim knowledge of particular domains.[18] Thus there is a corresponding focus in the chapters that follow on forms of knowledge and regimes of truth within programs. Second, rationalities comprise changing discursive fields within which the exercise of power is conceptualized: the moral reasons for the particular ways that diverse authorities exercise power; notions of the appropriate forms, objects, and limits of politics; and the right distribution of governing duties within secular, religious, military, and familial sectors, among others.[19] Rationalities are not simply theories, philosophies, or ideologies; they are broad, historically developed discourses of rule.[20] Both liberalism and pastoral power are examples of rationalities. Finally, technologies of government are the material and intellectual means, devices, and mechanisms that make different forms of rule possible.[21] Examples include everything from maps to accounting methods to architectural forms. In this context, a case in point is the Refugee Documentation Centre, which has made information about refugee conditions abroad accessible in Canada since 1989 in a way that fits liberal rationalities (see Chapter 3). Technologies come to be assembled within particular programs by rationalities, and specific technologies emerge to serve different functions depending on the specific rationalities with which they are linked.[22] These three overarching concepts – especially the first two – are used throughout the present study.

At least four theoretical issues have emerged within and in relation to this rapidly expanding body of scholarship. These concern how rationalities relate to one another as well as to sovereign power, law, and method. Each is addressed in the course of seeking to explore sanctuary in Canada in the chapters that follow, and each requires elaboration.

The first of these issues pertains to how liberal and nonliberal rationalities relate to one another.[23] A theme of Foucault's later writings is that governance in the modern West is not a singular process of instrumental rationalization[24] but a process shaped by the simultaneous presence of rationalities.[25] A central and explicit aim of governmentality studies from their inception has been to move away from totalizing and, in particular, neo-Marxist and state-centred accounts of governmental domains.[26] The shift to a new terrain – evinced by the dramatic growth of governmental studies across the disciplines – has been a remarkable success. Yet, in the process, and to the extent that nonliberal rationalities have been ignored, governmentality accounts risk becoming similarly totalizing and/or systematizing.[27] Liberalism as a rationality of rule has been elaborated upon in an array of contexts in the governmentality literature. Even a tacit admiration of liberalism in these studies has been noted.[28] Such a rationality has several distinguishing features. Liberal government establishes limits on political intervention and presumes a realm of freedom and action outside the acceptable reach of politics.[29] It identifies subjects in civil society and private realms assumed to possess rights that are not to be violated by formal political authorities.[30] Liberal government therefore entails a perpetual suspicion of formal political authorities who might impose their decisions throughout a nation or demarcated jurisdiction.[31] Although all liberal rationalities share these features, several forms of this logic are found in the literature: classical liberalism,[32] liberal welfarism,[33] and advanced liberalism. Of particular relevance to the Canadian sanctuary context are liberal welfarism and advanced liberalism.

Taking their lead from Foucault,[34] theorists writing about governmentality have argued that since at least the 1970s, a new governmental rationality has been taking shape in the modern West, evident in a wide range of domains from health care to higher education to policing. Although in each case the application of this rationality follows its own trajectory and is subject to specific conditions of possibility, these domains are said to be changing in a manner consistent with the onset of the logic of advanced liberalism. On occasion this logic is also called neoliberalism.[35] Although their meanings overlap, the two terms are not synonymous. Nikolas Rose, who coined the term "advanced liberalism," suggests that this logic "shares many of the premises of neo-liberalism."[36] Advanced liberalism is the preferable term since neoliberalism tends to connote specific writings, such as those of

Friedrich von Hayek and Robert Nozick, as well as the notion of a totalizing ideology consistent with the political-economy tradition rather than a rationality that encompasses critiques from the Left and the Right.[37] Nor is advanced liberalism limited to economic life. In what follows, therefore, "advanced liberalism" will be used most often (see Chapter 3), and "neoliberalism" will be reserved for governance that more specifically relates to the economic sphere – that is, the market, taxation, and the like. Advanced liberalism differs from liberal welfarism, discussed shortly, in imagining responsibility for governance shifting toward agents operating beyond the state, such as professionals, private corporations, and individuals, and a corresponding move toward these agents governing through their freedom.[38] The former has been explored in some detail within a variety of contemporary governmental domains and has much purchase where changes in refugee and immigration policies over the last two decades are concerned (see Chapter 3).[39] That said, it is a central point of this book that advanced liberalism or any other form of liberalism is problematic to the extent that it is understood and invoked as a totalizing or systematizing concept used to refer not to a particular rationality in a specific context but to something approaching a new epoch or societal condition. It is one thing to deploy advanced liberalism in reference to a configuration broader than neoliberalism; it is another thing to use it to signify a totalizing, seamless condition that blankets all other governmental logics and powers in a way that is at odds with the spirit of the later writings and lectures of Michel Foucault.

In contrast, liberal welfarism (which Nikolas Rose refers to as "social liberalism")[40] has rarely been investigated in context. Broadly characterized by what is commonly understood as welfare-state arrangements, this rationality has instead been deployed in the literature as something of a self-evident foil for and immediate predecessor of advanced liberalism, a use consistent with what Nikolas Rose, following Jean Baudrillard, calls the "death of the social."[41] Foucault never elaborated liberal welfarism but instead wrote in precious few passages of a pastoral power that had become institutionalized as welfare-state provision for individuals' needs. In particular, in the Tanner Lectures on Human Values given in 1979, Foucault traced the key themes of pastoral power within several of its historical incarnations and suggested that the modern "Welfare State problem" was but a recent recurrence of the "tricky" tension between the "city-citizen" game, associated with Greek political thought, and the "shepherd-flock" game of pastoral power.[42] Since Foucault's lectures, the latter game has been neglected by scholars.[43] It undoubtedly continues to be less celebrated in part because it has been subsumed within the term "liberal welfarism." It is my contention that liberal welfarism should be understood as a temporary coupling of liberal and pastoral rationalities – that is, as a coupling of governing through freedom and governing through need. The gradual unhinging of this coupling, which is consistent with the decline of the welfare state, raises an integral question: If there has occurred a degovernmentalization of the state as a result of the rise of advanced liberalism, has pastoral power and its corresponding discourse of needs[44] become obsolete, or can it also be found outside the state?[45] Just where can one find pastoral power today?[46] Certainly, there are remnants of this power in the welfare-state arrangements that remain.[47] Across nations of the modern West, however, much residual welfare provision by the state has been transformed into workfare and has otherwise adopted a neoliberal, marketized form.[48] Perhaps, then, better examples of pastoral power might be found elsewhere. It is thus germane to note that sanctuary is partially about identifying and providing for migrants' needs (see Chapter 5) and foremost about fulfilling a primary need for protection from an insecure life or even death as a result of deportation to a dangerous place. However, sanctuary seeks to accomplish this neither with the bureaucratic structures and expertise of the welfare state nor through newer hybrid or marketized agencies arising in conjunction with its gradual decline.[49] Consistent with the prospect of alternative genealogies of sanctuary that may yet reveal that sanctuary-like spaces, discourses, and practices have not in fact vanished but have proliferated in civil society since the eighteenth-century decline of church sanctuary, and in conjunction with the rise of a variety of social movements, pastoral power can perhaps be regarded as thriving today in unexpected and heterogeneous sites (see Chapter 7).

Empirical investigations of nonliberal rationalities such as pastoral power remain few.[50] This is perhaps because these logics are thought to be either largely nonexistent, little more than peculiar anachronisms, or all but irrelevant to rule in Western societies. If liberalism as a governmental rationality is not to be understood as having surpassed or systematically incorporated all other logics, then nonliberal rationalities or powers may still be present and, through careful research, discernable in particular contemporary governmental practices.[51] Questions about their current character and relevance, and about how they complement, resist, or otherwise relate to liberal rationalities, warrant empirical attention. Sanctuary serves as a special context in which to seek answers to these queries.

A second but related issue concerns sovereign power, particularly how it is to be understood and its relationship to governmental rationalities. It has been increasingly recognized in the literature that sovereign power cannot be easily dismissed as archaic or as altogether superseded by governmentality.[52] Yet, with few exceptions,[53] when it is invoked, sovereign power tends to be narrowly conceived. Specifically, it is assumed to be essentially coercive and to adopt the form of symbolic punishment, violence, or exclusion.[54] With some notable exceptions,[55] however, this coercive power also tends to be imagined to flow from a single source and space: the modern nation-state.[56] This issue, too, demands more attention. And sanctuary, as a form of symbolic salvation from coercion whose power emanates from other sources and territories, provides an opportunity to meet this need.

Recent scholarship has begun to suggest the relevance of a governmentality approach to understanding the governance of international migration.[57] All manner of governmental practices, including those pertaining to economic wealth, natural disasters, unemployment, health, crime, and national and international security, may be increasingly governed *through* migration. That is, migration may be less the central focus of governance projects, if it ever was, and more a useful tactic through which to govern other domains, subjects, and forms of conduct. Yet several writers have recently noted that the governance of migrants by nation-states may also be a key site through which the relationship between governmentality and sovereignty can be made intelligible.[58] To this end, this study of sanctuary in Canada seeks to shed light on the refugee and immigration domains to which it relates, as well as on how the diverse powers – liberal, pastoral, and sovereign – can be distinguished and potential relations among them better understood.

How the first two issues are dealt with in this book raises an intimately related but largely unacknowledged third issue: the role of law in governance. It is this issue that brings the current study more securely into the realm of socio-legal studies. The governmentality literature has sought to replace the idea of law as command, which is tightly tethered to a concept of sovereignty found in Foucault's writings, with the idea of law as governance.[59] According to this understanding, law is typically regarded as an integral mechanism of liberal governance.[60] Although deployed with other expert knowledges and techniques,[61] this kind of law ultimately promises to achieve the "conduct of conduct" in a liberal way. Through deployment of various technologies, it seeks to constitute legal subjects whose freedom will not be simply crushed by the state. But if the presence of other powers is evident in particular domains, such as the sovereign and pastoral powers that bear upon migrants in sanctuary incidents, then what is the role of law in relation to such powers? If one seeks to avoid totalizing conceptions, it would seem that law could be expected to adopt diverse roles. At the level of the subject, it could be deployed as a body of heterogeneous legal narratives that exist in complex relation to these powers rather than manifesting only as a component of an apparently limitless liberal repertoire. Indeed, in merely glancing at contemporary discourse on sanctuary incidents, one is almost immediately struck by the invocation of law in intricate and varied ways, which suggests the promise of sanctuary to shed light on this issue.

Governmentality studies have also come up against several critiques that warrant consideration, thus suggesting a fourth issue. Bruce Curtis has pointed out that Nikolas Rose and Peter Miller's influential 1992 article in the *British Journal of Sociology* uses two conceptions of the state that "do not

have the same ontological status; used interchangeably, they confuse empirical situations and political concepts ... [and refer] to both 'conditions of
forces' and a 'linguistic device.'" Here the governmentality program is
claimed to ignore "situated social relations and relations of causation."[62]
Subsequent critiques have tended to share this concern about an avoidance
of "the real."[63] In response, Nikolas Rose has demarcated a "new sociology
of governance," separating it from an "analytics of governmentality"[64] by
arguing that "analyses of governmentality are empirical but not realist. But
studies of governmentality are not sociologies of rule."[65] This implies that
the new sociology of governance is realist. Given this distinction, in periodically referring to the real, the present (empirical) study is closer to this
sociology of governance. However, it remains somewhat dubious that drawing such a firm distinction would be either possible or beneficial. Others
writing in the governmentality vein appear to think likewise.[66] Alan Hunt,
for example, refers to his recent work as the sociology of governance while
paying close attention to discourse and avoiding the above division throughout.[67] As well, in what is likely the most sympathetic critique of the
governmentality literature to date, Pat O'Malley, Lorna Weir, and Clifford
Shearing similarly avoid Rose's distinction and acknowledge appearances
of the real in governmentality analyses.[68] As they see it, the problem is not
so much inclusion of the real as the fact that "what actually happens" tends
to be treated as "merely obstructionist," when it ought to be thought of as
"constitutive."[69] Like Curtis, these critics lament that "the messy actualities"
of "social relations" are ignored,[70] suggesting that "many programmes exist
only in the process of messy implementation."[71] This understanding of programs resonates with the approach of the present study, which assumes
that many programs in the refugee realm are little more than tentative pilot
projects (see Chapter 3) or, in the case of sanctuary, made up on the spot
(see Chapter 4) and created and adjusted within short bursts of time as they
encounter and gain discerning knowledge of the real.

   A more important point is that there are two strains within these critiques, one focused on how to conceptualize resistance and the other centred
on the ontological status of the object of empirical research. The first strain
concerns whether resistance is either merely obstructionist, a seemingly irrational (or messy) source of program failure, or constitutive in the sense of
resistance becoming incorporated into liberal government.[72] It is my contention that to properly move away from totalizing tendencies, systematiza-
tion, and the like in governmentality studies, the issue ought to be less about
whether resistance is obstructionist or constitutive and more about whether
and how resistance is constituted by relatively distinct powers, such as those
investigated in this book. Approached in this way, resistance might be understood instead as relative to the specific form of power or rationality at work.
Yet this issue is even more complex since the present study of sanctuary will

reveal in the chapters that follow that nonliberal forms of power, such as sovereign and pastoral power, also encounter resistance – and not only from liberalism.

The second strain of these critiques focuses on the ontological status of the object of inquiry, which is an altogether different matter and one necessarily linked with questions of methodology. The preferred method in governmentality studies has been a form of discourse analysis of programmatic texts, often those produced by the state. In fact, most research in the governmentality area has concentrated on such state texts rather than on everyday discourse, or talk. The techniques of governmentality studies inspired by Foucault have tended to be directed at forms of discourse that show the structured regularities of statements, regularities that are perhaps less obvious in everyday discourse. While anthropology is a discipline that is influenced by governmentality studies and that focuses on talk, even here studies can be found that focus exclusively on texts. The common preference for texts over talk in this and other disciplines is also linked to the fact that some governmentality studies have investigated nineteenth-century or earlier contexts consistent with Foucault's own histories, thereby obviously making investigations of talk derived from interviews impossible. Yet the preference for programmatic texts over talk is, as well, undoubtedly linked to the comparatively greater time and expense required to arrange, conduct, and analyze interviews with social agents. At the same time, state texts are increasingly available via the Internet and are thus more accessible than talk. However, that everyday discourse is made up of a multiplicity of types of discourse and that it is difficult to analyze (given its lack of regularity and accessibility) are hardly adequate justifications for its avoidance. As Kevin Stenson notes, "mentalities of rule are embodied in texts and also in orally transmitted discourses."[73] The latter is true for a fundamental reason: in certain contexts, subordinate powers – indeed *because* they are subordinate at a particular juncture – may present themselves primarily in oral discourses. The first three theoretical issues above are thus related to this fourth issue, for it may be that some neglected powers beyond liberalism are apparent mostly in talk. In particular, if pastoral power is increasingly found outside the modern nation-state, its intimacy and immediacy are such that, as a rationality, it may not instantiate itself in texts to the same degree as liberal rationalities. More to the point, adopting traditional sociological methods (i.e., interviews) does not imply that the object of inquiry automatically becomes "the real" and that, by definition, it is therefore placed outside the purview of governmentality studies. Admittedly, this study relies on programmatic texts to make sense of changes in refugee resettlement and determination during the period that sanctuary incidents occurred (see Chapter 3). However, in treating the specific issue of sanctuary, this study pools textual and interview data to better identify, access, and make intelligible the diverse powers that constitute it. In the course of doing so, this research reveals several instances of talk finding its way into more systematic, programmatic texts – where such texts exist at all – and elements of these texts spilling into talk. For example, the United Church's sanctuary guidelines (see Chapter 2) have been informed partially by what previous providers said to its authors about sanctuary. Conversely, several interviewees in the present study noted they had reviewed their files (some of which were collected and analyzed) prior to their scheduled interview about a sanctuary incident. This suggests that there may not be a firm distinction between texts and talk. As well, sanctuary incidents were generally not associated with a specific programmatic text. Undoubtedly, providers in incidents occurring after 1997 benefited from sanctuary guidelines made available by then. However, although these guidelines are relevant, it is evident that they were often obtained by providers after their sanctuary incident had commenced. This general dearth of programmatic sanctuary texts is likely related to the uncertainty of sanctuary's legal status. But this does not mean that sanctuary has not been programmatic. It is my contention that sanctuary programs, informed by particular powers, can be glimpsed in talk. Due to talk's apparent relevance, as well as to the centrality of discourse in a governmentality approach more generally, excerpts of talk appear in abundance in the chapters that follow.

The present study of sanctuary in Canada, then, seeks to counter US sanctuary research implying that contemporary sanctuary was an exclusively US-based phenomenon that has now expired.[74] It does so by exploring the prevalence, trajectory, and features of sanctuary incidents in another national context. The Canadian sanctuary context also serves as a forum in which to address at least four theoretical issues pertaining to governmentality studies. This evolving research program, drawing on Foucault's later work, promises to yield illuminating accounts of governmental regimes that allow for historical contingency, specificity, and the performative role of discourse. Yet, given the outstanding issues above, this program seems to require further refinements, especially concerning the role of nonliberal powers and law. A key challenge facing this study of sanctuary in Canada is to contribute to such development. In so doing, this book draws upon insights of influential writers such as Giorgio Agamben (see Chapter 4), Susan Silbey, and Patricia Ewick (see Chapter 6), who have written since Foucault, but ultimately in a manner largely in keeping with the spirit of his legacy. If this challenge is successfully met, such refinement and an alternative account of contemporary sanctuary in a neglected context will be this study's primary contributions. Before the organization of this book can be discussed, previous accounts of sanctuary, definitions, and research procedures require elaboration.

Previous Sanctuary Research

Published accounts of sanctuary in Canada are few; comprehensive research is nonexistent. There are only two extended popular accounts of sanctuary in a Canadian context, both authored by religious authorities who played a central role in the single incident described.[75] One recounts the extensive efforts of a pastor to secure legal status for a migrant family facing deportation in an incident in Vancouver in 1992. The other is an account of the Southern Ontario Sanctuary Coalition incident that commenced in 1993. Although these accounts are detailed, both incorrectly imply that the incident depicted was the first of its kind in Canada and appear to be written primarily to appeal to a faith-based or popular readership rather than to address theoretical issues or to provide a comprehensive scholarly account of sanctuary.

Two prominent Canadian refugee advocates – Gunther Plaut and David Matas – have also written separately about sanctuary as a potential Canadian social movement.[76] Although these texts are thoughtful, they are exceedingly brief, mentioning but a few incidents and leaving out meaningful details. The only other published scholarship on sanctuary in Canada appears to be a little-known piece by Charles Stastny and Gabrielle Tyrnauer that refers to two incidents.[77] These various truncated and now largely outdated reflections on sanctuary share two major features: they imply that sanctuary in Canada has been limited to no more than three incidents,[78] and they are devoid of systematic reference to social theory. Collectively, these accounts also suggest that sanctuary's capacity to realize positive legal outcomes for migrants is limited by its apparent illegal nature (see Chapter 6) and the corresponding risk that it generates for churches and providers who choose to engage in it.[79] As discussed in Chapter 2, sanctuary's supposed limited effectiveness is incongruous with its outcomes. Although not without important qualifiers, the majority of resolved incidents yielded legal status for most migrants involved. Besides the few Canadian contributions above, and the US research below, there is virtually no other published English-language research about contemporary sanctuary.[80]

In contrast to the Canadian context, sanctuary in the US has received exhaustive study.[81] But this US literature, too, has a fault: it implies that contemporary sanctuary has been limited primarily to an *expired US religious movement*. These accounts – including those published since the mid-1990s – make virtually no mention of similar occurrences elsewhere. The US sanctuary literature fails to mention, for example, that in Britain contemporary sanctuary activities were manifest as early as the 1970s[82] and that through the 1980s, 1990s, and indeed into the 2000s, media accounts reported sanctuary incidents in Germany, France, Belgium, the Netherlands, Norway, Switzerland, and Australia. Sanctuary in Western and undoubtedly other contexts outside the US has been neglected. As noted, documenting

the Canadian context since 1983 reveals that sanctuary incidents have occurred and continue to do so outside the US and that, far from having expired, they are increasing prevalent.

This is not to suggest, however, that the US sanctuary literature is unwor-
thy of consideration. For comparison purposes, some findings are discussed
in Chapter 2. Yet my purpose is not to conduct a review of extant sanctuary
theorizing in this book. Rather, it is to contribute to the refinement of
governmentality studies. Therefore, reference to theorizing in the US literature is irregular and limited to the varied works of Susan Coutin, Hilary
Cunningham, Kirstin Park, Gregory Wiltfang, and Doug McAdam, which
share with almost all previous US research a more or less explicit view of
contemporary sanctuary as a US religious movement or form of activism
positioned against the state.[83] Typical are Wiltfang and McAdam's insistence
on the "centrality of religious groups and the salience of religious ideology
to the movement" and their claim that "the origins of the movement are
firmly rooted in religious groups."[84] Cunningham similarly investigates sanctuary in the US as an instance of conflict between church and state, an
approach best reflected in the title of her major work, *God and Caesar at the
Rio Grande*. Understanding sanctuary as conflict between political and religious authority is not new. A historical account of sanctuary in England
published in the early twentieth century, for example, notes that "in considering the question of sanctuary in England right through these pages, it
must always be borne in mind that the whole matter involved a perpetual
conflict between the State and the Church."[85] Although this approach sheds
considerable light on sanctuary in the US context as an instance of a religious movement, or on the church, positioned against the state, this dynamic applies only loosely to sanctuary in Canada. For one thing, compared
to church-state relations in the US, those in Canada have traditionally held
a different place.[86] In the US, church-state separation is mandated in the
constitution, and although there is a guarantee of religious freedom in
Canada's Charter of Rights and Freedoms, there has never been the same
legal or cultural emphasis on this division. This is evident, for example, in
the organization of education that continues today, particularly in the existence of state-funded Catholic schools. But more important, early in the
process of conducting this study, sanctuary in Canada was discovered to be
less a sustained national or regional religious movement – that is, less a
particular organizational form entailing some level of continuous communication among those involved – than a collection of local incidents that
were disconnected socially and geographically from one another, temporally limited, and surprisingly, often not primarily religious in orientation.[87]
For this reason, seeking to understand sanctuary in Canada as a religious or
social movement and correspondingly drawing concepts primarily from
social movement theories (including theories in resource mobilization and

new social movements),[88] as valid as such an endeavour is in other contexts,[89] was intentionally avoided. In place of a broad *movement*, the present study approaches sanctuary discourses and practices as *incidents*. The term "incident" better connotes an event that is limited in both time and space and is about confrontation. Sanctuary incidents defy the regular goings on in refugee and immigration domains, momentarily laying bare the otherwise routine practices of communities, churches, and immigration authorities, including resettlement, determination, and deportation practices, and therefore permit closer examination of the diverse powers at work. But this study steers clear of approaching sanctuary as a social movement for another, perhaps more controversial, reason. Although the term "movement" is usually understood to denote a specific organizational form, calling a phenomenon a movement also commonly implies the presence of agency. However, doing so in this context would raise questions: Are those providing sanctuary to migrants more or less agents than the immigration officials seeking to deport them (or, indeed, agents more so than the migrants themselves)? Why would sanctuary providers' language and efforts constitute a movement while those of immigration authorities do not? Are not the discourses and practices involving each kind of agent made possible by rationalities? In addition to focusing on those powers and legal narratives that constitute sanctuary, this book elaborates the changing rationalities within the discourses and practices of immigration and related authorities (see Chapter 3). Is not the agency of *both* providers and these officials, as Foucault suggests, "scheduled and programmed through rationality"?[90] This question points to a key theme of this book, which is that sanctuary is not alien to rationality, sovereign power, and notions of law typically associated only with the nation-state but is instead constituted by them. It therefore makes sense to approach providers and officials in a similar way, something that invoking the term "movement" for only one of them would not accomplish. Although drawing on theories in new social movements could potentially highlight the role of language in forming sanctuary providers' identities,[91] and although theories in resource mobilization might provide insight into how mass media are mobilized to serve movement goals – facets of sanctuary that are discussed in a different register in the chapters that follow – it is my contention that approaching sanctuary primarily as a movement is misleading and would not add significantly to our understanding of the phenomenon.

The present study, then, takes a different theoretical tack, one that seeks to identify the powers and legal narratives – among other aspects comprising contemporary sanctuary – that render possible the agency of sanctuary providers. Consistent with this approach, it is my contention that sanctuary is not so much a majestic and eternal conflict between two monolithic entities – church (or a national religious movement) and state – as a short-lived tension between two historical rationalities of government: the liberal and the pastoral. Conflict is thus conceived here in a less essentialist and more historical and local manner than is the case in much previous sanctuary research. To be sure, liberal and pastoral logics have come to complement one another in particular domains. Yet disagreement between these rationalities can also occur within local contexts, and this disagreement can overlap with conflict between sovereign powers that concurrently manifest themselves in such situations and that thus entail varied roles for law. Previous research has perhaps focused too much on sanctuary as a religious movement situated against the state or as an instance of church-state conflict to the neglect of elements that may shed light on theoretical issues in governmentality and socio-legal studies. Sanctuary promises to be a window on these issues, but it first needs to be better framed.

Defining and Researching Sanctuary
Contemporary sanctuary is less than a uniform space and set of discourses and practices. Writing briefly about sanctuary in Britain in the 1980s, Paul Weller distinguished between "exposure" and "concealment" within the provision of sanctuary,[92] a dichotomy that resembles the distinction between "overground" and "underground" railroads present in some US accounts of sanctuary.[93] Exposure entails purposively gaining the attention of mass media, communities, and political authorities; the latter involves avoiding such attention. Closer scrutiny of the Canadian context, however, reveals this dichotomy to be less than watertight. In the first documented Canadian instance of sanctuary in Montreal in 1983, for example, five weeks of concealment preceded exposure. The trajectories of incidents in Toronto, St. John, and Edmonton similarly reveal both aspects. As well, in several instances, specific churches publicly *threatened* to grant sanctuary, in which case migrants did not enter sanctuary to achieve a reprieve of some kind.[94] In addition, since 1983, at least one instance of concealed sanctuary was exposed after the fact, but this was not enacted as a strategy to aid the specific migrant threatened at the time.[95] Examples of churches helping migrants to fight deportation orders by providing resources for legal fees are also evident.[96] As well, community groups, such as Vigil in Toronto, formed (and disbanded) in Canada during this period expressly to aid migrants subject to deportation. A sanctuary provider from Toronto interviewed for this study recounted in passing that the group Vigil

> would go to the [immigration] minister ... and most of the times it worked
> [to stop the deportation or to secure the migrant's legal status]. So ... they
> had a lot to do, and they did it well. And the minister ... solved the like
> twenty to thirty cases that were really critical.[97]

More recently, groups of migrants in Montreal, such as the Action Committee of Non-Status Algerians, formed to fight their own deportation through efforts that at one point in 2002 overlapped with one sanctuary incident discussed later in this book. These latter three situations – threatened sanctuary, concealed sanctuary lacking strategic exposure, and antideportation campaigns of churches or other groups not involving physical protection – are comparatively rare. For this reason, while not entirely excluded from the discussion that follows, they are neither referred to nor studied as sanctuary incidents. This book, then, defines sanctuary as those incidents in which migrants actually entered and remained in physical protection to avoid deportation and that entailed strategic efforts to expose this fact to mass media, communities, and political authorities.

Although discovering sanctuary incidents involving exposure is by definition easier than researching concealed sanctuary, the former nevertheless proved methodologically challenging for three reasons. First, with the possible exception of national-security and intelligence agencies, no Canadian governmental or nongovernmental body systematically collects (or publishes) information about exposure incidents. Second, as noted, sanctuary incidents are at times purposively concealed immediately prior to or after periods of exposure. In these cases, researching sanctuary runs up against barriers similar to those encountered by researchers studying undocumented or illegal migrants more broadly.[98] Third, early in this research effort, as noted earlier, the local and disconnected nature of sanctuary incidents in Canada – that is, the fact that such incidents were primarily tied to particular local churches and communities rather than linked to a much broader network or movement – became apparent. Overcoming these challenges required the following research procedures.

Internet search engines and indexes covering major newspapers and national popular and church periodicals from the mid-1970s to 2003 were first systematically and exhaustively searched. A difficulty with this procedure was that "sanctuary" means protection or shelter in everyday parlance, de facto protection based on the accepted or at least perceived inviolability of a place where a fugitive has sought such protection from authorities, and a location within a church building. The first two meanings are often used interchangeably with "safe haven," "safe harbour," "refuge," and on occasion, "asylum." This necessitated sifting through a large volume of material to discern only those texts pertaining to sanctuary incidents so defined and to provide a comprehensive picture by ensuring that all such incidents were identified.

For some incidents occurring after 1998, websites were erected on behalf of migrants to expose their plight and to instruct visitors on how to lend support to the sanctuary effort. Also located on the Internet were brief television and radio news broadcasts or excerpts thereof regarding two 2003 incidents in the Montreal area that featured interviews with sanctuary providers. These were subsequently transcribed and analyzed. The presence of sanctuary texts on the Internet, however, is minimal. Two national or regional refugee-specific newsletters or periodicals that originated in the 1980s, *Refugee Update* and the *Inter-Church Committee for Refugees Bulletin,* which are not indexed, were also examined in their entirety. Following this, several indexes covering local newspapers from smaller cities – those in the 100,000-200,000 population range – were searched using a commercial service called Infomart. As well, two detailed and popular accounts of single incidents, noted earlier, were analyzed.[99] Other sources included one-hour videotapes of two local phone-in television broadcasts concerning two sanctuary incidents that featured interviews with sanctuary providers. These, too, were transcribed and analyzed. Finally, the few available Canadian church-sanctuary guidelines, which can be considered programmatic texts in the sanctuary context, were located and examined.

To more adequately explore the thirty-six incidents and to access sanctuary discourse, forty-six open-focused, confidential, personal interviews were conducted over four years with those persons discovered to be intimately involved (see Appendix).[100] These persons are referred to as "sanctuary providers" throughout this book, and their names and identifying information, to ensure confidentiality, have been removed from the interview excerpts displayed in the chapters that follow. These audiotaped interviews are crucial to this study for two reasons. First, they provide considerable detail about sanctuary incidents omitted from popular and secondary media accounts and from the few programmatic texts in existence. This information was not only purposely concealed from mass media and authorities, but it was also not documented anywhere. Second, the interviews facilitated access to collections of articles from smaller and somewhat obscure local newspapers of a kind typically excluded from major indexes as well as access to unpublished documents assembled and maintained by sanctuary providers in a third (or twelve) of the incidents, including the four incidents of the longest duration.[101] Some providers kept meticulous records of their efforts; others did not. As a result, these unpublished documents vary considerably but include at least some of the following: correspondence, leaflets, press releases, chronologies, petitions, texts of relevant legal decisions, and minutes of sanctuary groups' meetings. Taken together, these research procedures generated more than sixty-five hours of interviews and some 1,600 documents directly pertaining to thirty-six Canadian sanctuary incidents.

Chapter Organization
Chapter 1 has discussed major objectives, theoretical issues, previous sanctuary research, and research procedures. The remainder of the book is

organized with the two previously mentioned purposes in mind – revealing features of sanctuary in the Canadian context and providing insight into issues in governmentality studies. First, however, a comment about the title – *Sanctuary, Sovereignty, Sacrifice* – is necessary: "sanctuary" refers to the thirty-six incidents; "sovereignty" to Michel Foucault's notion of sovereign power; and "sacrifice" to pastoral power, specifically to the practices of providers who interrupt their lives and risk prosecution in order to draw attention to and care for migrants in need. Sacrifice is perhaps more pronounced here than in other pastoral practices because of the risk of legal prosecution and because the requirements of daily care for migrants' wellbeing that sanctuary situations create are often initially met by strangers. Yet "sacrifice" also highlights precisely what is absent in the exercise of sovereign power, thus contrasting the two forms of power that are of interest in this book. Consistent with the recent work of Giorgio Agamben, I argue that, as objects of sovereign power, migrants facing danger or death through deportation *cannot be sacrificed*.[102] Upon their desperate arrival at the doorstep of a local church or of the offices of immigration authorities, their lives are assumed to have already been stripped bare of any sacrificial potential (see Chapter 4).

Chapter 2 is largely descriptive and attends to the purpose of documenting the features of sanctuary in Canada. It first briefly discusses US sanctuary activities in relation to the Canadian context as well as four developments related to the idea of a distinctive Canadian sanctuary movement. Those interested more in the book's broader argument, especially as it pertains to theoretical issues, and less in these developments and the characteristics of sanctuary in Canada should proceed to Chapter 3. That said, in Chapter 2 sanctuary in Canada is found to differ from the much-researched US sanctuary activities in several respects. As suggested earlier, sanctuary in Canada constitutes less a sustained national or regional social movement or network and more a collection of contingent and temporary local incidents that, while sharing some features, have been mainly disconnected socially and geographically from one another. Equally important, many incidents have involved the efforts of persons from the larger secular communities in which they have occurred at least as much as the efforts of clergy and members of local churches. This suggests that sovereign and pastoral powers (discussed in Chapters 4 and 5), the powers that make sanctuary possible, are not necessarily of a faith-based or religious character. The major features of the thirty-six identified sanctuary incidents – their prevalence, durations, origins, providers and supporters, recipients, denominational affiliations, locations, and legal outcomes – are then discussed. A further noteworthy feature is that the vast majority of the approximately 261 persons who actually received sanctuary in these incidents were refugee claimants, and often their immediate family members, who had failed to gain legal status through official means.[103]

It is less than self-evident why contemporary sanctuary would be granted mostly to these failed refugee claimants rather than to fugitives fleeing, for example, criminal justice and threats of imprisonment or other state or nonstate authorities and sanctions. Certainly, those accused of criminal offences were granted sanctuary in the distant past. Why contemporary sanctuary has centred on migrants needs to be explained in relation to changes in refugee and immigration domains during the period of its emergence. Although only a partial explanation, the return of sanctuary in this form nevertheless corresponds with these changes, which, in Canada at least, have adopted an advanced-liberal character. Chapter 3 describes these programmatic changes by discussing the context of Canadian refugee determination and resettlement – and to a lesser extent immigration policy, with which this context overlaps – during the period in which sanctuary incidents began to appear. This discussion is necessary in order to begin to reveal, among its other aspects, sanctuary's conditions of possibility. Integral developments here include a complex movement of responsibility for determination and resettlement away from the state. Correspondingly, there has been an incursion of administrative law into refugee determination and a formal introduction of private sponsors and community volunteers into resettlement.

Chapter 4 discusses sanctuary as an instance of church and community sovereign power, a power understood in part as the monopoly to make the exception, rather than only as exclusive authority to punish or exclude. In so doing, this chapter raises questions about the typical understanding of sovereign power in governmentality studies, particularly its conception as essentially coercive, exclusionary, and violent. Sovereignty, however, also refers to territorial control; therefore, how sanctuary is constituted as a territory with fluctuating borders is elaborated upon. The spectacle of sovereign power, a key feature of its operation, is then discussed. Finally, what sanctuary reveals about the issue of how sovereign power can be distinguished from and how it relates to governmental power is taken up.

Sanctuary is also an instance of pastoral power. Chapter 5 thus pays close attention to pastoral power's knowledges, techniques, agents, objects, and spaces. It begins by considering community within sanctuary discourse. Sanctuary imagines enlisting members of a broader and often secular community, which implies that pastoral power is neither equivalent to Christian church governance nor obsolete[104] and that this rationality has purchase in specific contexts within other contemporary domains where the care and wellbeing of marginalized populations is sought.[105] This is contrary to some recent accounts of pastoral governance that draw upon Foucault's writings. The discussion then turns to needs, intimate knowledge, watching and visiting, and education in the sanctuary context as integral elements through which pastoral government is exercised. Next, consistent with this form of power, imaginings of sanctuary providers as "shepherds" and of migrants as "sheep" are discussed. Subsequently, and in more detail, the forms that sacrifice adopts are considered, these being a key aspect of pastoral power. The spaces of sanctuary constituted by pastoral power that facilitate the generation of intimate knowledge and the fulfillment of migrants' needs are then taken up. This is followed by a discussion of the resistance to pastoral power that is encountered in relation to sanctuary. Finally, in light of the foregoing, this chapter considers the issue of how pastoral power is distinguished from and relates to liberal rationalities.

Chapter 6 explores the crucial relation between sanctuary and law in light of the presence of sovereign and pastoral powers documented in Chapters 4 and 5. Both as a space and as a set of discourses and practices, sanctuary is usually thought to be beyond the reach of law. Yet, upon closer inspection, sanctuary is shown to be saturated with legal discourse. There are at least three legal narratives that partially constitute sanctuary. Two of these narratives reveal how law makes pastoral sacrifice by sanctuary providers possible, while a third authorizes sanctuary as consistent with the exercise of church and community sovereign power. Time is demonstrated to be a key dimension of these narratives in the sanctuary context. These narratives are shown to be not so much contradictory forms of ideology, consistent with the tradition of critical legal studies from which they are drawn, as instantiations of sovereign and pastoral powers at the level of the subject that complement one another in a manner that makes migrants' ultimate escape from deportation possible. The implications of this analysis for both governmentality studies and critical legal studies are considered.

Chapter 7 discusses the implications of the current study for previous sanctuary research and governmentality studies. Sanctuary, contrary to the claims of previous research, has occurred in nations outside the US, has not expired, and has been as much about local community as about religious efforts. Although previous research has pointed to sacrifice in sanctuary provision, sacrifice is better theorized as an element of a particular historical rationality. Rather than being regarded as religious or transnational political activism, sanctuary is better seen as the convergence of two neglected yet significant nonliberal powers: the pastoral and the sovereign. This account suggests that pastoral power outside the state continues to be relevant and argues that sovereign power is neither limited to the nation-state nor necessarily coercive. Consistent with a specific rationality, sovereignty may well make exceptions for situations that are outside the imagination of a given program. However, sovereign power may well be *constitutive of,* rather than simply a technique *within,* programs shaped by specific rationalities.

Implications for the concepts of resistance, hybridity, responsibilization, moral regulation, and program in relation to governmentality studies are also discussed. Sanctuary is also partially constituted by legal narratives in a configuration that is consistent with the two powers that make it possible, suggesting the potential for a more complex account of law as governance. Issues pertaining to pastoral power as an alternative form of need provision, as a longstanding challenge of governance, and as constitutive of welfare-state arrangements are then discussed. Finally, the notion that a more complex long-term genealogy of sanctuary is possible is raised. Ultimately, this study of sanctuary suggests that governmentality studies have to move beyond an almost exclusive emphasis on liberalism to allow for a plurality of powers and for corresponding roles for law in specific contexts. If this is done, the grand and mundane forms of governance, resistance, and exception that make up our lives may be made intelligible.

2
Features of Canadian Sanctuary Incidents, 1983-2003

This chapter describes known characteristics of the thirty-six sanctuary incidents that have occurred in Canada during the past twenty years. To provide insight into these incidents and by way of contrast, US sanctuary activities, their relation to the Canadian context, and four developments since the early 1990s relevant to the prospect of a distinctive Canadian sanctuary movement are first discussed. Then the prevalence, durations, immediate origins, providers and supporters, recipients, denominational affiliations and locations, and outcomes of the thirty-six incidents in Canada are elaborated upon. The vast majority of the thirty-six incidents are found to be isolated, having few links with previous or concurrent incidents or with the providers and migrants involved.[1] Nevertheless, these incidents share several key attributes: they have been local and temporary phenomena rather than elements of a distinctive and sustained national network or movement; they have resulted as much from efforts of the secular community as from faith-based efforts; and in delaying deportation and gaining legal status for migrants, they have yielded outcomes that are more positive than has been previously acknowledged.

By June 1987, more than 440 US sites had been declared public sanctuaries open to migrants fleeing US-supported war and oppression in Central America.[2] Indeed, US sanctuary activities were an element of a broader antiwar movement positioned against US foreign policy in this region. The sanctuaries formed a relatively integrated and organized national network (many sites never physically protected migrants, but supporters helped migrants in other ways).[3] Yet what became known as the "US Sanctuary Movement" is something of a misnomer.[4] The movement was not exclusively US-based but, rather, presupposed liberal Canadian refugee policies that provided Central American migrants with a greater likelihood of legal acceptance as refugees. Although they have converged of late, a trend perhaps best evinced by recent implementation of the Safe Third Country provision in Canada,[5] Canadian and US immigration and refugee policies concerning deportation and refugee determination have differed over the past two decades. Generally, Canadian policies have been more liberal than those of their US counterparts during most of this period.[6] Unlike their counterparts in the US,[7] Canadian immigration authorities have not typically imprisoned undocumented migrants awaiting refugee determination.[8] As well, since 1993 migrant women fleeing persecution and abuse have been more likely to receive status in Canada than in the US because of the introduction of gender guidelines for refugee determination.[9] Canada has also developed more progressive policies for accepting migrants who are fleeing "generalized violence" in civil-war regions and who have had difficulty fitting the longstanding United Nations refugee definition. Recognizing Canada's more liberal policies, a faction of the sanctuary effort in the US sought to aid the transportation of migrants from Central America to and through the US-Canada border so that they could enter Canada's refugee determination process.[10] A lawyer interviewed for the present study, one of the few interviewees who showed considerable knowledge of US sanctuary activities targeting Central Americans, recounted:

> There were a lot of others that were coming through that were really trying to get to Canada ... there were those who didn't want to stop and confront the [US] government in the same way among the refugees. They didn't want to be in sanctuary that way. They wanted to find it quietly ... [T]hey were trying to get to Canada and so some of the folks that were working around the Sanctuary Movement and with refugees there started trying to help them get to Canada as well.[11]

This division of the US sanctuary effort presumed considerable cooperation of Canadian nongovernmental groups. Efforts to resettle and support migrants immediately after their entry to Canada from the US were essential to the efficacy of US sanctuary activities. The same lawyer noted that members of the sanctuary effort in the US

> would notify ... the Committee to Aid Refugees or various other refugee groups across Canada saying: "Hey there's some Guatemalans or Salvadorans coming and they're going to cross the border at such and such a place. Can you be there to meet them just so that you can accompany them with their dealings with Canadian Immigration?"[12]

The Detroit-Windsor Coalition on Refugees, for example, formed to organize these migrants' legal passage through the busiest international border crossing.[13] The lawyer also noted: "So that was ... happening ... a lot within the Niagara Falls area, St. Catharines ... around Montreal and ... Vancouver."[14] The practices of these Canadian groups, and of the faction of the broader

US sanctuary effort of which they were a part, were independent of the thirty-six sanctuary incidents discussed in this book. However, through a comparison of these thirty-six incidents with US sanctuary activities, the localized nature of sanctuary in Canada is thrown into relief. Indeed, another provider noted this difference during an interview:

> The underground railroad ... was an *entirely different thing* because ... a large number of people needed sanctuary ... and that took organization and all that. But here in the case of sanctuary in Canada ... it's *very much a local affair*.[15]

The US sanctuary effort also serves as a useful reminder that from within Canada's borders, if legal status cannot be gained by migrants, there has been no nation to which they can migrate to apply for legal status. From at least the early 1980s onward, transporting migrants to the border to enter the US determination process from Canada, in hope of fairer treatment, has not been a serious option for refugee advocates and migrants. Unlike Central Americans fleeing persecution in the 1980s, migrants faced with deportation from Canada over the past twenty years have had to presume that there is "nowhere to go."[16] As a member of the Southern Ontario Sanctuary Coalition (SOSC) remarked: "But where would we, or could we, move refugees from Canada? To Greenland?"[17] There is no nation in close proximity that migrants facing imminent exclusion can enter in order to secure legal status (although many migrants enter the US from Canada illegally to live, including several at the centres of the thirty-six incidents who eventually exited sanctuary to "go underground"). The remaining legal option for migrants has been to return to their nations of origin.

Before the features of the thirty-six incidents can be discussed, four developments since 1983 relevant to the notion of a distinctive Canadian sanctuary movement require brief mention. First, following a sanctuary incident in Vancouver in 1992, the 34th General Council of the United Church of Canada, the largest Protestant denomination in Canada, now comprising 3,677 congregations,[18] endorsed "the moral right and responsibility of congregations to provide sanctuary to legitimate refugee claimants who have been denied refugee status."[19] Following this, the United Church commissioned research to develop guidelines for sanctuary due in part to the lack of success in securing status for the migrant at the centre of the Vancouver incident. These guidelines were first drafted in 1993 and subsequently published and made available to local churches beginning in 1997. Yet, since 1992, a United Church of Canada program has not appeared that imagines organizing sanctuary on a national or regional basis. This denomination, consistent with its decentralized structure, has sought only to offer advice about sanctuary to local congregations requesting it,[20] including detailed information about avenues for migrants once in sanctuary and, in at least one incident, about the potential of private-sponsorship arrangements as an alternative.[21] A provider from a local United Church recounted contacting the national church office about the prospect of offering sanctuary:

> The Toronto office, the person we spoke to there who works with refugees said, "You don't want to be offering sanctuary ... We don't offer sanctuary. It's illegal." So we said, "Well we understand that, but if they ask for it, can we grant it?"[22]

Despite the General Council's endorsement and the involvement of local congregations in sanctuary, the national (i.e., Toronto) office of the United Church of Canada has never advocated on its own a national or regional sanctuary program involving its local congregations.

Second, a separate development was the formation of the ecumenical SOSC in 1993.[23] While the coalition's name suggests a regional presence (i.e., southern Ontario), in practice the coalition has been primarily Toronto-based (e.g., meetings are held in a historic downtown Anglican Church). The SOSC's creation was premised on an awareness of the drawbacks of physical sanctuary in churches:

> When we initially set up the sanctuary thing, we had refugees hiding in various places, not in churches, but in different places ... We deliberately did not inform ourselves as to where everybody in this group was. The [Church of the] Holy Trinity was the symbolic centre, so we had a little corner of the church room. Basically we would light a candle and have a vigil on behalf of the various people in the early period ... It's far from an ideal situation for a refugee family to be stuck in a church somewhere, and I'm not even sure that in some [of our twenty-three] cases religious communities were used.[24]

However, despite physical sanctuary's assumed limitations, another SOSC member revealed: "We did investigate an emergency fall back in a church in this area with a very fine priest. And their congregation is supportive and there is a place and a priest. If we ever need it, we know where we're going to go."[25] While some support came from elsewhere in southern Ontario,[26] a SOSC member noted: "Well at this point the local group is Toronto. Back in '93 it was a bit more stretched out. It involved people in Hamilton, Kitchener, [and] Waterloo ... There were people all over in hiding."[27] By 2001 the SOSC comprised only about ten members,[28] and although it remained active in refugee advocacy after 1993, it never expanded its sanctuary efforts much beyond protecting the original migrants whose legal status – despite repeated promises from immigration authorities – remained in limbo for years, the last one receiving status only in 2002.[29] After 1993 the SOSC shifted its attention to broader issues affecting refugees.[30] Securing legal status for the original migrants who had been granted sanctuary

> was a continuing agenda, but there were always new things coming up that we got involved [in], a lot in public policy and various commissions that we set up, status reports, various proposed changes to legislation. We were always making various presentations to the IRB [Immigration and Refugee Board] or to the [federal Immigration] Standing Committee.[31]

Another current SOSC member noted:

> The Thursday morning SOSC meeting effectively has become a roundtable on refugee issues for the city. So there will be people from Citizen's for Public Justice, from [the] ICCR [Inter-Church Committee for Refugees], from [the] Coalition for a Just Immigration Policy. We know when and where the meeting is, and ... that's where you network. So ... in the last three years the Thursday meeting has become the forum for the city.[32]

In the analysis to follow, the SOSC's activities in granting sanctuary to migrants (albeit not necessarily in church buildings), which commenced in 1993, are treated as one of the thirty-six incidents.

While not an instance of sanctuary, as defined earlier, a third development is also noteworthy. Following the appearance of several sanctuary incidents in the early 1990s, the Inter-Church Committee for Refugees (ICCR), a now defunct national ecumenical organization that was funded by the major Canadian Christian denominations (including the United Church), sought to organize a national sanctuary-like network. The ICCR attempted this through a pilot project formally called Keeping Faith and informally referred to as "anonymous" sanctuary, an alternative to what it called "physical" sanctuary (of which the thirty-six incidents, including the SOSC's efforts, are examples).[33] It was foreseen that local churches and other supporters from across the nation would pledge financial and moral support for specially chosen (i.e., exceptional) migrants facing deportation. Neither the migrants' locations (as in the SOSC's program) nor their identities, which was a new adaptation, would be revealed to supporters.[34] In the months and years following its inception, however, no migrants actually received "anonymous" sanctuary. Therefore, this sanctuary-like program was never organized on a national or regional basis either. Its inability to protect migrants in this way is a point returned to in Chapter 6.[35]

Fourth, and finally, after commencement of several incidents in the Montreal area in 2003, a second sanctuary coalition was inaugurated. Yet this group, too, has had a definite local, rather than a national or regional, emphasis. A coalition member, whose church became a member after granting sanctuary, noted that similar to the SOSC in recent years, the coalition's "focus is not sanctuary. In fact the sense is that if they do the rest of it [i.e., refugee advocacy] well, sanctuary will be less an issue."[36]

Therefore, although a national or regional sanctuary movement comparable to US sanctuary activities could form in the future, such a movement has not developed in Canada.[37] This is not to suggest that sanctuary has been an unorganized, irrational, or merely spasmodic reaction to immigration authorities' threats to exclude particular migrants from the nation. On the contrary, an examination of sanctuary across the thirty-six incidents reveals its decidedly rational character, one that is exemplary of a pastoral rationality. As is discussed below, the sanctuary efforts seen in the thirty-six incidents have been almost exclusively organized at a local-community level rather than on a national or regional basis. Sanctuary in Canada, as a consequence, has not taken the form of a railroad. Rather, it has served as the last possible stop for migrants nearing the end of the line.

Prevalence

Table 2.1 shows the years during which sanctuary incidents commenced from 1983 onward. There were only two incidents in the 1980s. Sanctuary incidents began to appear with more frequency in 1992. Two-thirds (24) of the 36 sanctuary incidents occurred in the six years from 1998 to 2003. Significantly, the year in which the most sanctuary incidents (7) were set in motion was 2003, four of which continue at the time of writing, plainly suggesting that sanctuary incidents are increasing in prevalence.

Duration

The average duration of sanctuary incidents (excluding the SOSC incident) was 150 days ($N = 35$), or about five months, although this was highly variable ($s = 178$).[38] For one-sixth (6) of the incidents, more than a year passed

Table 2.1

Occurrences of sanctuary incidents, 1983-2003

Year commenced	N	%
1983-87	1	2.8
1988-92	4	11.1
1993-97	7	19.4
1998-2002	17	47.2
2003	7	19.4
Total	36	99.9

(the longest being 630 days) before either an official decision eventually leading to legal status was rendered or the migrants went underground or surrendered for deportation.

Immediate Origins

Although the sanctuary incidents involved clergy and members of a congregation or parish, the vast majority tended to be initiated by migrants themselves, their lawyers, or community and familial supporters. Usually this took the form of inquiring of local churches about the possibility of receiving sanctuary as a deportation date loomed, in some cases only hours before the migrant was expected to report for deportation:

> We tried to intercede in a whole variety of ways on their behalf and basically what it came down to was that we did everything we could possibly do and the calendar kept advancing and all of the sudden the next thing we knew it was ... deportation day and so we got caught between a rock and a hard place and we just said, "Well, what are we going to do?"[39]

A sanctuary provider drawn into an incident involving a relatively large number of migrants described how "the end arrived":

> Some of them through intermediaries found lawyers who ... in good faith ... tried to postpone it [i.e., deportation]. Sometimes they would say, "Well my father's sick." Okay Quebec Immigration would give them three months. "Yes I couldn't make it" – the lawyer himself or herself – [so they received an extension for] another three months. So ... the end arrived. This is the call that I received and it said, "Well what do we do? They are deporting ... 12 or 15 guys." Now ... these guys were not organized and [their] ... education level was limited. They got together some people who knew things and ... this lawyer called me and said, "Well, could we possibly have your help?"[40]

In another incident:

> We tried everything ... [including] crazy things like the daughter in the family had chicken pox at the time and there's no chicken pox in [nation]. You couldn't deport somebody who's got chicken pox. So ... we even went to the point of dragging this poor kid in her pajamas with her teddy bear covered in chicken pox down to the [immigration office at the] border to say, "Listen can you at least extend it [i.e., the deportation order] by a week until she's noncontagious?" ... We tried everything.[41]

Sanctuary discourse and practice, of course, invoke tradition. One provider noted, for example: "I knew about sanctuary as a very early *tradition* for churches and for universities. It goes back centuries."[42] Tradition is integral to understanding both how sanctuary can generate spectacles and how it is authorized. That said, the *immediate* and local origin of the idea of sanctuary as a potential tactic varied considerably across the incidents.[43] In some instances, it was due to vague knowledge of one or two previous Canadian incidents. In one case, it stemmed from a recommendation to a church pastor by a well-known local radio talk-show host and former Cabinet minister of the provincial government:[44] "During a commercial break, Mr. Mair suddenly turned to me and said, 'Have you ever considered offering the M's sanctuary in your church? It has been done over the centuries, you know!'"[45] Interestingly, and consistent with deference to lawyers in defining the legality of sanctuary discussed in Chapter 6, the same sanctuary provider added: "As we drove in the car that day, I turned to the others and said, 'We have to find another immigration lawyer of considerable reputation ... I need a second opinion!'"[46] Indeed, in three other cases, immigration lawyers representing migrants in determination hearings passed along the idea of seeking sanctuary.[47] In two others, the idea of sanctuary originated with the advice of an officer with the Royal Canadian Mounted Police and a member of the provincial legislature respectively.[48] Community supporters and family members were plainly the source of this option in other incidents:

> There's a woman in a church here named R, and R and M were friends and the possibility of M being deported had come up previously in some legal situation. I didn't hear about it until the last minute. So M had received some help from the International Centre. A woman named J had said, "Well this is an option ... and R, do you think that your church would be willing to put her up?"[49]

A provider from a separate incident remarked:

> The original idea for sanctuary came from the family... They wanted to take sanctuary but they didn't want to leave. But they had no choice. As of Friday they were to be [deported] out of here [i.e., Canada]. And this is like Wednesday and so then ... someone we know called around to different churches to see if any church would be receptive to this and [name of church] was.[50]

In still other incidents, the origin of the tactic stemmed from the migrants themselves: "Sanctuary was something they came up with on their own."[51] Significantly, each of these sources was decidedly secular. What is known of sanctuary incidents' origins suggests that they have been neither limited to nor primarily about religious activism:[52] twenty-seven of the thirty-six incidents were not initiated by churches in the sense that a developed sanctuary program had previously been in place or that the possibility of granting sanctuary had been collectively discussed beforehand. Even in a rare instance of the latter, the church committee had only "sort of talked about that issue ... We had kind of a philosophy of an open-door approach and receptivity."[53] More typically, a local church would be appealed to as a last resort, which often meant that church officials had to render a decision to grant sanctuary with little time to reflect or to consult the congregation, parish, or existing guidelines:[54]

> Occasionally you hear snippets on the news about it, but it's not something we had researched or actively pursued because we weren't going looking for an opportunity to provide sanctuary to somebody. *It was a situation that presented itself to us.*[55]

Consistent with these findings, interviews and texts reveal few and, even then, usually only vague references to previous US sanctuary activities. The few evident connections are best characterized as fleeting and indirect, such as the attempted duplication of some practices based on knowledge gleaned from previous media accounts. A Unitarian sanctuary provider noted:

> So we turned to sort of colleagues in the US for information ... But what we found was ... in many cases the information wasn't relevant to us exactly. For one thing, there was no Unitarian congregation in the States – that we discovered – that had actually taken a person into sanctuary.[56]

To be sure, one direct link with the earlier sanctuary movement in the US was uncovered. In this incident, a woman learned that a migrant had entered sanctuary in her community and offered to help. She remarked:

> My familiarity with sanctuary came about many years ago when I was going to a Unitarian church in El Paso, Texas. When there were refugees coming out from El Salvador, the Unitarian churches that were kind of along the way from El Paso up to Canada were involved in helping, almost like ... in the old days helping move them through and up to Canada. My early involvement and understanding of that as a movement to help people happened way back then.[57]

But, as noted, references to US sanctuary events such as this were extremely rare.[58]

Also consonant with the immediate origins of sanctuary and the lack of links with previous US sanctuary activities is the fact that there was little contact among sanctuary providers from different Canadian incidents. In one instance, a provider intimately involved referred to another incident that later occurred in the same city:

> And whether this city would ever do it again, I couldn't tell you that ... I don't know what kind of support the T's [another migrant family] had. I have no idea because I wasn't [involved], and I've thought about that afterwards, and I felt bad because I remember the T's case going on, and at the time I never bothered to really find out what the T's were all about. In hindsight [I thought] I should go down there in person. I didn't do it. I didn't. That was another community, and they were doing their thing.[59]

A provider in a different city where several incidents occurred within a few months of each other similarly noted:

> We understand the T's situation and the Q's situation [two incidents that occurred in the same city] but didn't really take that into account ... This was M, R, T, and N [they] were in need of sanctuary, and we granted it.[60]

A provider from another community where two incidents had taken place likewise remarked:

> My ... Unitarian Church did contact him [i.e., another sanctuary provider involved in a separate incident] and said, "You know what guys? We have done this before, we may be of a little help here if you would like just to talk through some things. We're here. We're available." There was a little bit of gentle animosity from the Unitarians towards the Catholics because during the time that M was in sanctuary at the Unitarian Church they had asked the Catholic churches for support and received none. So [our Unitarian pastor] felt that it was very generous ... to reach out to the Catholic Church during this time and, although they were not immediately rebuffed, they were certainly never contacted for assistance or help.[61]

In a more recent instance, limited contact was initiated between providers and migrants from two simultaneously occurring incidents:

> I have met with the pastor R and their lawyer. We've met several times ... as sort of a small working unit just to check in with each other, and we have the girls in contact every day to support them.[62]

But providers and migrants had no knowledge of one another beforehand. In another case, there was also evidence of temporary contact between two providers, but here, too, one provider involved noted:

I never entirely trusted some of the other people that had been involved in other situations. I didn't know them, and I didn't understand where they were coming from, and I was getting confusing information sometimes.[63]

In the minutes from one sanctuary group's meeting two years after their sanctuary incident had been resolved, there is mention of another incident. However, this mention entails only passing notice of a news article describing the second incident,[64] and there are no evident allusions to other incidents in three years of minutes from their meetings. In any given sanctuary incident, the participants' knowledge of previous US sanctuary efforts or of other Canadian incidents was exceedingly limited, as was their contact with the providers and supporters involved. Fitting this attribute, the single most noteworthy feature of sanctuary in Canada in the twenty years since 1983 is that only one congregation, parish, or sanctuary group has been centrally involved in more than one incident. Sanctuary in Canada, therefore, has not operated through a national or regional sanctuary movement over the past two decades. Instead, it has been decidedly local in character.

Providers and Supporters
Typically, providers were middle-class, middle-aged, white Canadian citizens of a class, age, race/ethnicity, and legal status similar to that of members of the US sanctuary effort.[65] Providers were members both of the congregation or parish and of the broader community. One sanctuary group's membership list reveals thirty active members, two-thirds of whom are women.[66] In another incident, the gender composition of sanctuary providers was said to be about "50-50."[67] Care for migrants in sanctuary was carried out mostly by women, whereas media relations and other efforts to expose the plight of migrants were handled mostly by men. This is consistent with the gendered division of labour in US sanctuary activities.[68]

Those most intimately involved in care and exposure efforts were rarely clergy. Indeed, in many instances clergy remained aloof from sanctuary provision.[69] Based on interviews, besides permitting use of their church buildings, in some incidents church congregations or parishioners were also distant from sanctuary provision and related exposure efforts.[70] In an incident involving a church mission: "The reality is that members of the congregation didn't become that involved. It was primarily the [mission] staff."[71] Another provider noted: "The church was not involved as an entity [although] the minister of the church attended that first [sanctuary group] meeting."[72] In yet another incident: "The church said nothing. The church had no spokes[person] role. They did not seek one. They wanted to be an invisible partner except for the obvious fact that these people are in the [church] basement."[73]

Some sanctuary support groups that formed were actually comprised mostly of people from the community. For example, in one incident, a provider remarked about her group, the "M Committee":[74]

> We brought together a number of different people from the community. Not just our own congregation. When the sanctuary stretched on into twelve months and then eighteen months, we had ... [a] support team which was *primarily composed of people outside our own congregation.*[75]

In some instances, the local church had but a single representative present at the relevant sanctuary group's meetings.[76] Another provider related:

> I was the only person on the ... committee who was also a member of that church [in which the migrants had been granted sanctuary] ... I was elected to be the liaison between the committee and the vestry. So I attended a number of vestry meetings and tried to keep people up to date on what was happening and what was the status of whatever application we were trying to work with at that point and tried to keep them informed of upcoming demonstrations or press conferences or whatever was being anticipated.[77]

Across the thirty-six incidents, sanctuary providers variously included representatives of labour, student, women's, and human-rights groups, members of other community organizations with no religious affiliation, and legal professionals who volunteered their time. Regarding the first sanctuary incident involving "Raphael," a provider noted that "there were some [providers] that would not have said they were religious at all."[78] In another: "Many of the people were not even religious at all. So it was a group of people from different walks of life that were really concerned."[79]

Exposure events designed to draw attention to sanctuary incidents also at times entailed only limited involvement of church members and clergy:

> We learned that supporters of M had planned to attempt to contact [Prime Minister] Chretien [who was visiting the city to mark the opening of a local historical park] at Y to seek his support. Some members of our congregation agreed to participate on the condition that the event *be kept low key and nonconfrontational.*[80]

A member of the congregation involved in the incident related that this effort was intentionally limited:

> We're just providing sanctuary in order for the authorities to think about this case and reconsider it so we weren't directly involved in the advocacy.

And that was important. In other words, we were providing a sanctuary ... And we worked hard actually to try ... and make sure that there was a separation between that group of people who were the outward advocates and this congregation who were providing sanctuary ... *I personally have difficulty about demonstrations, and I often wonder how effective they are.*[81]

In a separate incident, religious leaders were entirely absent during a march:

It was very interesting, for the record, that when they had the candle light parade in the city, the Christian churches were conspicuous by their absence ... We went out, and then we had a reception down in the basement, and people went in and met the family and everything. *But there were no religious leaders present.*[82]

To be sure, some providers and supporters were drawn from the clergy or from the congregation or parish concerned, but across the incidents, many providers were not necessarily of any professed faith, nor did they possess any previous relationship with the local church or with the migrants receiving sanctuary. Representatives of a variety of community groups were involved in organizing and participating in public protests, rallies, and pickets outside immigration offices and the offices of other federal political authorities. Such community support was substantial and not restricted to relatively low-risk or low-cost activities,[83] such as signing petitions or writing letters to political authorities on behalf of migrants. In some incidents, like members of the congregation or parish, community members regularly visited migrants in sanctuary, provided material support such as food and furniture, organized fundraising events, became centrally involved in visible protests, marches, and vigils, and met with immigration officials to discuss alternatives to deportation.

Although the ecumenical SOSC's activities have been primarily Christian-based, even these have involved individuals from secular community organizations. For example, at its initial meeting, in addition to members of the Roman Catholic Church, there was "a representative of Vigil, Amnesty [International], ... the Toronto Centre for Torture Victims, and ... a lawyer or two."[84] Indeed, the later SOSC public declaration dated 7 October 2002 calls on "church groups and *people of good will* to help refugees cross borders to safety."[85]

Most incidents (90.9 percent, $N = 33$) also entailed publicly announced support from political authorities at the municipal, provincial, and/or federal levels of the state who represented the communities where the sanctuary incidents were occurring. In some cases, representatives of all three levels were publicly supportive.[86] At the provincial and federal political levels, help for the migrants stemmed mostly from members of opposition political parties. However, support – sometimes of an intensive nature that went well beyond mere public declarations – from local members of the sitting government in the federal Parliament was also evident.[87]

Overall, 29 of the 36 incidents (80.6 percent) reveal sanctuary provision of a broader community character that would be impossible to exclusively or even primarily characterize as religious activism. Six of the 7 other incidents received decidedly sympathetic coverage from local media beyond the support of members of congregations and parishes. Four of these lasted only a few days and either were perhaps not thought to require additional community support to achieve the desired outcome or were so brief as to not attract it.

Looking across the incidents, however, the nonreligious character of sanctuary should not be overstated. All but one incident – that of the SOSC – involved individual migrants or migrant families actually physically entering churches to live, many for extended periods. These were churches with active clergy and members as well as with ongoing religious services and programs. At least some level of support from religious agents was therefore present in every incident. Nevertheless, the present study's findings are at odds with the depiction of sanctuary in previous research as primarily or exclusively about religious activism. Rather, sanctuary is shown to comprise activity of a broader, yet local, community character. This is especially significant since it implies that the sovereign and pastoral powers and legal narratives that have shaped and made sanctuary possible are not necessarily limited to churches and religious authorities but can also stem from communities, however varied these communities may be.

Recipients

In the 36 incidents, a total of 261 migrants were granted sanctuary.[88] As Table 2.2 shows, three incidents – one in Toronto and two in Montreal – involved several families and individuals, accounting for most of this figure, or 63 percent (166) of all migrants granted sanctuary since 1983. Although an average of 7 migrants were directly involved per incident, sanctuary typically involved either an individual migrant (36.1 percent) or a migrant family that comprised 2-7 individuals (55.7 percent) but that was most often made up of 4 individuals (16.7 percent).

The average age of individual adult migrants (those at least 18 years of age) at the time of entering sanctuary for whom information is available was 34.7 ($N = 47$).[89] The oldest adult migrant granted sanctuary was 71, and the youngest was 18. The overall average age of the migrants, reflecting the presence of a large number of children (including infants) accompanying adults into sanctuary as family units, was 22.2 ($N = 87$). Table 2.3 reveals that one-quarter of the incidents involved only men ($N = 36$). Fewer involved only women (11.1 percent, $N = 36$). However, the majority of

Table 2.2

Number of migrants granted sanctuary per incident, 1983-2003

No. of Migrants	N	%
1	13	36.1
2	2	5.6
3	5	13.9
4	6	16.7
5	4	11.1
6	2	5.6
7	1	2.8
34	1	2.8
65	1	2.8
67	1	2.8
Total	36	100.2

Table 2.3

Sex of migrants involved in sanctuary incidents, 1983-2003

Sex	N	%
Male and female	23	63.9
Male	9	25.0
Female	4	11.1
Total	36	100.0

incidents (63.9 percent, *N* = 36) involved a mix, again reflecting involvement of more migrant families than individual migrants.

Sanctuary recipients in Canada were decidedly multinational, as is evident in Table 2.4. Although there were sanctuary incidents that involved migrants from Central American nations (as in sanctuary activities in the US), such as Guatemala (8.3 percent) and Nicaragua (8.3 percent), others involved migrants from Chile, Peru, Colombia, Turkey, Iran, China, Bangladesh, Fiji, the former USSR, Poland, Romania, Serbia, Zimbabwe, Algeria, Nigeria, and Somalia, among other nations. Only the SOSC incident involved migrants of more than one nationality. Remarkably, 28 different nationalities were represented in the 36 sanctuary incidents. The notable variation in migrants' nationalities is consistent with the local character of sanctuary in Canada since 1983 or at least incongruous with the notion of a Canadian sanctuary movement or network responding to failed refugee claimants from specific regions or nations.

Table 2.4

Nationalities of sanctuary recipients involved in incidents, 1983-2003

Nationality	N	%
Chilean	3	8.3
El Salvadoran	3	8.3
Guatemalan	3	8.3
Polish	3	8.3
Colombian	2	5.6
Nigerian	2	5.6
Multiple other nationalities*	1	2.8
Other single nationalities	19	52.8
Total	36	100.0

* The SOSC incident included Eritrean, Sri Lankan, and Iranian migrants.

Migrants in all 36 incidents had previously attempted to gain formal legal status in Canada through official processes. None had entered the host country illegally, a common practice among Central American migrants at the centre of US sanctuary activities.[90] All but two incidents involved failed refugee claimants or their immediate family members. More than two-thirds (67.4 percent) of the incidents for which this information is known ($N = 34$) involved migrants who had applied, usually after being denied refugee status, to the Federal Court for a review of a decision affecting their status at least once and had been denied. In addition, migrants involved in 74 percent (23) of the incidents for which this information is known ($N = 31$) had applied for further "humanitarian and compassionate" consideration and had been refused,[91] and another 12.9 percent (4) of the incidents involved migrants with pending humanitarian and compassionate applications. Thus migrants were granted sanctuary after most legal options had been exhausted, which clearly suggests that sanctuary was a last resort.

Religious Denominations and Church Locations

The religious denominations of the local churches in which migrants were granted sanctuary were exclusively Christian: migrants were not granted sanctuary in synagogues, mosques, or temples. As shown in Table 2.5, more than two-thirds of the churches serving as physical sanctuaries were United (30.6 percent), Roman Catholic (25 percent), and Anglican (13.9 percent).

Unitarian, Baptist, Pentecostal, and other Protestant denominations, with much fewer members nationally, comprised the remaining 11 incidents (30.7 percent). Therefore, represented in the 36 incidents was a denominational mix involving churches that are traditionally conservative (e.g., Baptist and Pentecostal) and liberal (e.g., Unitarian) as well as hierarchically structured

Table 2.5

Religious denominations of churches in sanctuary incidents, 1983-2003

Denomination	N	%
United	11	30.6
Catholic	9	25.0
Anglican	5	13.9
Unitarian	3	8.3
Baptist	2	5.6
Pentecostal	2	5.6
Independent	1	2.8
Seventh-Day Adventist	1	2.8
Maronite Catholic	1	2.8
Mennonite	1	2.8
Total	36	100.2

(e.g., Roman Catholic and Anglican) and decentralized (e.g., United). The dominance of the three Christian denominations (69.2 percent) in Canada with the largest memberships[92] is not surprising, as their churches would have been the most available at the local level when migrants and their supporters sought out a last resort as deportation day loomed larger.

Table 2.6 shows that the churches at the centre of the incidents were widely dispersed across 16 cities in 7 provinces but were concentrated in Canada's largest cities (72.3 percent): Montreal (8), Vancouver (5), Winnipeg (4), Calgary (3), Toronto (2), Edmonton (2), and Ottawa (2). The remainder of the incidents occurred in churches and communities in other port cities (e.g., St. John, NB) or in cities near the US border (e.g., St. Stephen, NB, and Langley, BC). The wide geographical dispersal of incidents once again speaks to the local, rather than national or regional, character of sanctuary. The dominance of Canada's largest cities as sites of sanctuary is not unexpected, as this is where hearings on legal-refugee determination have been held since 1989 and where claims would have been rejected, possibly culminating in the issuance of deportation orders. This is true of cities near the US border as well. A provider commented: "They have a border entry point there ... [and] that's where the crunch comes in terms of these deportations."[93] Nevertheless, there was an unexpectedly small number of incidents in Toronto, which is Canada's largest city and the traditional destination of more international migrants than any other. Although the dearth of incidents in this city is undoubtedly due to various factors, a major influence has been the SOSC from 1993 onward. As noted earlier in this chapter, this group gradually moved from granting migrants physical sanctuary to dealing with refugee issues in Toronto in a manner that limited the necessity of

Table 2.6

Cities where sanctuary incidents occurred, 1983-2003

City	N	%
Montreal, QC	8	22.2
Vancouver, BC	5	13.9
Winnipeg, MB	4	11.1
Calgary, AB	3	8.3
Toronto, ON	2	5.6
Edmonton, AB	2	5.6
Ottawa, ON	2	5.6
St. John, NB	2	5.6
London, ON	1	2.8
Dieppe, NB	1	2.8
North Hatley, QC	1	2.8
Sydney, NS	1	2.8
Langley, BC	1	2.8
St. Stephen, NB	1	2.8
Kingston, ON	1	2.8
Halifax, NS	1	2.8
Total	36	100.3

sanctuary. For instance, the well-organized SOSC began to reroute many failed refugee claimants facing deportation in Toronto back to the US so that they could reenter the Canadian determination process anew, often with legal representation better than that retained the first time around.[94] For migrants facing deportation in Toronto, the home base of the SOSC, which had lawyers able informally to refer them, this latter tactic promised to be less arduous (albeit not necessarily more successful) than seeking and living in physical sanctuary in a local church for months on end.

Outcomes
In all thirty-six instances, arrest and deportation of the migrants concerned was effectively delayed by their entering sanctuary. A fact sheet published and circulated by a local Unitarian church that was involved in one incident asserted that sanctuary "give[s] immigration [officials] time to reconsider."[95] Buying time was one of sanctuary's central and, within the early stages of some incidents, only purpose. This precious time permitted: (1) church, community, and political support to grow through carefully managed public exposure of the plight of migrants; (2) funds to be raised through donations and other activities with which to pay for superior legal representation, private-sponsorship applications, "humanitarian and compassionate" claims, and additional Federal Court appeals; and (3) some level of

negotiation with immigration authorities to be initiated. No Canadian sanctuary incident between 1983 and 2003 saw immigration officials or police enter a legitimate[96] church to arrest those granted sanctuary on immigration charges or to charge their providers with an offence.[97] The broad community character of sanctuary mentioned above was undoubtedly a factor in successful outcomes, rendering it difficult for immigration officials to publicly dismiss a sanctuary situation as one of peculiar or even radical religious interests and then to use coercive force to make arrests. The perception by previous commentators in Canada that granting sanctuary in local churches has been ineffective or that it is overly risky for those involved contrasts with the reality of sanctuary incidents in Canada.

As shown in Table 2.7, most sanctuary incidents also brought positive results in that migrants eventually gained (or are still expected to receive) permanent legal status or were otherwise granted long-term permission to remain in Canada. Available information also reveals that in one of the three incidents involving a relatively large number of migrants, several received permanent legal status.

The outcome of 5 of the 36 incidents, in terms of migrants' legal status, is either undecided (4) or unknown (1). Nine incidents involved migrants leaving sanctuary after a period to be deported, to return to their countries of origin, or to illegally enter the US or another nation to live. However, excluding incidents involving mixed, undecided, and unknown outcomes, a full 70 percent (21 of 30) yielded legal status for the migrants involved.

This road to permanent legal status or long-term permission to remain in Canada varied considerably. In 11 incidents, sanctuary recipients were required to temporarily and "voluntarily" exit sanctuary (and Canada), legally enter nations such as the US, Mexico, and Peru, and then either reapply for immigrant status abroad or reenter the refugee determination process after a designated period consistent with Canada's immigration regulations. In these instances, providers' and migrants' cooperation was attained usu-

Table 2.7

Legal-status outcomes of migrants granted sanctuary, 1983-2003

Outcome	N	%
Permanent/long-term legal status expected/gained	21	58.3
Deported/went underground	9	25.0
Undecided/unknown	5	13.9
Some gained status/some deported	1	2.8
	36	100.0

ally through immigration officials' promises of special or expedited consideration of applications. Such promises remained unofficial and verbal to allow immigration and relevant political authorities to avoid declarations tantamount to announcing a general amnesty or to establishing a legal precedent that would potentially affect other migrants in similar dire situations. Other cases ended with the granting of a minister's permit or with a Federal Court ruling.

Although plainly difficult to measure precisely, the direct positive effects of sanctuary were not limited to the 261 migrants to whom it was granted. For example, in Montreal over the twenty-year period, in five separate incidents – which involved a Guatemalan migrant (1983) as well as migrants from Turkey (1988), Chile (1998), Zimbabwe (2002), and Algeria (2002) – blanket temporary stays in deportations as well as special arrangements made by the Quebec provincial government pertaining to hundreds of migrants destined to be deported to the same nations as those of sanctuary recipients clearly resulted from public exposure that flowed from the spectacle of granting sanctuary to migrants from these nations.[98] With respect specifically to the Guatemalans, Turks, and Algerians, these stays of deportation directly affected – at least temporarily – more than 2,000 migrants scheduled for deportation.[99] In Canada, therefore, the numbers of migrants positively affected by sanctuary have also been more significant than previously acknowledged.

Claims about positive outcomes of sanctuary have to be tempered with recognition of the psychological and physical toll on individual migrants and migrant families confined to buildings not designed for habitation for months on end amid considerable uncertainty concerning when and whether they might leave with legal status. Yet relative to the possible severe consequences of deportation – which varied by incident but which could have included a return to conditions of extreme economic insecurity or physical harm, imprisonment, or even death at the hands of authorities or other parties – the negative effects of prolonged sanctuary for most recipients likely paled in comparison.

Assertions about positive outcomes also potentially overlook the at times extraordinary efforts and sacrifices of some individual providers who risked arrest and not only attended to the daily material, physical, and psychological needs of migrants within sanctuary's walls, but also worked to expose sanctuary incidents and maintain mass media's sympathetic attention to the plight of migrants throughout the months that followed. In some incidents, such work was required even after officials had promised legal status and migrants had exited sanctuary as a consequence. Nevertheless, the positive outcomes that were generated only highlight the need for a deeper understanding of sanctuary and how it has been constituted.

Conclusion

Contemporary sanctuary has not appeared only in the context of US sanctuary activities that began in the 1980s and concluded in the early 1990s. Nor does sanctuary elsewhere or since necessarily share features revealed by studies of the US context. In Canada sanctuary shares some attributes with but also differs from earlier US sanctuary efforts. Most important among the divergences are that the thirty-six Canadian incidents do not add up to an integrated national or regional movement and that both the immediate origins and the local-community and political support of incidents refuse a primary characterization as religious activism positioned against the state. That sanctuary was usually a last resort is especially relevant to understanding sovereign power, as it suggests that sanctuary was granted and sustained only in exceptional cases. That these incidents have entailed the efforts of a larger community as much as those of clergy and members of local churches suggests that both sovereign and pastoral powers are not necessarily of a religious character but instead have a wider relevance. The characteristics of the migrants at the centre of the incidents – who were mostly young adults, often with families, and who had to wait in sanctuary an average of five months – help to provide insight into how the migrants were perceived and cared for by providers. That only one church or sanctuary group has granted sanctuary more than once is undoubtedly linked to the sacrifices, as an element of pastoral power, that sanctuary provision requires.[100]

Sanctuary in Canada has been more significant in the numbers of migrants that it has affected and more successful than previously thought. Although its increasing prevalence is undoubtedly due at least in part to a vague recognition of this success by other migrants and their supporters as they fast approach the end of the line, this is only part of the story. Sanctuary must also be understood in relation to changes in Canadian refugee and immigration policies beginning in the early 1980s that are consistent with advanced liberalism. These modifications are taken up in the next chapter.

3
Advanced-Liberal Refugee Determination and Resettlement

International migrants have become the central objects of sanctuary efforts in many Western nations, including Canada. Why migrants, rather than fugitives from criminal justice or from other kinds of state authorities, should become the target of contemporary sanctuary programs is far from self-evident. Anyone feeling unfairly treated by a state justice system or by the other state bureaucratic processes that can detrimentally impede the course of individuals' lives *could* seek the protection of churches and set in motion what is understood as the sanctuary tradition. Yet this has not transpired. Therefore, why migrants have become the focal point of sanctuary activities requires explanation. Broadly speaking, that this has occurred is insepa- rable from the rise of national refugee and immigration policies as governmental domains in Western nations as well as from the refugee's ascendancy throughout the twentieth century as an object of government.[1] More specifically, however, in Canada in recent decades the appearance of sanctuary incidents focused on migrants is linked in complex ways to the juridification of inland refugee determination and to the increased involve- ment of churches and communities in refugee resettlement (as well as to some extent in refugee selection abroad) as the state has retreated from these realms.

Canadian refugee programs that appeared in the early 1970s imagined protecting refugees from immediate physical damage and death through selection and determination and from moral and mental dangers through resettlement. Sanctuary incidents in Canada from the early 1980s onward must be seen in relation to developments in these two overlapping realms. What follows is not an exhaustive history but a discussion of some key changes in these realms that is intended to provide insight into the appear- ance of sanctuary incidents in Canada. Attention is paid to how refugee determination and resettlement as well as related programs and practices were problematized and to the rationalities and technologies from which they were reassembled during this period. Attempts to govern particular realms, once problematized, are always limited to the constitutive elements available at the moment. In particular, this chapter points to a shift toward an advanced-liberal rationality, one that is consistent with a greater reliance on administrative law in the determination process and on local agencies, communities, and refugees themselves in resettlement efforts.

Advanced liberalism has several key attributes. One is that expertise in the management of specific populations is no longer assumed to be located within the state.[2] Expertise is to be "purchased" by careful consumers exercising their choice in a marketplace. Among these consumers are authorities of a kind previously located in the state but who are now placed further from the reach of political authorities.[3] Because of this shift, a kind of marketization has been developing.[4] In advanced liberalism, trust in authorities claiming expertise comes to be replaced by techniques like the audit.[5] Such a rationality also entails localization and responsibilization,[6] or the movement of responsibility to more local levels of authority.[7] This has taken the form of a new emphasis on the language of community.[8] Here community comes to displace the social (associated with liberal welfarism) as the field through which conduct is both thought about and governed.[9] There is also a shift of responsibility to the level of subjects themselves, perhaps best exemplified by the proliferation of empowerment discourses.[10] Therefore, an advanced-liberal rationality presupposes more active or enterprising actors[11] – that is, "subjects of responsibility, autonomy, and choice."[12] Advanced-liberal rule generally involves the introduction of more distance between the decisions of formal political authorities and the conduct of a variety of more local authorities and actors,[13] which is evident in both refugee determination and resettlement.

Refugee Determination and Advanced Liberalism

In the decades following the Second World War, the Canadian federal Cabinet decided which nationalities would be recognized as refugees eligible to come to Canada to live permanently. In 1969, after Canada signed the Convention Relating to the Status of Refugees of 1951 and the Protocol Relating to the Status of Refugees of 1967,[14] refugee determination – that is, the question "who is a refugee?" – emerged as a new governmental domain. In the 1970s determination remained largely hidden from the Canadian citizenry, but as thousands of claimants not previously screened and selected abroad by state visa officers began arriving and then staying for extended periods during the early 1980s, determination became the object of extensive mass-media coverage and public concern. A much greater reliance on administrative law first emerged in 1989. This was facilitated by the installation of Refugee Documentation Centres in major Canadian cities that promised to allow effortless access to information and expertise about refugee conditions abroad in order to produce the "truth" about refugees. Refugee determination has since burgeoned into a significant area of legal practice and scholarship.

Although no specific provisions regarding determination appeared in the new immigration regulations in 1967, the Immigration Appeal Board was created that year to deal with deportation case appeals launched by noncitizens.[15] Canada's signing of the United Nations Convention and Protocol two years later announced that a regular, visible refugee-selection program was forthcoming. This fit well with Canada's renewed attempt to assert itself among other Western nations, especially those without such a policy. But now what Canada required under the UN Convention and Protocol was a determination program targeting those who had fled to Canada to escape persecution, one that would be in line with its *non-refoulement* principle, which dictates that refugees should not be removed to nations where they may be in danger.[16] At that time, a Canadian determination program was merely an afterthought, little more than a minor consequence of Canada's obligations under the convention. Thus it was largely hidden from the Canadian citizenry within the state and potentially relevant to only a handful of migrants annually.

New guidelines were subsequently established in 1970, and in 1973 an amendment was made to the Immigration Appeal Act, an amendment that explicitly recognized refugees and that allowed – but did not require – members of the Immigration Appeal Board to quash deportation orders if they deemed that the noncitizen in question was a refugee under the convention.[17] As this was not a requirement, refugee status remained a privilege rather than a right in Canada.[18] Also established in 1973 was an ad hoc interdepartmental committee to review refugee claims and make recommendations regarding status to the minister of immigration.[19] This program imagined a two-stage process, responsibility for which was located solely within the corridors of the state.

A new determination program, which was made possible through the programmatic Green Paper and followed by the 1976 Immigration Act, foresaw a four-stage process involving a newly created Refugee Status Advisory Committee (RSAC).[20] The guiding rationale for these new arrangements was a reduction in the Immigration Appeal Board's discretionary power.[21] Here refugee claimants were assumed to have a right to legal counsel and to a copy of the written transcript of their claim during an interview with immigration officials.[22] Under these arrangements, refugee claims were not necessarily expected to refer to refugee-producing conditions from which claimants had allegedly fled.[23] From there it was imagined that RSAC members would examine written transcripts and present advisory opinions regarding status to the minister of immigration. For them to do so, it was foreseen that the RSAC would draw on knowledge of refugee-producing conditions in mostly non-Western regions, knowledge generated through experience with previous deportation cases or through specific ad hoc inquiries of a small research unit.[24] The quasi-diplomatic representative of the United Nations High Commission for Refugees, who began operating in Canada in 1975, was to be a resource person who would review and provide an opinion about specific claims – but who would not vote – during RSAC sessions.[25] At this stage, expertise regarding refugee-producing conditions abroad was still clearly situated within the state. Still absent in programmatic texts was any suggestion of the need for better access to outside expertise or for better knowledge of refugee conditions generally. Significantly, this new determination program foresaw the refugee-status determination process commencing before a deportation order was made. This was to be an improvement that would reduce "tribulations of a person who may indeed be a refugee and eliminate unnecessary work for the Immigration service and Immigration Appeal Board."[26] From the outset, determination was seen to be creating problems for ongoing immigration schemes. A few years later, this alleged improvement would be deemed to have led to difficulties that were more far-reaching than the "unnecessary work" that it had been intended to prevent.

Thus, immediately following release of the Green Paper and enactment of the Immigration Act, Canadian determination programs envisaged RSAC officials deciding whether noncitizen claimants were indeed refugees. Beginning in 1980, the numbers of claimants entering Canada's refugee determination process began to rise from a few hundred to thousands annually, and by the late 1980s the figure had reached more than 10,000 annually.[27] This enormous increase in refugee claims constituted a crisis of resources.[28] It was imagined at this point that future increases in claims could be avoided by deploying a proportionate volume of staffing and funds and that with a few minor reforms, the existing system could be made to work.[29]

This crisis arose under certain conditions of possibility. Among them were a decrease in the cost and an increase in the availability of international air travel from non-Western regions to North America via Europe, thus making populations in these regions more mobile and Canada more accessible during the mid-1980s. Claimants travelled through Europe because there were (and remain) few nonstop flights to Canada (or the US) from many regions outside the West.[30] Another condition was extensive Canadian and international mass-media coverage of the sudden introduction of Canadian programs in July 1979 to select and resettle more than 50,000 Indo-Chinese refugees by the end of 1980, efforts subsequently touted as the most generous among Western nations.[31] Mass media widely and sympathetically displayed dramatic images of impoverished Indo-Chinese migrants from nations such as Laos, Vietnam, and Kampuchea in crowded, dilapidated boats helplessly adrift on the open ocean, followed by images of their salvation and subsequent arrival in Canada. As a result, Canada appeared more than ever as a haven for refugees.

Sudden, spectacular decisions to grant legal status to migrants, and thereby to include in the Canadian polity tens of thousands of newcomers facing death and peril, remain unanalyzed as instances of sovereign power. Exclusionary decisions and their accompanying images – although important – have received exclusive scholarly attention instead.[32] This neglected aspect of sovereign power is evinced in reprieves granted by the minister of immigration to migrants as well as in parallel decisions by churches and communities to grant sanctuary to those facing deportation. The 1979-80 event concerning the Indo-Chinese refugees was followed several years later by a reduction in planned levels of immigrants and state-sponsored refugees from 1983 to 1985 and by the introduction of categories of business-class immigrants, who could effectively purchase legal status with an investment of several hundred thousand Canadian dollars. As a result, the numbers of immigrants were reduced to their lowest levels since the Second World War, potentially extending the waiting time to immigrate by years.[33] As the queue swelled with migrants of modest means, new forms of resistance emerged, particularly an array of unconventional and ever-mutating ways of migrating to Canada to live. After 1985 the situation was further exacerbated by the introduction of new provisions that restricted access to determination in Western European nations. One such provision was the Schengen Agreement,[34] which encouraged those seeking entry to Europe to continue on either to Canada or to the US and then to Canada. Although these conditions of possibility by no means fully explain sanctuary incidents involving migrants since 1983, it is nevertheless interesting that the first such incident, which commenced on 23 December 1983, coincided with the appearance of this crisis of resources in refugee determination.

The continuous mass arrest and deportation first of hundreds and then of thousands of would-be refugee claimants as they arrived at Canadian ports of entry (i.e, airports, inland border crossings, and harbours) during this crisis would have been a spectacle and, on its face, inconsistent with liberal government. Such undertakings, in which the naked force of the state is wielded by formal political authorities on Canadian soil, have an inherent potential to upset the citizenry. Their effects can be unstable if continually used on a mass scale.[35] It was widely thought that similar dangerous effects would likely result from sanctuary incidents if immigration authorities or police stormed the churches to arrest migrants and their providers. Of course, immigration officials eventually removed some failed claimants during this period, but at least initially, liberal government proved to be much more resourceful and experimental than it would have been if such measures had been the norm.

A task force on determination was created in September 1980, which ultimately produced the Robinson Report.[36] Its recommendations included making the RSAC independent of the Department of Immigration and External Affairs and granting every refugee claimant an oral hearing as a central feature of the existing determination process. It was further suggested that although oral hearings for all claimants would come at a greater cost than an administrative review, minor amendments in the process would make up for this increase through improved efficiency.[37] In February 1982 the minister of immigration convened a National Symposium on Refugee Determination in Toronto to announce structural changes that would effectively remove the RSAC from the Immigration Department.[38] The earlier creation of the RSAC had already placed determination farther from the department's influence than it had been when the ad hoc committee was in operation. This new arrangement promised to reduce the department's influence even further. However, the head of the RSAC was still foreseen to be reporting to the minister of immigration.

Following the introduction of these reforms, determination continued to be deemed problematic for ongoing immigration programs. This problematization prevailed even though the practice of delivering Adjustment Assistance Program benefits to refugee claimants in the Quebec region was terminated in October 1982.[39] By 1983 this same region had received the most claimants in Canada.[40] In 1984 another major report observed that determination "has been the subject of abuse by some claimants with little chance of success, who claimed refugee status in order to be permitted to remain in Canada while their claims were being processed. The laborious procedures imposed by the Act, together with a dramatic increase in claims, have created serious delays in the disposition of cases, *with repercussions throughout our system of immigration enforcement.*"[41] Nevertheless, in the same report, the pilot projects were judged to have led to fewer adjournments and to have improved efficiency overall.[42]

The Plaut Report, the third major programmatic statement on determination, was commissioned in 1984. When released, its many recommendations included: allowing refugee hearings to take place before a refugee board that would be part of a larger Immigration and Refugee Board (IRB) operating independent of political influence; training members of the board mostly through an education division; allowing two oral hearings and an appeal; and allowing public access to hearings before the board unless the claimant requested otherwise.[43] As determination became visibly problematic, liberal government demanded that it be intensively and continuously scrutinized through increased production of expert knowledge by the education division; public display; a decision-making board freed from arbitrary intervention by political authorities; and most significant, liberal administrative law in the form of oral hearings and legal representation.

In April 1985 the *Singh* decision was rendered in the Supreme Court of Canada, marking the beginning of a deluge of law that would flow into the refugee determination realm.[44] At this point, it was decided that "everyone" described in Section 7 of the Canadian Charter of Rights and Freedoms, which happened to have been entrenched in 1982, referred to everyone physically present in Canada as well as to "anyone 'seeking entry at a port of entry.'"[45] The decision required that Canadian refugee determination be brought in line with the notion of "fundamental justice."[46] In practical terms, this meant that at least one oral hearing had to be granted to refugee claimants in place of an administrative review of a written transcript representing the claim.[47] Thus, by 1985, refugee claimants, upon reaching Canadian territory, had become juridical units with rights that had to be respected by formal Canadian political authorities. In other words, refugee determination underwent juridification, necessitating the provision of legal representation for refugee claimants through legal-aid programs.[48] This development has plainly served as a condition of possibility for the growing prevalence of sanctuary incidents. In the sanctuary context, aspects of this change are evident in the heavy reliance on lawyers and in the sacrifices that providers must make to cover the fees required for migrants' adequate legal representation.

Another task force was subsequently created to begin drafting legislation for a new system of refugee-status determination.[49] At this moment, new efforts were also suddenly launched to limit access to determination from abroad. Explicitly intended to restrict the numbers entering the existing system, transit-visa requirements were put in place in June 1985 for fourteen mostly non-Western nations.[50] These new provisions allowed state visa officers abroad to prescreen prospective visitors to Canada in order to determine whether they might claim refugee status upon their arrival. Despite this measure, in the months that followed, the backlog of refugee claimants entering the old system continued to grow. Considerable mass-media coverage of the crisis continued between 1981 and 1985, but starting in 1986 and until new legislation was passed in the summer of 1988, the backlog increased significantly.[51] The image of the crisis became that of Canada's territorial borders being flooded with noncitizens making refugee claims in order to collect welfare or otherwise gain status to live permanently in Canada. During this period, the focus of the crisis became the 4,000 Portuguese and 2,000 Turkish migrants who arrived in 1985 and 1986 respectively, the 800 Brazilians who landed in early 1987,[52] the 155 Sri Lankan Tamils who made a more dramatic arrival off Newfoundland's coast in lifeboats in August 1986, and the similar number of Indian Sikhs who landed on the shores of Nova Scotia in July 1987.[53] Following their arrivals, these and other groups were thought to have made fraudulent refugee claims, to have travelled to Canada using fraudulent documents, or both. Emerging was a general public picture of refugee claimants as "welfare burdens," "criminals," "security risks" (i.e., unidentified terrorists or their supporters), and "queue-jumpers" (i.e., persons who unfairly move ahead of those waiting patiently in the immigrant line by entering a faster-moving refugee line to receive status).[54] Refugee determination was again seen as a problem for ongoing immigration schemes. But at this juncture, it also began to be perceived as increasing the pressure on Canadian provincial and municipal welfare programs by adding undeserving individuals to the rolls;[55] weakening national security programs by potentially permitting entry of security risks; and exacerbating Canada's urban crime problems more generally by importing foreign-born criminals or those with criminal propensities.

It was in 1986, then, that perception of the crisis began to change. From mere concern over the arrival of increasing numbers of refugee claimants and the lack of available resources with which to respond, the focus shifted to a profound questioning of the rationality guiding the determination process itself: the crisis of resources began to be identified as a crisis of governability. The latter is not tantamount to something as momentous as a state crisis.[56] Consonant with the way that determination had been defined – that is, with the problems that it was assumed to be creating for various external program realms, such as welfare, immigration, national security, and the criminal-justice system – a crisis that had previously centred on a need for allocation of more staff and funds to the RSAC to deal with increased volume now centred on the capacity of the determination process to identify bona fide refugees. As more instances of claims deemed fraudulent became known and were dispersed through mass media, the prevailing questions became: Did these claimants have no other choice but to flee to Canada to enter the process because they feared persecution? Had they merely travelled to Canada to collect welfare (welfare burdens) or to gain Canadian status (queue-jumpers)? Had they fled to Canada to avoid prosecution by political authorities elsewhere (criminals) or to establish clandestine terrorist operations (security risks)? Or were they an amalgamation of these immoral and dangerous entities? The system was increasingly deemed to lack the capacity to make such distinctions.

In March 1986 a new effort foresaw dealing with the backlog resulting from an increase in appeals of the RSAC's determination decisions by expanding the Immigration Appeal Board from eighteen to fifty members. This expansion was to be completed by the fall of 1986 through passage of the new refugee legislation announced in May.[57] Simultaneously, a newly introduced administrative review envisaged transferring all refugee claims from the RSAC's backlog to a temporary ad hoc body.[58] Such a program imagined immigration authorities deciding whether claimants demonstrated at least the potential for successful establishment in Canada. The criteria to be used were: employment stability, length of time employed, frequency of

and reasons for changes in employment, present income and future prospects, and family obligations.[59] This review, therefore, was not to be a new
refugee-determination program. Those receiving positive decisions were to
be selected and categorized as immigrants, and those given negative decisions were to reenter the regular process of refugee determination in order
to have their claims decided by the RSAC.[60] Nor was this a wholesale amnesty program. Instead, it sought to circumvent the now pressing question
"who is a refugee?" while awaiting the effects of coercive measures used
abroad that promised to reduce the numbers of claimants accessing the
determination process. These measures involved increased interdiction efforts, coupled with threats of arrest, detention, fines, seizure of travel documents, and seizure of airliners and sea vessels transporting undocumented
migrants. This administrative review sought to deal with claimants in a
manner comparable to that adopted by state visa officers working abroad.
That is, it regarded claimants as potential citizens of a liberal order and
based refugee determination on standardized point-system criteria (e.g.,
education, age, etc.) and on family ties. Simultaneously, it attempted to
avoid a full amnesty – "amnesty" being absent from programmatic statements[61] – in order to "avoid creating incentives for a new influx of claimants in the transition period."[62]

More than 20,000 claimants were eventually dealt with in this manner.
Persons from one of eighteen nations on a list assembled by formal political
authorities (known as the "B-1" list) who were not covered by the temporary administrative review (i.e., claimants arriving after May 1986) were
imagined to be entering a process involving the automatic granting of
minister's permits and work permits. This would allow migrants to remain
in Canada while preventing their entry into the already backlogged determination process. The "B-1" list was claimed to include nations deemed to
be refugee-producing in the past, to which Canada did not deport persons.
In effect, the answer to the question "who is a refugee?" would now be
based on past RSAC practices. This development was equivalent to making
an exception to the regular determination process. Those persons not covered by the review and whose nationality was not on this special list were
seen to be entering a fast-track determination process, to which additional
resources were to be allocated. Resources expected to be required for several
years for determination and the Immigration Appeal Board were finally increased, but by now it was too late – the character of the crisis had already
shifted. The problem was no longer centred on a lack of resources but on
the rationality guiding determination.

Despite the introduction of the various measures mentioned above and
several new programs, by the summer of 1986 another backlog was quickly
forming. Indeed, the number of claims, in particular those associated with
the "B-1" list, continued to increase.[63] In February 1987 a further expansion

of coercive measures was announced. Persons from those nations whose citizens were required to obtain visitor visas – now numbering ninety-eight – were also required to present transit visas, which allowed persons to enter Canadian territory by aircraft to temporarily await travel elsewhere. This was to "reduce the number of non-bona-fide visitors who abuse the transit privilege to claim refugee status."[64] Another measure was then announced that foresaw training private international-airline personnel to detect and halt travellers with fraudulent documents en route to Canada, which would also enable airlines to avoid fines or the seizure of airliners for carrying such passengers upon their arrival.[65] At this juncture, a distinction between claimants represented on the B-1 list and those entering the fast-track process was also removed, thereby requiring that all claimants be dealt with in the same way. The rationale for the elimination of this distinction was the failure of the previous blanket approach to determine the motivations of individuals entering the process, "as people from unaffected regions of a country benefited from the policy. Case-by-case review will allow the government to remove people where there are no personal consequences from this action ... it recognizes that we need to view each individual's need within the specific context of the country to which they might be returned. Case-by-case procedures will allow the government to remove those who are not genuine refugees, i.e., economic migrants, or those who are undesirables because they are criminal offenders or security risks."[66] The program had failed; thus visible exceptions could no longer be made.

This failure centred on the system's incapacity to generate consistent answers to the question "who is a refugee?" and, by implication, to determine who should be quickly expelled. Sufficient answers to this question were now deemed to require considerably more detailed, systematic, and up-to-date knowledge of the specific political and economic conditions from which individual claimants had fled. The notion of allowing political authorities and immigration officials to dictate answers on the basis of past practices or personal whim was deemed to have failed after eight months, only reinforcing perceptions that a new process was required. Refugee determination now had to be reassembled from what was available at this moment.

The Refugee Reform Act[67] was passed in the summer of 1988 during an emergency sitting of Parliament that followed extensive mass-media coverage of the arrival of the Sikhs mentioned above. After its passage, another temporary administrative review was created to deal with the backlog of over eighty thousand claims that had appeared by the end of 1988.[68] This review, which expired three years later, likewise managed to avoid the question "who is a refugee?"

The continuing crisis of governability throughout this period encouraged the introduction of a new program. It was to involve a three-stage process that would replace the RSAC with a large quasi-judicial decision-making body: the Immigration and Refugee Board. The latter was to begin operations in 1989.[69] The Convention Refugee Determination Division (CRDD) of this independent, "nonpolitical" body would oversee legal oral hearings. This program imagined legal professionals assisting refugee claimants by providing legal aid and by developing claims prior to presentation at the oral hearing. Hearings would be attended by a refugee-hearing officer and overseen by two members of the CRDD, only one of whom was required to decide in favour of a claimant in order for status to be granted.[70] Formal political authorities would appoint CRDD members for multiyear terms.

Within the RSAC and earlier, there had been little emphasis on the need for formal knowledge of refugee-producing nations and of the specific contexts from which refugee claimants had fled.[71] In contrast, the new process was to be highly reliant on this knowledge, which would now come from experts situated in universities and in an array of human-rights and non-governmental organizations operating outside the state. This shift in emphasis is consonant with the rise of advanced liberalism. A new technology, the documentation centre, would make this change possible. It would permit not only IRB members, but significantly, also refugee-hearing officers, refugee claimants' legal counsel, and the Canadian citizenry, access to this knowledge with which to scrutinize claims. Considerably more resources would be made available to the CRDD for the staff and materials required to run these centres than had been allotted to the RSAC to respond to the crisis of resources prior to 1986.[72] The facts would now be assembled and provided by documentation centres and then subjected to legal judgment in oral hearings. The new process therefore sought to tame the unruly political question "who is a refugee?" by transforming it first into a technical question (e.g., which information databases or publications should now be accessed through the documentation centre to construct or critique a refugee claim?) and then into a legal question to be answered in the oral hearing (i.e., is this a credible and valid refugee claim?). Formal knowledge and law would seek the "truth" regarding who should be deemed a refugee and, by implication, who should be regarded as merely a criminal fleeing prosecution, a welfare burden, a security risk, a queue-jumper, or some combination of these entities assumed within a liberal order to be worthy only of efficient expulsion. Once claims were determined, the refugee claimant would be either granted immigrant status and resettled or, following appeals, encouraged to leave and if necessary physically removed from Canada. Such a program promised to render determination governable once again.

In anticipation of the new determination process of 1989, coercive measures to reduce the numbers of persons accessing the process in Canada from abroad were stepped up. The Refugee Deterrents and Detention Act[73] was passed, as was the Refugee Reform Act. The former included provisions for expanding the measures deployed abroad, which had first been announced in February 1987; more severe penalties to be levelled against private international airlines that transported inadmissible passengers to Canada;[74] and new discretionary powers for immigration officials to board and turn around sea vessels thought to contain undocumented migrants without status.[75] During this period, only one more sanctuary incident occurred (i.e., in 1988),[76] but it was accompanied by other churches' threats to grant sanctuary to migrants[77] and by the Canadian Council of Churches' launch of a Charter challenge to this legislation, which ultimately failed.[78]

Efforts to reduce access to determination continued after 1989. In 1990 the Operation Shortstop program was launched explicitly to deter thousands of migrants from arriving on Canadian soil in order to enter the new system. It imagined the enforcement branch of the Department of Immigration monitoring patterns in the use of fraudulent documents to travel to Canada's borders as well as coordinating the education of private international-airline personnel in identifying and "stopping" travellers destined for Canada who were using such documents.[79] By 1994 visa restrictions first launched in 1985 had been applied to over one hundred nations.[80]

After three years of operation, the determination system continued to be altered. Through passage of Bill C-86 in 1992,[81] the initial credibility stage of the new process was removed. This legislation also permitted deferring the landing of refugees until they had been satisfactorily identified and entering into agreements with other nations over responsibility for the examination of refugee claimants.[82] The former measure sought to deter those who would otherwise travel to Canada with fraudulent documents to enter the determination process. This amendment to the Immigration Act came into force in February 1993. It was intended to "improve the efficiency and effectiveness of the refugee status determination system without compromising the protection which Canada has provided to refugees. The Minister hopes to avoid future backlogs which weaken the determination process and delay the acceptance of genuine refugees."[83]

In March 1994 another temporary administrative review – again rather than an "amnesty" – was announced. This Deferred Removal Order Class (DROC) program was foreseen screening the thousands of claimants who had been rejected but who had been stuck in a backlog for more than three years – a situation similar to that which had become a barrier to the RSAC process in the early 1980s before a crisis of governability emerged. Significantly, and consistent with the resourcefulness of liberal government, both the DROC program and the appointment committee mentioned above managed to circumvent, in one way or another, the political question "who is a refugee?"[84]

More recent changes in determination are noteworthy but not as integral as those noted thus far. The new Immigration and Protection Act, which came into effect in June 2002, provided for a refugee-appeals division that would permit appeals based on the merits of a refugee claim. However, after more than two years, it has still to be implemented.[85] Not inconsistent with juridification, this is a legal appeal process for which the Canadian Council for Refugees (CCR) – the nongovernmental umbrella group representing church groups and various organizations concerned with refugee advocacy, immigrant settlement, and human rights in Canada – had been advocating for at least a decade.[86] Sanctuary providers across incidents consistently referred to its absence and, more recently, to frustration over failure to implement the process as promised in the legislation as being among the reasons migrants were forced to seek sanctuary.

The more recent introduction of the Safe Third Country provision renders Canadian policy more reliant on the fairness of US refugee and immigration policies than ever before and is consistent with broader policy shifts toward the securitization of migration[87] in the aftermath of 11 September 2001, although these shifts had commenced prior to this event.[88] Such a provision would have been a near deathblow to the faction of the earlier US sanctuary effort discussed in Chapter 2. As for failed refugee claimants in Canada since 1983, many Central American migrants who entered the US to flee persecution and death in the 1980s and early 1990s would have had "nowhere to go." For the first time in ten years, implementation of the Safe Third Country provision has led the Southern Ontario Sanctuary Coalition (SOSC) to threaten to return to its sanctuary roots.[89] Yet it would be a mistake to view either this provision or securitization generally as the defining features of recent Canadian refugee-determination and immigration policies. Both are noteworthy developments, but both remain consistent with the earlier shift to advanced liberalism described above.

With respect to sanctuary, the more important development has been the earlier move toward a greater reliance on law as a central component of a new determination program that foresaw restoring order to a specific crisis of governability. This crisis began to emerge not as a matter of course but in response to circumstances that converged during this period, including the entrenchment of the Charter. Once in crisis, Canadian determination could be reconceived only in terms of an advanced-liberal rationality, which includes administrative law in its repertoire, and with reference to knowledges and technologies that were available at that historical moment. The new system has not simply aided the search for the "truth" or "untruth" of refugee conditions – and thus the search for answers to the question "who is a refugee?" Rather, legal oral hearings and the documentation centres have created the very possibility of "truth," "untruth," and refugees.

This key change in determination coincides with the period in which sanctuary incidents became increasingly prevalent. As noted, one result of this much greater reliance on law in refugee determination is that claimants have required legal representation as never before, giving rise to a situation that imagines lawyers playing a central role in sanctuary incidents. This juridification of refugee determination, coupled with the gradual movement of responsibility out of the hands of immigration officials and their political masters and into those of an independent "nonpolitical" body, is consistent with the rise of advanced liberalism. Like another facet of Canadian refugee policy that underwent considerable change during this period – refugee resettlement – refugee determination was now to be "governed at a distance."

Refugee Resettlement and Advanced Liberalism

The onset of an advanced-liberal rationality is also evident in refugee resettlement. A liberal subject must have the capacity for choice,[90] and it is precisely this feature that refugees are assumed to lack. Because of persecution, or fear of it, refugees are assumed to have no choice but to migrate to Canada and no choice but to stay after arriving. Recognition of this fact is assumed to be vital to their proper integration into Canadian society upon their arrival. The liberal subject contrasts starkly with the refugee: whereas the former is the stable Western figure characterized by reason and normality, the latter is an entity defined by nonreason and abnormality who flees illiberal government by migrating to the West. Liberal government insists that devices be present to foster a capacity for choice among those deemed to lack such power. Refugee resettlement is such a device. During a more or less discrete period, it attempts to mediate between the Canadian citizenry, who are thought to be established and civilized, and the migrating, marginalized refugee.

Refugees are presumed to be resettled when they have become "self-supporting."[91] In resettlement, refugees' active capacities are not to be crushed or annihilated; they are to be nurtured, promoted, and in a sense, brought into being. Far from being assumed to adapt naturally after arriving in Canada, refugees are thought to require considerable care and investment as well as the inculcation of skills and knowledge if they are to develop into self-governing entities able to exercise choice. (Such intensive care is also evident, although to a greater degree, within the confines of sanctuary.) Resettlement programs therefore imagine an undifferentiated mass mined from remote refugee camps or crisis situations metamorphosing into self-regulating citizens – that is, entities at Canadian society's conceptual margins who lack a capacity for choice being converted into liberal subjects who freely exercise choice at its centre. Resettlement programs have envisaged delivering to refugees financial assistance and special services that promise to foster such dramatic change. As with the overlapping domain of refugee determination, the facets of Canadian refugee resettlement have been problematized, producing significant change since the mid-1970s. In particular, there has been a shift toward greater reliance on local agencies, communities, and refugees themselves.

Following release of the Green Paper in 1974, the Immigrant Settlement Adaptation Program (ISAP) and the Adjustment Assistance Program (AAP) appeared. The former was to constitute a system of "contracting out" to immigrant-settlement agencies in order to provide services to immigrants and refugees.[92] The latter was to provide direct financial support to destitute immigrants and refugees for a discrete period following their arrival.[93] The AAP was distinct from provincial welfare programs, but like them it foresaw serving those deemed to require concentrated services when and where other resources were unavailable rather than seeking to provide for all immigrants and refugees.[94] All state-sponsored refugees were foreseen receiving AAP payments.

These new state funding arrangements were to be monitored by the settlement branch of the Department of Immigration. There and within the newly funded immigrant-settlement agencies,[95] expert counsellors were to deliver special orientation and counselling services to immigrants and refugees and make referrals to manpower/employment centres for work placement, labour-skills acquisition, and language training as deemed necessary.[96] Following release of the Green Paper, the multiculturalism branch of the Department of the Secretary of State was also foreseen funding ethno-cultural organizations for immigrant and refugee integration but over a longer term.[97] Although immigration authorities, which at this juncture operated within a large department comprising both manpower/employment and immigration, were assumed to have responsibility for resettlement of refugees for three years, but after the first year, this responsibility was to be shared with the Department of the Secretary of State.[98] This latter federal-level department of the state, however, was not anticipated supplying direct financial support similar to that provided by the AAP.[99] Among state agencies, the Immigration Department has dominated the refugee-resettlement realm since the release of the Green Paper.

Localization

The ascendancy of an advanced-liberal rationality is evident in resettlement in the appearance of the ISAP. In the early 1970s state agents carried out refugee resettlement from within a bureaucracy that was organized across the nation and that was politically directed: the settlement branch of the Department of Manpower and Immigration. In contrast, the ISAP foresaw nonprofit organizations providing "basic social services in a more personal, integrative and less bureaucratized way than government."[100] Six basic services would now be "purchased" from these newly created settlement organizations across Canada: reception, information, orientation, expert counselling, interpretation and translation, and referral.[101] Employment-related services, the sole preserve of a nationwide system of employment centres staffed with employees of the Department of Manpower and Immigration even after introduction of the ISAP, were later added to this arrangement.[102] Through the ISAP, each of these services was converted into hourly cash terms. A monetary value was assigned, thus making their purchase and audit possible. State settlement officers were now imagined merely monitoring the new ISAP-funded organizations by occasionally visiting their sites to conduct audits of their records in accordance with ISAP agreements.[103] This increased reliance on the audit is also consistent with the onset of advanced liberalism.[104]

Through the ISAP, resettlement of immigrants and refugees was shifted out of the state's purview. Immigrant-settlement agencies became quasi-autonomous nongovernmental organizations (QUANGOs),[105] or "special agencies,"[106] which comprised neither a state bureaucracy subject to the direct commands of political authorities nor, in the strict sense, a private corporation in that their potential customer base was ostensibly limited to the Department of Immigration. This development was accompanied by the introduction of specialized training in larger Canadian cities that imagined fostering self-identity and organization among settlement workers.[107] Consistent with advanced-liberal rule, the ISAP created considerably more distance between political authorities and those who during this period increasingly claimed expert knowledge about how to bring immigrants and refugees in line with the requirements of liberal citizenship.

In 1995 it was decided that the settlement branch of the Department of Immigration, which had continued to monitor delivery of the ISAP and the AAP, would be completely dismantled. The remaining responsibility for resettlement would be transferred from the federal to the provincial state level. Professional "private" settlement agencies would now receive funding directly from the provinces and be policed by provincial state agents. Consonant with the rise of an advanced-liberal rationality, refugee resettlement would now be further localized.

Within resettlement, it had become clear by 1986 that those claimants already in the determination process or arriving at ports of entry every day would – in one way or another – be granted permanent status (thousands had already received status) without having been previously screened by state visa officers using point-system criteria (e.g., education, age, etc.).[108] It was recognized that these claimants had been or soon would be granted status without having been examined to determine whether they possessed qualities and character consistent with emergent liberal citizenship. This reality, coupled with the recognition that during the early 1980s large numbers of family-class immigrants had also bypassed immigration-point selection screening (as noted in the section on determination, immigrant levels began to be significantly reduced in 1983), became the subject of considerable concern.[109] An administrative review subsequently announced in May 1986 promised to address this problem in relation to refugees.

Private Refugee Sponsorship
Provisions for private refugee sponsorship materialized in the 1978 immigration regulations.[110] Immigrants were sponsored to come to Canada through private sponsorship before 1978, but when European refugees were resettled during World Refugee Year in 1959, from Czechoslovakia in 1968, and from Chile in 1973, to mention but three examples, most were financially provided for by the state.[111] These new provisions anticipated groups of at least five Canadians providing financial support to refugees for one year after their arrival or until they became self-supporting, whichever was of shorter duration.[112] In addition, sponsors were envisaged providing refugees with "moral support and general orientation."[113] This program also foresaw established national nonstate organizations guaranteeing sponsorship of large numbers of refugees on behalf of smaller affiliated groups. This was to be realized through special umbrella contracts known as master agreements, with these organizations becoming master-agreement holders (MAHs).[114] MAHs would be left to govern the resettlement activities of their constituent groups without interference from political or immigration authorities. The appearance of this program is consistent with the rise of an advanced-liberal rationality in that it also moved responsibility for refugee resettlement away from political authorities. This legal arrangement was to eventually result in private sponsors having some input into state visa officers' decisions about which individuals would be selected as refugees from camps and crisis situations abroad, decisions previously made by state agents alone.[115] Thus there is a sense in which responsibility for refugee determination affecting migrants *abroad*, in addition to responsibility for inland refugee determination and refugee resettlement, also shifted farther from the reach of political authorities.

Friends and Hosts in the Community
In the early 1980s, shortly after introduction of this private-sponsorship program, concern began to be voiced about the resettlement experiences of state-sponsored refugees.[116] At this point, these refugees were provided on arrival with temporary accommodations as well as basic orientation classes that included information on shopping, banking, home budgeting, modes of dress, and personal hygiene.[117] Refugees were to be aided by Canada Employment Centre (CEC) counsellors in arranging housing, furniture, food, clothing, and various basic household needs as well as in enrolling children in school and making medical or dental appointments.[118] They were also to receive language and employment training through CECs[119] and AAP

support until employment was secured.[120] Yet a 1981 announcement in *Refuge*, "Canada's National Newsletter on Refugees," reads:

> CECs Often Not Enough [headline] ... newcomers needed a greater degree
> of support and personal attention than most CECs in Toronto could pro-
> vide.... For many this is sufficient for them to find their way in their new
> home ... [but] some personal contact with members of the older commu-
> nity seems essential to full integration into society. In some areas the Man-
> power Officers have taken this role on themselves, going into the refugees'
> homes to show them how to cook cheap meals when they can't make ends
> meet on their allowance, running English conversation groups, inviting
> people to dinner in their homes. In other cases, sponsors have endeavoured
> to help the friends of the people they sponsored. But in many communi-
> ties, organized volunteer programmes evolved to meet this deficiency.[121]

In several Canadian cities, where the vast majority of state-sponsored refugees were resettling, various organized volunteer programs arose during this
period to address this "deficiency," programs such as Friendship Families,
Foster Friends, Be a Friend, Canadian Friends, and *Mes Amis de Partout*.[122]
These resettlement programs foresaw some responsibility for the conduct
of state-sponsored refugees during their first year in Canada – previously
assigned exclusively to state agents – shifting to volunteers: "We asked volunteers to work for one half day a week escorting people to medical appointments, helping to enroll children in school, explaining public transit
or helping a family with their shopping."[123]

Such programs sought to make up for the assumed shortcomings of state
refugee resettlement, which were increasingly highlighted in evaluations
of the newer private modes. In some cases, volunteers were to visit state-
sponsored refugees' homes.[124] Such intimate governance, particularly visiting migrants to instruct them on how to manage their private lives, and
related "friendship" discourses are clearly evident in sanctuary occurrences
as well. In other programs, such as the Home Placement Program in Sudbury,
Ontario, refugees were envisaged being placed in volunteers' homes to live
until alternative housing could be found.[125] In Toronto, Friendship Families
were to administer much of the program, including general office work,
social activities, volunteer recruitment, and giving media interviews regarding the program.[126] As private sponsorship was touted, so was the increased
efficiency of these new programs.[127] The newsletter *Refuge*, for example, notes
that "each host family is given $45 a week per person for room and board,
which represents an enormous savings to the government."[128]

In March 1985 a national pilot Host Program for refugee resettlement was
launched in seven Canadian cities.[129] Like earlier Friendship Families arrangements, this program anticipated volunteers aligned with Canadian

private groups and organizations – that is, the type of authority already imagined resettling privately sponsored refugees within the Friendship Families Program – also becoming involved with state-sponsored refugees.[130] It foresaw the transfer of AAP funds to cover costs and a coordinator to recruit hosts, matching them with newly arrived individual refugees or refugee families, and then overseeing hosts' subsequent resettlement practices, which were to include teaching English or French and helping refugees to secure employment.[131]

Besides reducing costs and CEC counsellors' workloads, this program sought to effect "more rapid adaptation to community life in Canada."[132] Refugee resettlement was to be enhanced "through community-based human resources" and to be conducted by "an established community organization."[133] Refugees were to be resettled within and through communities. This marked emphasis on "community," although not completely replacing "society" in programmatic statements,[134] is consistent with localization. Three years later, the Host Program was extended to ten Canadian cities in six provinces.[135] Again "community" was a principal signifier in programmatic statements and in the talk of Host Program coordinators.[136] An emphasis on community is also evident in sanctuary discourse, but there it fits with the presence of a nonstate sovereign and pastoral power rather than serving as the principal, if not exclusive, governmental element of advanced liberalism.

In 1990 it was announced that the pilot Host Program would be made permanent and expanded to target immigrants.[137] The rationale continued to be efficiency: the services provided by hosts in the community would be delivered "sooner," "faster," and "better" than those provided through state resettlement efforts alone.[138] Private-sponsorship and host programs promised to resettle refugees at a reduced cost that greatly appealed to the new neoliberal immigration economists who arose during this period to expertly identify the refugee category of migrants as more risky to the national economy than other Canadian migrant categories (e.g., the business, independent, and to a much lesser extent, family classes).[139] Similar programs continued through the 1990s and into the 2000s.[140]

Partnerships
Various authorities have become increasingly responsible for refugees, more involved in governing their conduct and fate in light of conceptions of what is normal, good, and efficient.[141] A new form of association has been emerging along with this gradual shift of responsibility from the state to an assortment of "nonpolitical" authorities. Together these varied associations have promised to allow refugees to be governed "at a distance"[142] and have enhanced the state's capacity to achieve particular goals, such as successfully resettling a designated number of refugees in Canada on the basis of

targets set for a given year. That state agents have become less involved in administering the lives of resettled refugees and that these other authorities have become more involved raises a question about the form that these alliances have been taking. To be sure, some associations, especially those between immigration authorities and professional immigrant-settlement organizations, are maintained primarily through ISAP funding arrangements and related audits, but for others, language, understood here as having a performative role, is crucial. The predominant form of association in refugee resettlement, as in many other contemporary domains,[143] is the partnership. Reference to "partnerships" was not present in early programmatic statements, such as the 1966 White and 1974 Green Papers, but since the mid-1970s this key signifier has become ubiquitous.

Advanced-liberal programmatic statements are to include the term "partner." At the Ontario Conference on Refugee Resettlement held in November 1984, the Inter-Church Committee for Refugees presented a brief that reads: "The resettlement of every refugee in Canada is the shared responsibility of the government and private sector, working in *partnership* to ensure the successful reception and integration of refugees in Canadian communities ... the several *partners* which contribute to the resettlement of refugees should be allowed to contribute what their particular organizational form, powers, insights, and limitations allow them to do best. *Partnership* responsibilities should be determined according to the skills, and limitations of each *partner*."[144]

Partnerships are to be formed within and between state departments and among nonstate agencies. The former is seen in an immigration report from the mid-1990s wherein it is suggested that departmental priorities are to include: "Supporting effective *partnerships* within the department and between the department and its key stakeholders. CIC [Canada Immigration Commission] will continue to work to identify opportunities to create and strengthen *partnerships* in each region and to work together with traditional and non-traditional *partners*."[145] The latter is evident in a 1997 issue of the *Centre for Refugee Studies Newsletter*: "This project has allowed the Centre for Refugee Studies [at Ontario's York University] to develop further *partnerships* with professionals in NGO settings."[146]

Within advanced liberalism, the term "partner" has acquired moral overtones. Partnering has become the proper, civilized way to relate. Good associations are those based on good partnerships, whereas bad associations are those involving bad partnerships. Alliances between authorities are increasingly problematized in terms of partnership. For example, responding to a policy change in sponsorship arrangements by immigration authorities in 1979, the Standing Conference of Canadian Organizations Concerned for Refugees, which later became the CCR, stated: "We demand recognition of our expertise and insist on our right to participate in decision-making. We want a regular process of consultation and dialogue before decisions are made if we are to be true *partners* ... In the light of the above we urge the government to reconsider its recent policy decision to change the nature of our *partnership*."[147]

The "partnership way" entails "really hearing" one another, and dialogue is crucial to such a relationship. It is not difficult to see how the concept of partnership fits an advanced-liberal rationality that presumes the state to be unfit to accomplish the "conduct of conduct" on its own. To be sure, state agents are to continue to be involved in forging habits but in a more distant and decidedly reduced capacity. They are now to be accompanied by a variety of other authorities who are seeking to accomplish specific goals. The concept of partnership corresponds to an advanced-liberal rationality that specifies this reduction in the reach and power of the state and that demands the state's commensurate alignment with other authorities in order to accomplish "government at a distance." Such a rationality imagines that there are more parts, or roles, to be filled. Partnering is also consistent with the more enterprising subject specified in advanced-liberal discourse: the rational, bold subject assumed to have an inclination to associate with like-minded entities in the fearless pursuit of particular goals. Partnerships are, of course, inconsistent with emotional devotion, spiritual obligation, social bonding, and rigid bureaucratic requirements. Partnerships, whether between management and labour, two individuals in cohabitation, or state and nonstate agencies to resettle refugees, are to be flexible, business-like ventures. They are foreseen as investments whereby everybody wins, undertakings wherein the implicated parties do not remain silent, subsist, and survive but rather consult, prosper, and thrive. Notions of culture, intimate needs, and oppression are, of course, absent in such a relationship. Meaning, feeling, and perpetual outcomes to the advantage of one partner over another are unthinkable here. Such notions are omitted from the rosy partnership pictures that are always framed a bit in the future, slightly out of reach in time, and according to any given project's quarterly business report, never quite accomplished. It is not with reference to these notions but rather through dialogue, flexibility, and adherence to their parts in the instrumental venture that partners will accomplish the larger goal next time around, perhaps even in the next quarter.

Since the release of the Green Paper, then, responsibility for refugee resettlement has moved farther from the direct reach of political authorities. There has been a move away from state agencies to a complex mixture of "private" community-based settlement agencies, church and community sponsors, host volunteers, and refugees themselves. This has been accompanied by the rise to prominence of "community" and a new form of association, the partnership.

Responsibilizing Refugees

Other evidence of the rise of an advanced-liberal rationality is seen in the appearance of programs that imagined refugees taking more responsibility for their own resettlement in a variety of ways. During this period, conferences began to be held in which the prevailing theme was empowerment,[148] such as the "Empower the Most Vulnerable" workshop: "Improving refugee programs implies using resources more efficiently, increasing the opportunities for refugees to assume responsibility for their own management and programs, and ensuring that programs benefit everybody in the community – men, women, children, and the most vulnerable."[149]

Advanced liberalism's rise is also seen in the announcement, in 1995, that refugees and immigrants would be required to pay a $975 right of landing fee.[150] This fee was in addition to the $500 fee for processing an application for landed-immigrant status for adults,[151] which doubled from $125 to $250 in the early 1990s and then doubled again in 1994.[152] If the introduction of these fees during this period appears trivial, it should be noted that by 1996 the right of landing fee was expected to generate more than half the total annual federal cost of resettlement programs (including the AAP, the ISAP, and the Host Program).[153] A refugee's future legal status became a right to be purchased. A fee would be paid in order to exercise a right. This is advanced-liberal rule *par excellence*. This imagined increase in refugees' responsibility is also seen in, among other changes, the fact that the Refugee Studies Program at York University began to encourage their participation.[154] Good research about the resettlement of refugees became "refugee-centred" research.[155] Increasingly, bona fide refugees were imagined resettling themselves.

Failed Refugee Claimants

By the early 1990s, sanctuary incidents were becoming more prevalent in Canada. Undoubtedly, this is due in large part to sanctuary's visibility and corresponding successes, but it is also partially a result of changes in Canadian refugee and immigration policies, trends that began in the early 1980s and continued through the 1990s and into the early 2000s. These changes have had implications for how numerous migrants – especially those unsuccessful in the refugee-determination process in Canada – have been perceived. Many have been regarded as incapable of taking on new (and proper) responsibility, as lacking purchasing power, and therefore as failed liberal subjects, which is to say, as burdens lacking both moral and financial potential to become active autonomous subjects once resettled in Canada. When deemed active, autonomous subjects, many of these migrants have been imagined to be of the wrong sort, in some cases to have actively marched so far down criminal or other immoral paths that there is no hope of their return. In other instances, consistent with the inadmissible categories of immigration law, they have been deemed unfit not only morally, but also economically, mentally, or physically,[156] and have been policed with the ostensible aim of securing the population's "wealth, health, and happiness."[157] Assumed to possess intractable deficiencies along these lines, these migrants have been assumed to be "hopeless cases"[158] or "chronically unimprovable"[159] and consequently worthy only of efficient, permanent removal from the nation and, by implication, from the communities supporting them. Clearly capturing such a neoliberal regard for one migrant at the centre of a sanctuary incident is a letter to a local newspaper editor:

> Romero's plight is exactly that – his plight. Our government deemed him unsuitable as a citizen and thereby ordered him deported back to his native El Salvador. That should have been the end of that, but ... Romero is determined to become yet another tax burden on us. The government does care about the welfare of people and families, which would account for their decision to deport someone who is admittedly in bad health and unable to contribute to society in a vital and constructive manner. With the funding cuts in the health care field and the cutbacks, the rest of us do not want the added responsibility of individuals such as Romero ... Whatever happens in El Salvador, so be it.[160]

The legitimacy of reductions in public health-care provisions is taken for granted here, as is the systematic rollback of the welfare state (i.e., "the cutbacks"). Yet, in such a context, reductions provide greater license to dispose of those deemed "unsuitable" as citizens and otherwise unable "to contribute to society in a vital and constructive manner." Responsibility for "his plight" lies not with society or "the rest of us" but with the migrant himself. Consistent with the reassignment of such responsibility, it is taken for granted that by seeking sanctuary he is "determined to become yet another tax burden on us." The local immigration manager involved in the incident echoed this: "As long as he stays in the church, he *doesn't cost taxpayers any money*, but if he steps out, he'll be arrested."[161]

Evident in sanctuary discourse is the unambiguous conflict between such liberal rationalities and pastoral rationalities. At times, this conflict has taken the acute form of a contrast between the business immigrant choosing to immigrate by investing in the nation and the would-be refugee "spontaneously" arriving at the airport in need of care and support. For example, consistent with neoliberal refugee and immigration policies, in one incident, a letter of support for a migrant in sanctuary from a member of the clergy in the same city contrasts the migrant's predicament with that of migrants within one of the relatively newer business-immigrant categories:

Had Ms. N come into the country with a quarter of a million dollars [the amount required at the time to establish eligibility for Canada's business-investor immigrant category] – either to invest in a country inn or to pay the retainer of a senior member of the bar – she would long since have been landed, and she and her children would have been able to get on with their lives.[162]

In the same way, during a Christian television talk show focused on a local sanctuary incident a caller noted: "The issue is if you have money, you can get into the country, and you can get a visa if you have $150,000. And they're all fronted with a lot of money, and these poor people don't have the money, and it simply boils down to the haves and the have-nots."[163] In another instance: "For Marchi [the immigration minister], *bucks obviously count more than need*. If Mauricio had a quarter of a million dollars to put into some spurious Canadian investment, the system would welcome him with open arms."[164]

Most sanctuary providers revealed little knowledge of the neoliberal nature of refugee and immigration policies and selection criteria *prior* to being drawn into an incident. This is perhaps not surprising since the vast majority of providers were citizens who, in the daily course of their lives, would not have been immediately aware of the broad shifts in refugee and immigration policies discussed above – unless their churches or other refugee-sponsor groups had encountered difficulties in sponsoring relatives or refugees wanting to immigrate from abroad. But these providers learned of the new nature of such policies shortly after granting sanctuary, as they commenced the complex search for alternatives to deportation of the migrants in their midst. Providers came up against policies that refused status through immigrant streams (as well as via refugee selection abroad) to persons who were deemed needful but who were also thought to be "improvable" and potentially "good immigrants": mostly young, physically healthy individuals and families who had worked and volunteered in providers' local communities for months or years or who had extensive family support there. Thus providers also recognized that the migrants they had come to know intimately in sanctuary had left their nations to seek legal status in Canada through the only means available: the refugee-determination process. As a consequence, whether the migrants were truly refugees whose experiences plainly fit the UN Convention on which this process is based was often not providers' foremost concern. Sanctuary providers typically sought a different "truth" with respect to refugees, one that was consistent with a pastoral rationality and that correspondingly focused to a large extent on migrants' individual needs.

Conclusion

Consistent with the onset of advanced liberalism since the 1970s, refugee resettlement has been moving out of the reach of formal political authorities and increasingly becoming the responsibility of communities and churches, a process that has included the increased input of communities and churches into refugee determination overseas through the private-sponsorship program. During the same period, as refugee determination has likewise moved away from the state, it has undergone juridification. This has led, among other developments, to a need for adequate legal representation of refugee claimants and a more prominent role for refugee and immigration lawyers. Failed claimants, in particular, have increasingly been considered incapable of taking on the new responsibilities accompanying these changes. These are among the conditions of possibility that explain the rise of sanctuary incidents involving these migrants since 1983.

4
Sanctuary as Sovereign Power

On 20 January 1984 "Raphael" twice became the object of a sovereign power, one emanating from church and community, the other from the nation-state. Sanctuary provides insight into this form of power. A close examination reveals that sanctuary is about making the exception and therefore is consonant with the notion that sovereign power is not always coercive. In this context, minister's permits, granted by the immigration minister to allow those about to be deported to remain in Canada, make a similar suggestion. As sovereign power, sanctuary also entails the control of territory and shows an affinity for spectacle. In these ways sanctuary indicates that sovereign power is not restricted to the nation-state but can flow from other spaces and sources. This chapter first considers sovereign power as making the exception in the sanctuary context and then proceeds to discuss sanctuary as territory and spectacle. Next, failed spectacles and hunger strikes – resistances to sovereign power from outside and inside sanctuary – are discussed. Finally, in the chapter's conclusion, how sovereign power is distinguished from and relates to governmental power is considered.

Making the Exception
When sovereign power (or sovereignty) is discussed in governmentality studies, it is often associated with coercion, consistent with the opening chapters of Michel Foucault's *Discipline and Punish*. In his horrific account of the "spectacle of the scaffold," it takes the form of extreme, symbolic punitiveness that flows from a central source and finds its corporeal target in the human body.[1] Since Foucault, this source has been typically assumed to be a monarch or, in the contemporary era, the nation-state. Less often noted, however, is that sovereign power is about making *and unmaking* laws. Foucault writes: "The sovereign was present at the execution not only as the power exacting the vengeance of the law, but as the power that could suspend both law and vengeance."[2] Although questions have been raised about Giorgio Agamben's more recent account of sovereign power, particularly its

claim to complete or correct Foucault's alleged insistence that sovereign power had been surpassed by bio-power,[3] its greater value may well lie in implying that sovereign power can be but is not *necessarily* coercive. Agamben borrows from Carl Schmitt's earlier account of sovereignty and, specifically, from his notion that a "sovereign is he who decides on the exception."[4] Thus sovereign power can be better understood as a monopoly to decide the exception rather than only as a monopoly to coerce, punish, or exclude. Coercion and salvation are two sides of the same coin. It is not the outcome of a decision but the capacity to make the decision and to have it obeyed that renders the decision sovereign. In the context of sanctuary, the exception can entail coercion and exclusion, but also sudden suspension and inclusion through the granting of sanctuary or the issuance of a minister's permit or other reprieves to migrants facing deportation and possible death.

As in the sanctuary incident involving "Raphael" in 1983, in 2002 a reprieve was granted to a migrant family in sanctuary. At a press conference, the minister of immigration announced this decision as "an exceptional measure for an exceptional situation."[5] As noted in Chapter 2's discussion of sanctuary outcomes, few humanitarian and compassionate applications yielded positive outcomes for migrants in sanctuary. Ministerial discretion in the form of a minister's permit is an exception and therefore can be sovereign in character. In the case of decisions made on humanitarian and compassionate grounds, this sovereign aspect is also reflected in the absence of an indication of the timing or reason for the decision. Announcements of decisions were bereft of explanations of when and why. Following a migrant's application on such grounds, the decision tended to appear suddenly and to adopt the form of a terse "yes" or "no."[6] The answer was: "Just no. No reasons were given. 'Your application has been denied,' and that was it."[7] In another incident:

> Provider 1: You get back a piece of paper that just says "no." It didn't say "no, sorry."
> Provider 2: "You're not good enough, no we don't believe you're story." "No" nothing. Just "no."[8]

Such decisions contrast markedly with routine legal decisions of the Immigration and Refugee Board (IRB) regarding refugee status, which correspond to a relatively coherent and extended schedule and are accompanied by lengthy explanation. (These excerpts also illustrate providers' perceptions of immigration law as arbitrary, as discussed in Chapter 6.)

Where more explanation is evident, it was typically used to highlight the exceptional character of the decision. Toward the end of one incident, a minister's permit was granted to allow the migrant in sanctuary to be privately sponsored to stay in Canada. Communication between a local immigration office and national and regional immigration headquarters about this private undertaking of assistance included draft "media lines": "We need to establish media lines as we will have to face media upon resolution of the case. I propose to work with our communications people locally with draft lines to be discussed with R [the migrant's lawyer]." The "lines" read:

> M's medical condition makes him medically inadmissible to Canada ... This section of the Act protects Canadians from having to absorb the cost associated with an illness that an immigrant has when they apply to enter Canada. *This case is unique in several ways*: None of Mr. M's immediate family live in [nation], they are living in Canada. New facts that were gathered revealed that although the medication Mr. M requires for his illness is available in [nation], the therapy that also helps to manage his illness is not. Nor is it clear whether or not Mr. M would be able to access the available medication. Despite these *new facts* ... Immigration still had concerns surrounding the costs associated with Mr. M's illness. Mr. M is fortunate to have a network of family and friends who brought these *new facts* to the attention of the department, and who have also taken a legal commitment to cover all costs associated with his illness.[9]

Precedent was to be avoided here. There is no reference to political persecution that would invite refugee claimants of the same nationality facing deportation to come forward with similar claims and reasons to remain in Canada. "New facts" are noted, but reference to "old" errors in related previous refugee determination proceedings or to subsequent risk assessments upon which both were ostensibly based are omitted.

Yet, in the sanctuary context, churches and communities have also decided who will be included or excluded from protection. What has gone unrecognized in previous US and media accounts of sanctuary[10] is that churches and communities have their own selection and exclusion procedures,[11] which are distinct from but nevertheless parallel to elaborate refugee-determination procedures and exclusion mechanisms administered by the nation-state. This fact reveals sanctuary as an instance of sovereign power and suggests that the exception does not necessarily always refer back, in a majestic manner, to the state, the Constitution, or as Carl Schmitt refers to it: "a case of extreme peril, a danger to the existent of the state, or the like."[12] Rather, the exception can refer to a specific program and to the law that enables it.

Chapter 2 notes that sanctuary is granted as migrants near the end of the line. Across incidents, decisions to grant sanctuary were consistently claimed to be "a last resort."[13] In 1998 a member of the Southern Ontario Sanctuary

Coalition (SOSC) noted receiving "a call every month from someone asking for sanctuary," and according to a founder of the SOSC, *most often the answer is no.*"[14] The only clergy member in Canada directly involved in more than one incident said: "I have turned people away because I didn't think their life was in danger ... but these two people's lives are threatened."[15] This pastor had "fielded almost weekly requests for sanctuary in the last 18 months, all involving refugees."[16] Regarding the 1993 SOSC incident, a provider remarked:

> We decided that we would be very careful about the cases that we undertake. We would ... not take on any cases that we thought would not be absolutely ironclad ... We did not want to be caught taking on a case that turned out to be obviously filled with distortions and perjury and all sorts of stuff. So we settled on twenty-three cases.[17]

Being granted sanctuary is the exception, not the rule. The SOSC stated at their press conference in 1993: "We are here today to say that *extraordinary* measures must be taken to protect the lives of genuine refugees."[18] Few migrants requesting sanctuary were granted it. Echoing the immigration minister's claim in 2002, the minutes of a sanctuary strategy meeting from another incident read: "This is *not a typical situation*, sanctuary *is not granted often*, [and] the case is *exceptional in all aspects*."[19] In a distinct instance, a lawyer for a church indicated:

> I've developed a three-tiered test. The first test: Has the IRB and Citizenship and Immigration Canada respected its own norms, its own standards, its own procedures? Okay. Secondly, have I received reliable information that perhaps the IRB did not have access to which would call upon a reasonable person to view the basis of the claim in a new way? And thirdly, are there *extraordinary humanitarian considerations* that justify the intervention on the part of the church?[20]

This lawyer added: "I must underscore the fact that as a result of that experience ... I have to say no many times."[21]

It is nevertheless worth noting that although attention to the IRB's processes would perhaps be expected from a lawyer more than from providers from other professions or from the clergy, it is significant that "humanitarian considerations" – that is, a focus on migrants' human needs rather than only on the "extraordinary" (or exceptional) character of migrants' predicaments – are included in his test. One implication of this inclusion, as was evinced in most other incidents, is that a migrant's solid request for sanctuary, a solid refugee claim in front of the IRB, and an exceptional situation, although perhaps often overlapping, are not equivalent. These represent differing "truths" of refugees, shaped by different powers and rationalities.

Significantly, precisely as immigration authorities seek to avoid precedents, so do churches and communities, whose members therefore deploy the language of exception and uniqueness in decisions to grant sanctuary.[22] A provider explained:

> Here's the dilemma. If these were not real refugees, would we be essentially condoning initiatives by different groups of claimants who might down the line decide to occupy church buildings or other public buildings? ... Were we giving a message that it's okay to engage in this kind of enterprise? What kind of message were we giving?[23]

Providers repeatedly expressed concern that granting sanctuary would encourage others to seek it. On a Christian television talk show, the lawyer representing the migrants in sanctuary noted: "So that's why I'm saying it's not a precedent-setting thing where you're going to have churches extending their arms left and right. *It's very unique.*"[24] In some instances, providers reported that migrants to whom they granted sanctuary had previously been refused sanctuary by other churches in the same community:[25] "And so part of that six days was used trying to find sanctuary. I tried ... six churches and [then] the Unitarian Church ... said yes."[26] Undoubtedly, partially due to the exposure that sanctuary generated, churches and communities were occasionally later contacted by migrants in similar predicaments,[27] and although they sometimes offered advice and encouragement, they ultimately refused these migrants similar protection.[28] In another incident, sanctuary was refused to migrants from another community:

> While the M's were in sanctuary ... there were phone calls that alerted us to the fact that there was a group [of migrants] in [Canadian city] ... who had heard about this situation and were interested in coming to Y and putting out feelers as to whether they could come to this church ... So ... it was during a meeting ... [that] R was on the phone for a long time explaining that the church could not afford, that we were not equipped, [that] we didn't have the facilities or the money [to grant them sanctuary]. It was a small parish in a small town, and there was no way that we could help them [i.e., the other migrants] out. So it didn't happen, but we were quite worried that they were going to come anyway. And there was this Sunday morning ... we had this sort of a watch at the church. R and I stayed outside, and one of the other ... [sanctuary group members] was sort of the vanguard ... What were we going to do if this crowd of migrants shows up?[29]

That sanctuary is about a form of sovereign power is also seen in the single instance in which a church decided to expel the migrants already in sanctuary.[30] The migrants

> wanted to take back all the rules. Basically, they broke every one of the three conditions that we set for them. They wouldn't cooperate with their lawyer ... There were lots of fights going on between the coterie and the [migrant] families, and the coterie was always [saying], "Well think of everyone else," and the families were saying, "No we want to think of ourselves." And then eventually it all sort of fell apart. I informed the police that we were going to have them kicked out and that they might not go voluntarily. I said that I wanted this done without force, that even if someone had to be removed, I wanted it done in such a way ... The police came, probably about thirty of them, and a very nice individual went down and negotiated them out ... What we had to arrange for them was that they were not going to be picked up by immigration [authorities]. They were just going to be asked to leave. And I managed to talk ... [to] immigration and say that ... I want them out of the place, but I don't want them picked up by immigration... This is not going to be an immigration raid. This is just a police action to have them removed from the building, and they are to be able to get into a vehicle and leave ... I negotiated this with them. And they left, and they were put into a van and taken away.[31]

Therefore, many migrants were undoubtedly rejected by the IRB and the minister of immigration *and* by churches and communities,[32] which is to say that these migrants received reprieves from neither sovereign.

Where the decision to grant sanctuary was concerned, as suggested above, a distinction tended to be made between the migrants who were seeking it. In one incident:

> You've got to really make sure it's a very solid request ... [and not] *just because someone doesn't want to go back to their country* because you'll squander the goodwill of your congregation because ... they could be there [in sanctuary] for years.[33]

Typically, where sovereign power was concerned, the initial distinction was between those whose "lives are in danger" and "economic refugees who can't prove they face physical danger."[34] In a different case, cited above:

> There are a lot of Colombians ... that want to become Canadian. But they don't all have these stories of torture and horror. Some of them have just come here because it's a much safer place to live than where they have been

living, and they've heard that there are work opportunities and that life would be better for them.[35]

The distinction here is consistent with Agamben's suggestion that sovereign power requires "bare life" – that is, life that can be "killed but not sacrificed."[36] Reference to migrants' sacrifice is entirely absent in sanctuary discourse. It is assumed that little remains of migrants' circumstances, identities, and lives that can be sacrificed. Providers' lives, rather than those of migrants, eventually become the sacrificial terrain of sanctuary incidents. When sovereign power excludes migrants (what Agamben refers to as "inclusion through exclusion"),[37] such as in immigration detention,[38] migrants are imagined neither as self-regulating nor as needy and obedient but instead as "bare life." But this is also true of sovereign decisions that make exceptions to *include* migrants in the polity or local community. These decisions, on which Agamben is silent, are ostensibly of more relevance here.

Sanctuary providers and immigration and IRB officials recognized one another's capacity to make the exception in this respect. In one instance, a decision by the Appeal Division of the IRB to allow a migrant family in sanctuary to remain in Canada explicitly recognized that granting sanctuary was also about making the exception. This fact was used to bolster the IRB decision and, more generally, to save face in light of "a lot of support from the Arab community in Canada, Toronto-area Members of Parliament, and members of the general public":[39]

> [I]f everyone sought to evade enforcement of immigration decisions by seeking sanctuary in church basements, the enforcement system would be rendered meaningless. Without condoning the actions of the applicants, their actions were influenced by their desperate situation. One can imagine that *not all persons trying to evade deportation* would evoke such sympathy and support from a church, and one can only assume that [c]hurch leaders in this country would reserve their church basements for only those deserving of sympathy.[40]

Conversely, in a separate incident, a sanctuary provider noted that

> we have a minister for a reason. The minister is there for when the system does not catch everything. This is one of the exceptions where the minister should have intervened ... She should have done it very quickly ... [and] said: "Look this is a humanitarian case. They are not refugees. I respect that the [determination] system said they were not refugees; however, I am giving them a minister's permit because of the *special situation of this family*."[41]

The recognition of other sovereigns is also evident in a sanctuary provider's personal letter to the minister of immigration that noted "the ostensible need (as reported unofficially from within the ministry) for you [i.e., the minister] to have some *unique reasons for making an exception* in this case."[42]

Another sovereign was thus recognized in sanctuary discourse, but this was tantamount neither to agreement with nor to an absence of moral indignation toward this other sovereign. In one incident, a provider noted regarding a migrant family:

> They were embraced by the community. Why don't [sic] the federal government listen – if a couple or a family lands in Y, and Y's willing to look after them, and Y is willing to help them – then why doesn't the federal government mind their own damn business? They don't know this family ... If a church takes a family in and the whole congregation rallies around that family, then why don't they trust the communities? ... Do you think I'm going to spend months in the church basement [protecting] ... the family if I don't believe in them? And if you ask anybody around Y about me, I'm a person that has integrity in this community. I've built it up all my life, and I would spend months in the basement of a church for a family that's not worthwhile to be in Canada? Come on. Give your head a shake.[43]

A provider from a separate community remarked:

> By refusing to engage in any dialogue on this issue, [Minister of Immigration] Elinor Caplan is thumbing her nose at a very broad range of the Y community. This issue is ... also about the government's lack of accountability to this community.[44]

In another incident, cited below, it was noted during a protest and blockade of an international bridge to the US that "the community feels it is totally unacceptable that the Minister of Immigration has not responded to our communications."[45] The exercise of sovereign power is directed toward opposing sovereigns who "thumbed their nose," acted in a "totally unacceptable" manner, and ought to have minded their "own damn business." In part, this exercise is an attempt to outflank the other (morally inferior) sovereign by granting an exception.

Territory

Foucault's seminal essay on governmentality notes that territory is the "very foundation" of sovereignty,[46] which is also a feature of orthodox conceptions of sovereignty.[47] The inclusion and exclusion of outsiders is about territorial control.[48] While nation-states such as Canada are defined in territorial terms, sanctuary is also about territory, as one provider noted:

In the Old Testament ... you have the tradition of people taking sanctuary ... if they grabbed onto the horns of the altar ... They were in some kind of sanctuary and the medieval concept of sanctuary, where people would go and place themselves in a church, and that would be *territory that the local king or prince couldn't infringe upon.*[49]

In another incident, immigration personnel were no longer permitted entry to what had become sanctuary. It had been taken over and rendered foreign:

There were people within the [immigration] border guards that go to that church that the family was in sanctuary. And some of them were not allowed to go to church. For the 388 days, they couldn't attend their own church because they couldn't be in the same building as the family.[50]

Sanctuary's territorial borders were to be protected, if necessary, in another incident:

And I eventually received the private phone number of the president of the [provincial] Federation of Labour that, if, by any chance, the feds should ever come in and try to take these children and take M, [we could] call this number and the [provincial] Federation of Labour would be here to *surround the church within minutes.*[51]

Church buildings did not entirely correspond to the territory of sanctuary (nor did these buildings directly correspond to pastoral spaces, as noted in Chapter 5). In one instance, a space within the church building was to remain secret because it was feared that immigration authorities might invade sanctuary's territory:

I took M and ... showed him a secret place where the family could go, a place in the church where they could go should something like that happen and if they had the time to get out of where they were ... It might buy them a little time, time for us perhaps to get in touch with the lawyer or something. And maybe it gave them a little feeling of greater security knowing that they wouldn't be quite so vulnerable in their quarters. So we left a flashlight there and maybe some blankets ... and no one knew about that. The children didn't even know about that. I told him not to even tell the children because I was afraid they might ... mention it.[52]

As well, the territory of sanctuary gradually expanded during some incidents. In one, sanctuary was at first limited to the walls of the church, but then "the [migrant] children were starting to play outdoors, at first under supervision, then as time went by, on their own. The church parking lot became a beehive of activity as children in the immediate neighbourhood also came to play."[53] In another, "sometimes, because we consider that the grounds are sanctuary [and] safe as the church itself, they go outside, and they can be seen playing on the lawn."[54] Consistent with this notion, another provider, following concern about immigration authorities entering sanctuary to make arrests early on, referred to "pushing the boundaries":

After they'd been with us for about a year, we just started taking liberties ... We weren't aware that anybody was sitting in an unmarked car watching the door, and so we started ... *pushing the boundaries* a little, and there's a paved parking lot just outside the basement windows here, and the kitchen windows actually are just above the counter space. So the kids would just be outside playing, going in and out through the windows and the door ... The kids got to go out.[55]

This flexibility of sanctuary's territorial boundaries was mentioned in a somewhat humorous light by a provider who was obviously aware of sanctuary's affinity for spectacle, discussed below. He recalled saying to another provider:

"I've got the answer ... We get one of the those big yellow school buses, particularly one with 'Christian Fundamentalist Church' [written] on the side, and we'll put a table in there ... and we're going to bless this, and we're going to turn it into an altar, and we're going to back that up to the door, and we're going to walk M out there, and we'll say [to the immigration authorities]: 'Will you contact [i.e., arrest] him? He's still on church property.'"[56]

Another provider related: "She would sit in the sun sometimes ... This is church property. This is sanctuary. It's outside, so you can sit out here."[57] But there was a clear concern that migrants *could* be arrested if they moved beyond sanctuary's territory. In one instance: "Sometimes they'd go out and sit on the steps, but they didn't go for walks."[58] In another:

We wouldn't let M out of the church because if they didn't want to invade the church, they might get him if he walks out. In fact, he took exercise in a little fenced-in place behind the church, which is outside, and there was a[n] ... oval path where he walked in the grass.[59]

Sanctuary's territorial borders became extended to an entire community during an incident mentioned earlier:

And at one point we caught wind that [a] ... whole whack of them were going to come down from [Canadian city] and were going to join in sanctuary in our church with our family. We understood that they were going to come down and ... get on the bandwagon while things were good. *We actually stood around town ... and guarded the church during the Sunday service and guarded the door to make sure that some [migrants] ... didn't enter into the sanctuary at the time of the church service. And we locked the church door.*[60]

This territorial aspect of sovereign power distinguishes it from (mere) discretionary power.[61] Yet it remains difficult to always distinguish sovereign and governmental powers on the basis of space,[62] which is especially evident when sanctuary's pastoral spaces are considered in detail, as in Chapter 5. Sovereignty's affinity for spectacle may be a more distinctive feature of this form of power.

Spectacle

For sovereign power to be consistent with Foucault's conception in *Discipline and Punish,* it requires an affinity for spectacle. Although thousands of migrants are "removed" from Canada annually,[63] it is exceedingly rare for these exclusions to be depicted in mass media. Deportation is almost entirely "withdrawn from the public eye."[64] In Canada expulsion of migrants often has not been accomplished by physical force and coercion. Rather, "departure notices" or their equivalent have been issued, provisions that are dependent on migrants' compliance. Only eventual failure to "depart" leads to a deportation order and to later physical arrest and removal. In contrast to the US context, in Canada very few of the thousands of failed refugee claimants produced by the refugee-determination system every year are held in detention facilities, such as Toronto's infamous "Celebrity Inn," to await deportation.[65] Whether or not migrants are detained, deportation orders can be suspended during their wait through a successful review on humanitarian and compassionate grounds that leads to issuance of a temporary minister's permit; through a positive preremoval risk assessment, which determines the likelihood that a deported migrant will undergo harm in the country of return; or through a stay of the deportation order by the Federal Court of Canada.[66]

This is not to say that the occasional mass detentions and deportations and other mass exclusions of migrants have not become spectacles, as was evident in 1999 when a boatload of Chinese migrants off Canada's West Coast was detained.[67] However, granting a minister's permit or reversing a deportation order either by sudden ministerial intervention on humanitarian and compassionate grounds or for other unique reasons may well possess as much spectacular potential. About the sovereign suspension of punishment, Foucault writes: "And it never appeared with more spectacular effect than when it interrupted the executioner's gesture with a letter of pardon. The short time that usually elapsed between sentence and execution (often a few hours) meant that the pardon usually arrived at the very last moment."[68] The timing of the issuance of minister's permits, like the pardon's interruption, as well as the fact that exceptions are by definition statistically rare, are among the sources of their affinity for spectacle.[69] The temporal aspects of such decisions help to make them spectacular. For example, if "Raphael" had not been granted sanctuary, his deportation would have been unspectacular, but, in January 1984 the minister of immigration *suddenly and publicly announced* that his and other scheduled deportations to Guatemala would be suspended.[70]

Sanctuary can similarly become a spectacle portraying the power of the local church and community to make an exception where members of the community are concerned.[71] Sanctuary's affinity for spectacle is intimately connected to its exceptional character, its uniqueness. Because it is rare, sanctuary can attract attention. It is also sanctuary's archaic aura, its tradition, that can contribute to its spectacle, to the cinematic production of a sense that it belonged to the distant past and ought to have been surpassed long ago by modern legal institutions and processes.[72] As discussed in Chapter 6, tradition was drawn upon to authorize sanctuary, specifically by invoking forms of "higher" law. With its peculiar rituals and implied divine power to keep minions of the nation-state at bay, sanctuary is tethered to both rarity and antiquity. Consistent with this fact, early on in some incidents, there were reenactments of the ritualistic accompaniment of migrants by providers into sanctuary and media opportunities to photograph or videotape migrants sitting safely in the pews, back-grounded by the churches' protective walls and ornate stained glass. Peculiar and arcane details of sanctuary were occasionally incorporated into these spectacles. For example, one newspaper reported: "Ecclesiastical law said that a fugitive who had touched the knocker on the church door was immune from arrest. For that reason, the knocker was called the sanctuary ring."[73]

A first strategic step to achieving such spectacle in sanctuary incidents was to alert mass-media outlets that the migrants in question had entered the protective territory of the church. An SOSC member remarked: "We had a press conference at the church to announce it. We made a statement. We said we would take a civil initiative."[74] In no instance was the granting of church sanctuary first discovered by mass-media personnel and then displayed.

Consistent with a division of labour in sanctuary provision, in most incidents, a sanctuary provider was assigned the task of programming media relations on behalf of the migrants.[75] One such provider noted:

I phoned the Immigration Department and told them unless they gave him a fair hearing [that] I was going to consider putting him in sanctuary ... I immediately had all the press involved – television stations, radio stations, papers, the works ... It was in the paper almost daily.[76]

In another incident:

He was desperately alone, and he was being pursued. So we found this place that would give him sanctuary, and we needed public opinion to help us pressure the government ministers to do something decent. And so ... I had a day with the press, mainly with the help of [the] CBC [Canadian Broadcasting Corporation] and with some people sympathetic on the [major newspaper], which is a right wing rag ... In moving M from his last place where he stayed to the church, we stopped at the CBC because our rationale was that if they wanted to capture him and deport him, they didn't want to do it under public view. And so I was honest with the reporters. I said, "two reasons we want to cooperate with you – one is we want the publicity, and two we think that you being here with us is a protection." And so they escorted us, and they followed in my car in taking him from the CBC to the church.[77]

Media coverage of sanctuary's spectacle was extensive. This extent is shown in a summary prepared by a group that had granted sanctuary to a migrant for only nine days:

During the period, there were more than 120 telephone calls ... and a continuous parade of television and radio crews with cameras and recording gear who beat a path to our church doors to interview M. All the major networks showed up time and time again as the complex story unfolded. As the days passed, the story got wider and wider attention across Canada. There were calls from as far away as Germany, Poland, and the United States.[78]

A priest noted in another incident: "I've gotten about 500 phone calls."[79] Another provider claimed to have received "400 phone calls."[80] Similar circumstances were echoed in another instance: "Our telephone line was swamped with calls ... We had to devise ways to immediately increase our telephone capacity."[81] In a different incident, a pastor travelled to Ottawa to negotiate with immigration officials and to call attention to the plight of the family that had taken sanctuary in his church. He held a press conference: "Like everything else on the [Parliament] 'Hill' the press room was impressive ... As I began my press release of the week's activity, there were representatives from CBC, Global Press, CJOH, CTV and ... the *Vancouver*

Sun."[82] The files of another sanctuary group reveal that press releases were sent to three television stations, three local radio stations, two national newspapers, a French-language newspaper, and four local newspapers as well as to religious and student papers and media outlets.[83]

On an ongoing basis, public press conferences as well as visible vigils, protests, and pickets outside the offices of federal political authorities and immigration officials were organized. This attempted visibility was central to the exercise of a nonstate sovereign power. In the various excerpts that follow, note the language of spectacle, with "visible," "view," "spotlight," "picture," "demonstrate," "notice," and "symbolic" featuring prominently in sanctuary discourse.

For the duration of sanctuary incidents – in a manner analogous to how immigration officials regularly publicly release information about policy shifts or decisions through specialized media-relations personnel and staged press conferences – media were encouraged, often through press releases, to cover spectacular events and protests as they developed. Once media personnel began to know the migrant or migrant family, they tended to become amenable to providing such regular coverage. Media were alerted to each protest, rally, or other event with aspirations to producing spectacle. The objective was to keep sanctuary constantly visible. A provider related in one incident that they took

> every opportunity to be as *visible* as possible. If the story seemed not to be in the news very much, we would put it back in the news or we would send stuff out to update on what was going on with the family so that it didn't kind of get lost in the shuffle.[84]

In a distinct incident:

> The *Calgary Herald* kept watch, and there was [*sic*] articles every day. And the CBC reported it, and other television stations reported it, and we sort of kept it in their *view*. And we had vigils and marches ... so that it gave them some reason to pay attention.[85]

Another provider noted:

> We were getting desperate ... to do something else ... to keep them in the media *spotlight*. They made national news, the whole nine yards. And so we were always looking for ways to not have the ... people just forget they were there.[86]

Spectacles varied dramatically. Some took the form of vigils, which were spectacles of a religious nature:

We had several sets of vigils... One was at Christmas. We had three, four, or five of them ... quite a number. And sometimes just religious services or whatever, and so people would come in from these different groups and sort of be part of it.[87]

Other spectacles did not adopt an overtly spiritual form. A provider described one such event that sought to display the migrants' ethnicity and culture to onlookers:

People came from as far away as the States, Vermont, and Montreal, and we had, by that time, been in touch with the Colombian community in Sherbrooke, and there is a significant number in Y as well, and they came. And they in fact provided a nice display of Colombian leatherwork to give a sense of the culture. They brought their flag and so on and a video about the human-rights violations in Colombia. And then they participated in the concern that culminated that day. So we had this mixture of talent, and it was an incredible outpouring of just artistic support. People came playing the cello, various instruments. The young woman in sanctuary played the flute, and she totally wowed the crowd. There were Colombian dancers in costume. They brought their food. So people really got a sense of widespread support, and this was so well attended it packed the church, and there were people outside who couldn't get in ... And it took the whole social hall next to the sanctuary as well.[88]

Other spectacles adopted the form of public protests. One provider recalled such an effort:

There must have been close to three hundred kids, as well as adults. And we had asked them to bring noisemakers, so we had like bells and whistles, and ... we had banners and just [made] a racket [and] went ... downtown and met ... at City Hall. Anyway we had a good *picture* that was in the paper, and we made a little speech down there.[89]

In another instance, providers took advantage of a local dedication ceremony involving political authorities and other prominent groups by staging their protest nearby:

The time that they had the opening of ... a little new park across from [the] immigration [offices] and all of the big groups were down opening the new park, and we did *demonstrate* with picket signs across from the opening when the TV cameras ... were there. And during the international parade, we built a church that was the same colour as the church that they were in, and we had little people looking out the windows.[90]

Relevant instructions to church and community members participating in one phase of this ongoing spectacle were recounted:

> We don't want swearing. We don't want disrespectful things. We don't want this, this, this, this ... We want to make a statement, but we want to make sure it's a statement that we wanted control of so that we could still do it in a respectful way ... and I can't remember how long we blocked the [international] bridge [coming from the US], at least a half an hour, maybe slightly longer. And we just stood there very quietly ... And we stirred them into a total state of confusion ... [and] by the time the police cars were circling and whatever, we politely withdrew, and we didn't cause an altercation, but I think we made our point. We made ourselves *noticed*.[91]

Providers were "noticed" in a spectacular blockade of an international border crossing between Canada and the US on behalf of migrants residing in a church nearby, the unambiguous "point" being that if immigration authorities would not permit the migrants to remain in the nation and their community, the church and community would not permit anyone else entry either. Similarly, after entering sanctuary in a church in another incident, migrants and their providers then

> decided to walk to Ottawa using overnight sanctuaries, community centres, and churches but not on the [main] highway [to Ottawa], on the Quebec side. It is the slow road, and it's linked with communities ... So we started walking from the bridge ... We were three [to] four hundred people, then a thousand people started ... It grew to thirteen [to] fourteen [hundred] including us ... marching. The cars behind would come, and then [we] stay[ed] overnight on the hospitality of these people, the churches in Quebec who were informed by the bishop to open their doors, and they did so. And the church ... was impeccable in the morning. People gave orders to each other not to leave paper or anything, to mop the floor, the rest of it. We moved on, continued. That was eight, nine days. And then ... [Immigration Minister] Barbara McDougall spoke to us.[92]

Although sanctuary possesses an inherent affinity for spectacle, here connected with the elasticity of sanctuary's territory, such display was not realized as a spontaneous reaction or as a matter of course. Rather, it was organized and programmed (e.g., there were "instructions" and "orders" to spectacle participants) to appear respectful, so as to speak to the good moral character of the sovereign. A sanctuary provider detailed another spectacle that was tethered to temporarily expanding sanctuary's territory:

They were doing renovations at the immigration offices down here, and so they were temporarily housed in a trailer. It was quite convenient for us because you can encircle a trailer quite nicely. So we marched around the trailer, and there was one poor immigration officer in the trailer. We didn't go in, but he found it very unpleasant. So ... the local immigration officers came to represent the Immigration Department and the minister. So ... because they were right here, it was easy to focus on them, and of course the media likes that sort of thing. If you're protesting, you can usually get a picture.[93]

Spectacle was connected with marking sanctuary's territory in another incident:

We had a rally here on Mother's Day, and we publicized it around the place ... We kind of turned it around and said ... "she has a mother who's back in [nation] in a displaced persons camp and maybe it would be nice to give something symbolic on Mother's Day" ... It was cold and it was wet, and a hundred people came out! They made this big ring around the church. One facing outward to kind of say ... it was a protective kind of stance, and the other was turned around facing inward – it was a *symbolic* kind of hug.[94]

Here there was both a protective stance, taken as though defending a territory, and a "hug," consistent with the intimacy of the exercise of pastoral power. These varied sanctuary spectacles effectively attracted the attention of the local community and immigration officials and, in most incidents, also captured the gaze of distant political authorities.

Failed Spectacles and Hunger Strikes

Despite programming, the spectacular aspects of sovereign power can be unruly.[95] Indeed, Foucault writes of "a political fear of the effects of these ambiguous rituals."[96] Like all aspects of sanctuary, spectacles sometimes encounter resistance of one kind or another. For example, in the first incident involving "Raphael":

We decided to have a press conference ... to get it out there what was going on and had the person there at the press conference, and then we were going to take him ... to the church where he was going into sanctuary. So that was all lined up, and I remember just as we were getting set for that press conference, I got a call from the archdiocese office here ordering me off, out, not having anything further to do with it, to not commit the Catholic Church at any rate. That happened two hours before the press conference, and so I couldn't sign anything on behalf of the Catholic Church, and so I went to it and was there but stayed in the background throughout.[97]

In another instance, normally welcome news media appeared at the wrong time:

> One local TV station ignored my plea [not to disrupt church services], and they arrived during our Christmas Eve service, and I was quite annoyed and told them so, but once they're here, they're here, so they continued to grind away.[98]

In a different incident, in which a protest was planned on behalf of a migrant in a nearby church: "We waited for Immigration Minister Caplan at a planned visit to Queen's University, but she cancelled that appearance at the last minute."[99]

Sometimes spectacles and sovereign power generally were challenged because of what occurred *within* sanctuary. Over the past twenty years in Canada, hunger strikes have become a desperate, but nevertheless common, tactic of antideportation politics.[100] A provider noted the difficulty that a migrant's hunger strike caused in one sanctuary incident:

> He was on the hunger strike ... we were concerned for him as a human being ... I went to my own physician ... [because] he wouldn't come [to the church]. And they then happened to find a fellow ... who was very familiar with Ireland [and] the hunger strikes ... and he came in ... We wanted to make sure that he was looked after from a health standpoint.[101]

In a separate incident: "Most [sanctuary-group] members expressed concern for Mr. M's health, should he carry out his plan to refuse to eat during his stay."[102] Hunger strikes are an instance of a sovereign power emanating not from the state, church, or community but from yet another source and space.[103] Here such power flows from the human body and represents the point at which "bare life" refuses to be such. Such strikes challenge – as a further last resort – other sovereigns. They are a bleak illustration of Foucault's notion of the "imperative to resist" or, as Alan Hunt and Gary Wickham aptly describe it, the "rationality of irrationality,"[104] which targets the human body and seeks a final escape. Such strikes also possess an affinity for spectacle. One hunger strike was justified *by the migrant* on a

> publicity standpoint because at that time the media already knew that he was in sanctuary, and then of course once they knew that he was in sanctuary, then well now he's on a hunger strike ... So that was *effective publicity*.[105]

Yet, as well as adding to sanctuary's spectacle, there is a sense in which hunger strikes potentially rival it. In an occurrence noted earlier, the migrants expelled from sanctuary violated a rule prohibiting such strikes:

Provider: The second rule [set out for the migrants in sanctuary] was that their threatened hunger strikes could not happen, that we weren't going to tolerate that, that if there was a hunger strike, if they called a hunger strike, we'd have them thrown out.

RL: Why would that be?

Provider: Why? Because there were children there. We were not going to have this *turn into a spectacle*. They want to do a hunger strike, let them do a hunger strike in the detention centre. Let them do a hunger strike somewhere else.[106]

The prospect of a hunger strike by migrants in sanctuary, the severe threat that such acts posed to migrants' very lives, constituted resistance to the ideal of passive, obedient, pastoral objects in need of others' life-affirming care and guidance *and* resistance to the overlapping exercise of other sovereign powers that demanded "bare life." The larger point, however, is that sovereign spectacles were incomplete and encountered resistance from outside and inside sanctuary's confines.

Conclusion

Among other purposes, this book aims to reveal the diverse powers in the sanctuary context, to provide insight into how to better distinguish them, and if possible to shed light on how they relate to one another. This chapter has shown that sanctuary is an instance of sovereign power that flows from church and community. Mitchell Dean writes that relative to exercising the right of death, which is a characteristic of bio-power, "sovereign power is manifest in the *refraining* from the right to kill" and in this sense reveals a kind of restraint.[107] Far less restrained in the context of migration is the systematic, although mostly invisible, deportation of migrants as well as exclusion in the form of refusals to accept would-be immigrants from impoverished contexts or to select refugees from camps or political-crisis situations for resettlement due to their assumed lack of potential to become self-regulating liberal citizens. Made possible mostly by evolving point-system technologies and by new specialized economic knowledge, such as human-capital theory, within immigrant-selection systems,[108] these are practices exercised at the level of populations.[109] However, that a decision is about who lives or dies makes it difficult to distinguish sovereign – whether flowing from nation-states, churches and communities, or migrants themselves – from either governmental or bio-powers. Nor do the spatial aspects of sovereign power always successfully make such distinctions, since liberalism and pastoral power also have spatial aspects.

Foucault writes that "popular agitations caused by punitive practice ... seldom spread beyond a town or even a district. Yet, they did have a real importance. Sometimes these movements, which originated from below, spread and attracted the attention of more highly placed persons who, taking them up, gave them a new dimension."[110] Foucault could have been describing sanctuary incidents, which rarely extend beyond a particular community and sometimes "attract the attention" of "highly placed persons." It is precisely this spectacular aspect that seems to better distinguish sovereign power from, especially, governmental power. Support for sanctuary incidents typically did not "spread beyond" particular communities to form a national or regional social movement in Canada, but most incidents effectively attracted the attention of those in high places. Strangers from churches and the broader community were often drawn to visit migrants in sanctuary. But local, provincial, and federal political authorities also became aware of incidents through the ongoing generation of spectacle and often came to publicly endorse the migrants in question.[111] Yet it is doubtful that all of this is best understood as "popular agitation," as though it were somehow irrational or spontaneous. Rather, although temporally and spatially limited, a specific power was evident in sanctuary incidents. It was exceptional, territorial, spectacular, and every bit as sovereign as the power commonly assumed to flow exclusively from the nation-state.

How sovereign power relates to governmental power is less clear. To a journalist's comment during a sanctuary incident that minister's permits granted on humanitarian and compassionate grounds are "few and far between," an immigration spokesperson responded: "That's because the system is good." "If the figures were higher, the exception would be the rule."[112] From the point of view of governmentality, making the exception is but a momentary acknowledgment of problematic but unique factors outside those originally foreseen from within a particular program. Granting sanctuary to desperate migrants deemed to be facing physical danger or death while denying sanctuary to others thought to be economic refugees or otherwise undeserving constituted an exception both to the regular pastoral practices of churches and communities directed at "the poor" and to the selection, sponsorship, and resettlement of refugees through private-sponsorship and host programs. But making the exception – in the form of granting either a minister's permit or sanctuary – is quantitatively limited: too many claims of uniqueness can cast a spectacular light on perpetual program deficiencies. Making the exception is therefore a step closer to widespread recognition of failure and the birth of a new program – although, until there are several such forced steps, programs can continue intact because, even though not perfect, they remain "good." One particularly astute provider noted a problem with this logic in a letter to the minister of immigration: "The requirement of uniqueness is itself unacceptable. It is equivalent to the principle that if an injustice or hardship is one of two or more such injustices or hardships, then it is not to be corrected."[113] Yet it is worth noting that this provider's observation would be true only from within an existing program that remained intact. New programs that replaced failed ones *could* appear, and by incorporating knowledge of such patterns of injustice or hardship, these new programs could make the exception into the rule.

Michael Dillon writes that "what is most interesting about the relationship between governmentality and sovereignty is not that it is competitive, much less that it is oppositional. Nor is it that they can be reduced to the same thing. What distinguishes the relationship between the two is their very complementarity."[114] For a governmental program to avoid failure by making an exception is consistent with Agamben's notion of the exception as an "inclusive exclusion."[115] By this, Agamben means that law's power comes from its capacity to maintain itself in relation to what is outside itself, and in this sense entails including what is excluded – the exception is not simply excluded, but instead only momentarily suspended or "taken outside" a program enabled by law.[116] If Agamben is right that a law or a program shaped by a specific rationality "nourishes itself on this exception and is a dead letter without it,"[117] then it would seem that the exception is the very moment at which sovereign power constitutes governmental power. While this assertion undoubtedly requires further refinement and empirical inquiry, at a minimum the foregoing analysis of sanctuary, minister's permits, and the like suggests that governmental and sovereign forms of power overlap, sharing irregular points of mutual constitution.

5
Sanctuary as Pastoral Power

These people are not "cases" to us. They are human beings with
names and faces.
  – Southern Ontario Sanctuary Coalition, press release,
    31 May 1993

Using the metaphor of the "shepherd-flock game," Michel Foucault elaborated a "less celebrated" rationality of government in his later writings and lectures.[1] Themes of this pastoral power are seen in early Hebrew literature and Jewish thought.[2] Such a rationality shows itself, but not in unmodified form, in Christian practices of the Middle Ages.[3] According to Foucault, this rationality later takes shape as the science of Cameralism and the theory of police in Europe in the seventeenth and eighteenth centuries.[4] Here "police" is something much broader than what is commonly understood as the modern public police. It refers instead to a domain of administration encompassing justice, finance, military, and diplomacy. Police was about gaining knowledge of and governing virtually all aspects of society; it "includes everything."[5] But police fell out of favour with the rise of liberalism in the nineteenth century, and its accompanying assumptions of the need for realms of privacy and freedom outside a central state. It is in the welfare state, however, that pastoral power became clearly observable once again, even as it was tenuously coupled with liberal rationalities.

Pastoral power is characterized by "constant kindness, for the shepherd ensures his flock's food; every day he attends to their thirst and hunger ... for the shepherd sees that all the sheep, each and every one of them, is fed and saved."[6] This is a power, Foucault notes, that seeks care for the "lives of individuals" and seeks "to constantly ensure, sustain, and improve the lives of each and every one."[7] Extending kindness and providing life-affirming care on a continuous, individualized basis is precisely what occurs inside sanctuary. Sanctuary therefore affords an exemplary opportunity to take a closer look at this neglected rationality.

This chapter considers sanctuary as an instance of pastoral power and attempts to provide insight into its knowledges, techniques, agents, objects, and spaces. It begins by discussing community within sanctuary discourse, suggesting that pastoral power is neither limited to church governance nor expired. The focus on needs, intimate knowledge, watching and visiting, and education are then discussed as integral aspects through which pastoral government is exercised in the sanctuary context. Next, the agents (i.e., shepherds) and objects (i.e., sheep) of pastoral power are taken up. Governing through need entails drawing in "shepherds" from church and community to identify and fulfill the needs of "sheep." Sacrifice, the medium through which this power operates, is then considered in more detail, followed by a discussion of the spaces of sanctuary. These spaces are at once both constituted by pastoral power and facilitative of the generation of intimate knowledge and fulfillment of migrants' needs that is so central to this logic's exercise. Finally, this chapter considers how pastoral power is distinguished from and relates to liberal rationalities.

Church and Community

> When we have the chance to reach out to somebody, or a family who is in distress, or in danger of tragedy right in our own back yard ... [we] reach out and do whatever we can.
> – CTV News, "Nigerian Mom, Girls Seek Refuge in Alta.
>   Church," 12 December 2002

Two aspects of pastoral power consistent with sanctuary are suggested in Foucault's oft-quoted statement about the welfare state being "one of the extremely numerous reappearances of the tricky adjustment between political power wielded over legal subjects and pastoral power wielded over live individuals."[8] First, this assertion suggests that in constituting welfare states, a pastoral rationality is not a leftover of the distant past, when Christian churches wielded considerably more power than they do today. Second, it implies that this logic is not equivalent to Christian church governance.[9] Foucault elsewhere aptly notes: "You will say; the pastorate has, if not disappeared, at least lost the main part of its efficiency. This is true, but I think we should distinguish between two aspects of pastoral power – between ecclesiastical institutionalization, which has ceased or at least lost its vitality since the eighteenth century, and its function, which has *spread and multiplied outside the ecclesiastical institution*."[10] Consistent with this assertion, as pastoral power, contemporary sanctuary imagines enlisting providers from local churches but also from broader secular communities.

As Chapter 2 revealed, local churches were involved in at least some capacity in the sanctuary incidents. Providing sanctuary was often consistent with these churches' concurrent practices of caring for "the poor" or privately sponsoring refugees from abroad through the program asserted in Chapter 3 to be consistent with the rise of advanced liberalism. Private refugee resettlement, in particular, shares many of the assumptions of the provision of sanctuary, and on some levels the two overlap. Private refugee sponsors attend to refugees' material needs by providing food and furniture upon their arrival in Canada. Private sponsors visit refugees in their new accommodations daily. From the moment they are met at the airport, through their first year, and sometimes beyond,[11] refugees' conduct is constantly monitored in a manner consistent with pastoral power: "Most sponsorship groups seem to have made a point to be sure that at least one member of their group visited or had some other ... activity with the sponsored refugee every day during the initial moments of resettlement [There was] a kind of *constant contact and guidance.*"[12]

Very similar practices comprised the daily operations of sanctuary. In sponsors' resettlement practices, there is little respect for refugees' privacy.[13] Indeed, sponsors sometimes sleep in a room within refugees' new "private" accommodations during the first days after their arrival.[14] The reason for this lack of privacy is that within sponsors' resettlement practices, refugees are simply not imagined to be capable of exercising choice. Similarly, sanctuary providers' determination of who deserves sanctuary is not unlike selection for private sponsorship abroad in that there is allowance for sponsoring groups to nominate individuals rather than a reliance on selection by state visa officers alone. Given these similarities –which will become clearer in the pages that immediately follow – there can be little doubt that the introduction of the private refugee-sponsorship program, which moved responsibility away from the state, was a condition of possibility for churches and communities later asserting themselves by granting sanctuary to migrants.

However, there were differences among churches in how they understood their involvement in sanctuary. These ranged from social justice to charity.[15] One provider claimed to be part of

a social-justice congregation. And we had had a number of other kinds of events in the past – not sanctuary – but other things where we took a stand politically and or socially in the community around certain issues, and so this was just one more of those kinds of issues.[16]

A provider from a church mission that served "the poor" noted: "We did it on the premise of how we run this place, and ... [sanctuary] was just an extension of what we were doing here."[17]

Chapter 2 revealed that support for sanctuary was rarely limited to churches but also extended to the broader community. And Chapter 3 argued that community, as part of localization within refugee resettlement, was a feature of the shift to advanced liberalism. Community is also evident, however, in sanctuary discourse that is shaped by pastoral power. It is important that adequate evidence of this assertion be provided since it is central to this book. The United Church of Canada's sanctuary guidelines note that "the initiating congregation in turn will need the support of the local community, secular and religious."[18] One provider remarked:

> So we had people bringing food and that sort of thing ... a lot of the people that would have not had any contact with the church. We had many people come to the fore who basically came alongside the International Centre ... We felt very much affirmed by the community.[19]

From a separate incident, a provider noted that there were "church and labour and community people who had something to do with the church and a lot not to do with the church all working together around the table to keep M in the country."[20] A priest in another incident said: "People in the community are convinced that these people are telling the truth."[21] In yet another incident, the migrant in sanctuary had

> worked at two coffee shops here in the city, and when the story first hit the paper, [we received] all kinds of phone calls from people, the sort that said, "Well M won't know who I am, but I go in there every Sunday morning and order a cappuccino or something or other, and she always brings it, and we have a chat." So the people who were customers at the two places have been extraordinary in terms of sending money, coming out for the rally that we had around the church, signing the petition, and turning up with little treats for her. So that's one group of people. The churches in the city have also been extraordinary as well in terms of putting up the petition in their churches, and ... as some of them have said, "This is the first time we've ever done anything like this." So it got some of them enlivened to pay attention to what's going on in the world. And then there are people in this *community*, the folks who work at the daycare and the folks who work at the lunch program ... The first day [they] came over and said, "Do you want the kid's lunch or the senior's lunch?" And so they've been bringing meals and food and stuff. Other people in the *community*, one woman just heard about it ... and she was coming downtown to visit her daughter, so she came and brought this big fruit basket, and she has faithfully, every week, sent a letter, a little note to encourage M to keep going ... She had never met M until she came the first time to

meet her. The people from the R Centre have been great. The president ...
came up. People who were formerly teachers there have come in or they've
sent letters off to the [immigration] minister. The kids in the playground
... they've been over.[22]

Providers from various incidents referred to support from "the whole community,"[23] an "entire community" of support,[24] "broad community support,"[25] and "massive community support"[26] in relation to sanctuary
provision. And if the community was not involved at the outset, it was
deemed to have become so over time:

> And so people stop by the church to visit them. There's a sense of welcome
> in the Y community for these two people, and it's grown as they've learned
> more and more about their story.[27]

> The general consensus of the community was very, very, very supportive.
> And ... the more educated people became of what was really going on, and
> the more people listened to what you said, went home, and found out for
> themselves what the reality was, it grew and grew.[28]

Only rarely were community discourses exclusively Christian or religious in character – that is, primarily focused on Christian communities.
Instead, the term "community" tended to signify something more varied
and complex. In sanctuary discourse, community took different forms. In
one occurrence:

> People in the Downtown Eastside are very welcoming to all, and they were
> very welcoming to her, and so many people are in a hurting community
> down here that ... they wouldn't misjudge her ... because so many people
> are hurting down here.[29]

Here, given the character of the community and its assumption of shared
harm, community members could immediately relate to a migrant facing
deportation. In other instances, community and its corresponding relations
were assumed to be ethno-cultural in nature, as is evident in the following
excerpts:

> We had a flood of people from the South American communities coming in
> here ... They came as support. On a Friday night maybe fifty or sixty people
> would sit down to supper ... That was the support ... We had a lot of people
> who had no church affiliation at all. They just felt this was a just cause, and
> they came.[30]

So over the course of the day ... there's people coming and going. Some of them are local people. Some of them are people from the Serbian community. Some of them are friends.[31]

There were a number of people from the Latin American community who knew M and who knew of the situation, and so there was a real connection for the time that M was here, especially with the Hispanic community. There was [sic] probably about ten to fifteen people from that community that would help and be emotional support.[32]

Similarly, a sanctuary provider noted that

the Arab Canadian community had taken an interest in this. In other words, it was not just this family in the church, it was not just the church ... the Arab-Canadian community had taken a very special interest in the case as well.[33]

In sanctuary discourse, then, "community" is a key signifier. Although such community clearly retains Christian faith-based aspects, sanctuary discourse suggests that these aspects are neither necessary nor sufficient to distinguish pastoral power. This community character of sanctuary implies, contrary to some accounts of pastoral power since Foucault,[34] that this form of power is not exclusively a form of Christian faith-based governance but is of wider relevance. That pastoral power has not "died" is consistent with the onset of advanced liberalism. Nor is community the latter rationality's exclusive offspring. Pastoral power and governing through needs can also be glimpsed in the concept of community, which is to say that in our present, community remains among the potential havens of pastoral power.

Pastoral Needs

In a book published in 1989, the social theorist Nancy Fraser claimed the following about needs talk: "Talk about needs has not always been central to Western political culture; it has often been considered antithetical to politics and relegated to the margins of political life. However, in welfare state societies, needs talk has been institutionalized as a major vocabulary of political discourse."[35] Consistent with the rise of advanced liberalism, governmentality theorists and other scholars studying profound changes in governance over the past two decades within nations of the modern West have provided good reason to doubt whether we any longer live in welfare-state societies. If they are right, what of needs talk? If sovereign power is about exceptions, territory, and spectacles, then pastoral power is a logic about care, sacrifice, and perhaps above all, needs. Foucault writes:

"The shepherd must be informed of the material needs of each member of the flock and provide for them when necessary."[36] By contrast, in liberal discourse there is little talk of needs. There is much more talk of rights, especially pertaining to privacy and freedom. Needs are central to pastoral power, and since sanctuary is an exemplary site of such power, "need" is seen to dominate in many of the excerpts of sanctuary discourse that follow.

Sanctuary went far beyond providing for migrants' needs for material shelter in a church building; considerable attention was paid to identifying and meeting migrants' requirements for daily survival, such as food, clothing, and hygiene.[37] In sanctuary, migrants' needs were many and varied. A provider observed:

> There was a lot of stuff to be done. I mean we had to feed these people for this entire year. We had to look after their medical needs, their spiritual needs, their psychological needs, their dental ... you name it.[38]

A sense of the variety and extent of migrants' needs is provided by an open letter to the community at the outset of one sanctuary incident:

> How you can help: Gifts of toys, books, videos; Spanish language videos and reading materials; educational tutoring ... ; English language tutoring; time shared in recreation and socialization; sheets, pillow cases; people who will shop and do laundry; financial contributions; prayers for M.[39]

There was a division of labour to satisfy these needs. A provider noted:

> And we had jobs within the group too. Like we had a lady who I expect is pushing eighty ... and she would do the family's grocery shopping. So ... they had a grocery-shopping day, and she knew ... that the groceries came Thursday, so she'd call and say, "What are you running out of, or what do you need?"[40]

Another provider remarked that

> there is a group that is responsible for bedding and linens ... another group that is responsible for personal laundry. We have a group that's responsible for groceries and another one for the finances. Another one is responsible for entertainment so that we make sure that these people have people coming in to visit with them or things they can do ... Others were teaching the daughter how to knit. So we've had all different [persons] who are working together to take responsibility for all these different areas to make sure that their needs are met as much as possible.[41]

Of course, through confinement, sanctuary created needs that would otherwise have been absent in migrants' lives, but such needs were always seen to be secondary to the primary need for protection from deportation by immigration authorities. Pastoral needs were to be fulfilled through intimate care and sacrifice. First, however, migrants' needs had to be known.

Intimate Knowledge

> There's lots of older people [who] ... certainly warmed to the
> children and then to the family. Lots of the people would help
> them out in various ways, once they got to know them.
>   – Interview 27

Governance demands knowledge of its objects.[42] According to Foucault, pastoral power cannot work without shepherds "becoming informed" of the needs of individual members of the flock by "making them reveal their innermost secrets."[43] In relation to the flock, the shepherd "must know what is going on, what each of them does – his public sins. Last and not least he must know what is going on in the soul of each one, that is, his secret sins, his progress on the road to sainthood."[44] An integral feature of pastoral power is this tendency toward individualizing and intimate knowledge, and such knowledge was exemplified in sanctuary.[45]

Chapter 2 suggested that the idea of seeking sanctuary on behalf of migrants often did not originate with church or religious agents. Chapter 4 asserted that granting sanctuary to these migrants was exceptional. But it is also necessary to note that sanctuary involved determination that differed from the newer refugee-determination process discussed in Chapter 3. "Truth" determinations about migrants, sometimes after their entry into sanctuary, were rendered in a manner antithetical to the formal determination process. Whereas the "truth" of refugees has been increasingly generated "at a distance," in sanctuary, when shaped by pastoral power, it emerged in an "up close and personal" way. That is to say, in sanctuary the distance – spatially and socially – between the authorities who decided and those whose fate was decided was minimal.

The United Church's guidelines suggest that congregations, "over two to three interviews, with at least one person present consistently throughout and a translator if necessary, find out the person's story."[46] Consistent with pastoral power's intimacy, sanctuary providers in most incidents spoke of gathering more direct, less mediated knowledge of the migrants in sanctuary:

> And actually on one occasion we interviewed them. We grilled them on
> their story because something ... had happened that caused us to ... wonder
> [about the veracity of their claims], and so we grilled them on their story.

And both of us came out of there with the same reaction ... They had answers to every question that we asked. "Why did you do this? Why did you not do that?" And we were satisfied at the end of it.[47]

In a distinct incident, generation of such knowledge typically came from intimate, trustworthy others:

They [i.e., the migrants] were clear on those accounts, and others knowing the case and dealing with them felt their case was plausible. [These were] people that we could trust ... I had known her for a couple of years ... [and] could trust her assessment.[48]

Personal experience with the potential conditions that migrants had fled mattered in another case:

My personal reason for assisting them is there was a young man from this area ... where I was the pastor before. He went to Guatemala as ... a social worker. And he was killed there ... That's one of the reasons I was kind of going to accept them into the church.[49]

A lawyer who had inspired another sanctuary incident had "heard about this case and was affected by it. [She] had been in South America for some time [and] ... it made it more relevant for her."[50] Moving toward pastoral power's extreme, one provider commented: "We're not going to have them be hurt. And we love them. They're us. We'll do anything we can to support them and have them be comfortable."[51] Here feelings of "love" in relation to providing sanctuary and the inclusive intimacy that these feelings were imagined to entail were of such magnitude that the migrants provided for were deemed self-evidently worthy – since "they're us."

This knowledge gathering associated with sanctuary was the antithesis of liberal "government at a distance," which entails the deployment of authoritative scientific or expert knowledges. Here knowledge stemmed from the efforts of intimate amateurs, not distant experts. Such intimate knowledge was evident in decisions about migrants' worthiness for sanctuary's protection and also provided the basis upon which to more generally discern and respond to migrants' needs. In this sense, it differed from elaborate legal-based refugee-determination efforts and sought a different "truth" of refugees. It attempted to establish not so much the nature and validity of claims of political persecution – a phenomenon that has rendered the refugee category so politically useful since its emergence in the early twentieth century[52] – as to determine the depth and kinds of needs that such persecution, forced migration, and necessity to remain in Canada at all costs created in the figure of the migrant in sanctuary. This intimate knowledge of migrants was not simply given but was generated through specific pastoral techniques. Chief among these were the watch and the visit.

Watching and Visiting Sanctuary

> They had visitors like me, and there were a number of other
> people ... who would go by and visit.
>   – Interview 36

Of pastoral power, Foucault notes that "everything the shepherd does is geared to the good of his flock. That's his constant concern. When they sleep, he keeps watch."[53] Providers literally kept watch over sanctuary's inhabitants, who were fearful of authorities. Having their fears calmed was migrants' initial need and the first aim of keeping watch:

> There was a lot of fear. The family was very fearful. The children were very fearful. They had been through horrible experiences with the police and the uniformed people ... they were terrified of them.[54]

In other incidents:

> RL: Was there someone with the family at all times?
> P1: At all times.
> RL: And why was that?
> P2: Just the fear factor ... on the part of the family.[55]

> For two or three nights ... [we] stayed right there with them. They were very fearful in the beginning.[56]

In most instances, one or more providers accompanied the migrants during waking hours within the church, and at times a twenty-four-hour rotating watch was established.[57] In one incident, a provider remarked:

> It wouldn't be uncommon for me to go this afternoon for instance and find that there would be five or six people there who just dropped in and decided to visit. But we always have one person prearranged to be there, and others who drop in just to be part of it.[58]

Keeping watch was intended to ensure that migrants were safe and secure. A provider related in a separate incident: "At the beginning ... [there] were people – females – taking turns and coming to sleep over. It was to give her company, to support her about whatever she needed to share and to help her be safe."[59] Other providers similarly noted that migrants' security was "our priority"[60] and "our responsibility."[61] Keeping watch entailed constant surveillance of the migrants, who were deemed incapable of making proper choices on their own.

Yet there were two primary targets of the watch: the fearful migrants in the church and immigration authorities, who might at any moment have entered to arrest the migrants. Providers kept watch as care givers and border guards. As noted in Chapter 4, it was somewhat unclear to providers, especially early on, whether it was necessary in practice for migrants to stay in sanctuary's spaces to avoid arrest and deportation. Regarding the watch, a provider in one incident related:

> It started off to be someone there at all times to represent the church if they attempted to enter. It has since evolved, just the people who dearly care for M wanting to be there, especially a lot of older women who just think the world of her and just want to be there to help her through this.[62]

Another provider explained:

> We had probably two hundred people involved in helping in one way or another, getting food, staying there overnight because they didn't leave him alone ... We always had somebody else there so that the federal [immigration] people knew that if anything happened, it would be resisted nonviolently if possible, and it would be reported.[63]

This dual purpose is perhaps best exemplified in the announcement of a future gathering to continue sanctuary's spectacle, also cited in Chapter 4:

> M is currently in sanctuary in the church. The plan is to form a circle around the church – once facing outward as a sign of protecting M, then facing inward as a symbolic big hug, from her Mom, since it is Mothers' Day, and from all her friends and supporters. There will be music, an opportunity to sign the petition in support of M, and [an] opportunity to contribute to the fund for her application and legal fees.[64]

Keeping watch required providers to face inward to look after migrants' intimate needs and wellbeing as well as outward to protect against immigration authorities who were possibly lurking outside. Perhaps more than any other facet, keeping watch reveals sanctuary as an instance of both pastoral and sovereign power and represents a point at which the two powers overlap.

Keeping watch went hand in hand with sanctuary visits, another pastoral technique. One provider noted that "there was lots of visiting that went on. There were people dropping in all the time."[65] Another recounted:

There was a surprising number of people that just came in to support the family ... that would just knock on the church and say, "Hi can we come for a visit?" ... People came from all over the place, and they built friendships ... It was just unbelievable ... People would just come out of the woodwork.[66]

In another occurrence:

There was always somebody coming in to visit M. There would always be people to come in and say, "Hello how are you?" Everyday there would be people coming in ... I'd always go check on her to see how she was.[67]

Visits did not just happen; they were imagined and arranged to happen: "Some of the women in the church ... *made sure* there were meals and people to come in and visit them and play with the kids."[68] Suggestions that support for the migrants was required and that donations or other aid would be welcomed from the community were disseminated through mass media. Visits were therefore programmed and often involved "schedules" and "rotations":

People would ... establish a visiting schedule. Different groups in the community would say, "Okay well we'd like to come in," and maybe they'd come in and bring puzzles, or they'd come in and bring arts and crafts, or they'd come in and do whatever. So we ... couldn't bring them to the community, [so] we brought the community to them... [On] Halloween they couldn't go out [trick or treating]. We had people coming to the church ... We had people knocking on the door saying "trick or treat" and giving them the candy.[69]

In another incident: "A rotation of thirty families divides their time with the M family, providing food, company, and stimulation."[70] That visits were programmed is also revealed by the fact that they were temporarily halted on rare occasions in order to give migrants time to themselves.[71] "Open houses" were also held so that visitors could meet the migrants:

As the church was sort of wide open, people were in and out all the time. So they certainly were visited ... like a big sort of open house. People came and went ... A lot of it was just people dropping in and gabbing.[72]

Similarly, in a distinct incident:

We were planning a weekend of community support because people have asked how can they help us. And since the sanctuary refugees can't go out to meet the community, we're inviting the community to come in and meet them.[73]

Yet, in part because of the need to manage the spectacle that involved visiting media representatives, sanctuary was never fully "open" to visitors:

We had people posted in the church ... for the security of the sanctuary because we anticipated a bunch of reporters coming in. As a matter of fact, myself and another chap stood at the door and made sure they didn't.[74]

Foucault suggests that pastoral power "cannot be exercised without knowing the inside of people's minds, without exploring their souls, without making them reveal their innermost secrets. It implies a knowledge of the conscience and an ability to direct it."[75] Through intensive conversation and continuous contact, visitors acquired intimate knowledge of the migrants in sanctuary. Some visits were religious or spiritual in their focus: "A few religious groups came to visit with her, and they were praying with her and ... reading the bible with her."[76] But visits to sanctuary were not typically such. As noted in several excerpts above, during these occasions, often long and intensive discussion would ensue between "shepherds" and "sheep." One provider noted: "I used to come over here on a fairly regular basis in the evening, and we used to sit there and shoot the breeze and have coffee and cookies."[77] Often first time visitors to sanctuary would ask the migrants about the story of how they fled their nation of origin:

The first few days were really hard [on the sanctuary recipient] because everybody wanted to know the story ... "Could you just tell me ... how you came to be in Canada?" And so she's going back over ... the bombing, and our house was burnt down, and we had to flee in our car, and ... the troops that were coming in ... and then following us.[78]

In these confessional moments of seemingly mundane visitation and "shooting the breeze" or "gabbing," pastoral power is at its peak: needs are self-examined, obediently revealed, and immediately followed up with providers' guidance.

The visits served not only to monitor and to provide knowledge of sheep, but also to draw in shepherds. That is, these stopovers made shepherds out of otherwise apathetic or distant members of the congregation and community:

M was sharing with me on Saturday as we were moving some of her furniture that she had gotten very depressed the last month or so because not very many people had come to visit them. The family really grows on you ... I didn't know them that well before that, but I tell you, you'd come over to the church for a visit or whatever, and the kids, they'd just latch on to you ... You just want to do something with them.[79]

A local physician described getting to know the migrants and, in so doing, becoming a shepherd:

I met this family about three weeks ago through notices in my church. After volunteering to teach reading skills to the children, I quickly became very familiar with the whole family, their story, their medical histories, their hopes, and their fears. I have seen the children daily for three weeks and have felt the extreme frustration of not being able to help them, knowing that ... the need is to be back at school and to be back in the stimulation of their community.[80]

Another provider similarly recounted:

And when he [i.e. the migrant] talks about ... little incidents of things that have happened to him that are part of their life down there [in South America], it's just horrifying. But we get the emotion from him ... And hearing little bits of their story just increased the level of passion that we had to help them.[81]

Language was not necessarily a barrier to these visits, as might be expected. A provider noted: "We have people that don't speak French either so that they feel very limited in their ability to do anything more than give them hugs, but there are certainly lots of hugs going on."[82] In another incident:

And so everyone in essence took the time to get to know them in their own way. For some people, the connection was simply providing for their basic physical needs, bringing food, and ... they need not only services, but human companionship at this point. And so ... when you come, you don't just drop off the food, [you] stay and visit. And it's particularly tricky with the language differences ... He speaks Spanish only and a few words of French now. He's learning, and she speaks fluent French. And so for those that only speak English, it's difficult to communicate. But the issue has been addressed in a number of ways ... We talked at one point, a group of us, about the importance of communicating beyond language.[83]

In one case, visits involved playing music with the migrants, thereby overcoming any anticipated language barrier:

Every day there is someone, and it could be a member of the congregation, coming for another reason, but they always stop and spend time with them. For instance, one of the more delightful developments is that various people play musical instruments, and when they realized that M played the flute, they made an effort to ... recover the flute from the apartment they had left and brought it down, and then those who play guitar or accordion or flute take time to visit and play with them.[84]

The notion that visits were a technique of governing through need was especially evident in the following two instances:

People came to visit M, and people would bring them food ... that she needed for herself and her children. And the church really provided all the support that she needed. I think she had everything that she needed at the time.[85]

Another older member [of the congregation], ninety years and holding, has decided that her role is to bring little gifts of ... French Canadian delicacies or ... a can of maple syrup – and here's how we use it – or fresh strawberries. And she always makes a point of visiting when she does. She's the person most likely to say, "Is there anything you need and how can we help?"[86]

In other occurrences visitors, "moved by the need," dropped off financial contributions:

Yesterday there was a woman who came into church. She [had] read the story in the paper, and she stayed for church, and then she handed somebody a $100 cheque to give to them. She didn't know them at all, but she just was *moved by the need*. And so there have been little surprises like that that come in that are very heart warming and encouraging.[87]

Individual people have been coming, like that fellow who just came in the door [i.e., during the interview], and he said, "I want to make a donation" and handed me twenty-five bucks and went down [to the church basement] and said [to the migrant], "You hang in there" and gave M one of his cards, and off he went.[88]

Spatially and socially, sanctuary is about the intimate or "close" government of pastoral power. Through visits, migrants were transformed from distant abstractions (i.e., desperate failed refugee claimants) into real entities in need. Capturing this notion was a lawyer involved with a family in sanctuary for more than 150 days: "They've become real people in our midst, a real family, not just a news story."[89] In the same way, in response to a journalist's question about the fact that some persons were still calling for deportation of the migrant in sanctuary, another lawyer noted: "But these are people who approach him in the abstract."[90] Intimate governance rendered the abstract real.

Of course, migrants became more real to some visitors than to others. That is, differing levels of intimacy were evident in sanctuary. Not all visitors were imagined gaining equally intimate knowledge of migrants. In one instance, migrants plainly related more to specific shepherds than to the congregation as a whole:

> It was kind of odd because even the family didn't necessarily feel that same attachment with the church; it was with certain individuals. They didn't even attend church every Sunday. It was just hysterical because they were in that church basement.[91]

Another provider noted: "M had very specific issues that she didn't want to vent. Many of those specific issues, she actually shared ... only with me ... [but] didn't say in the committee."[92] That certain individuals became more intimately involved is particularly evident when migrants understandably became frustrated. In a different occurrence:

> They would not share their doubts, or their real concerns, or their frustrations with just anybody ... People from the congregation ... would just drop by, and folks ... were real casual ... There was always food, and they would sit and chat. The conversations would often be: "How are the kids doing?" "How are you doing? Is there anything you need?" [But with] the small group of people that they were really close [to, they] would then share ... the[ir] frustrations and concerns.[93]

Another provider similarly noted:

> One of the things that M in particular felt real uncomfortable about was he was getting frustrated with [the] Canadian government. You got to think a lot of people don't want to hear this, but at this point ... he's thinking: "Damn this country, if you don't want me, then I'll just bloody leave. Just tell me you don't want me." That's not something M felt he could share with many people who would be really insulted as Canadians. To me, as an American, he knew he could just say, "Damn, if they don't want me, then why don't they just tell me, and I'll go home ... M felt a little bit freer sometimes because of that.[94]

Particularly integral to sanctuary visits was the provision of migrants' food needs: "There were people who always dropped by. Even ... after work they would come and ... bring food."[95] One such visit was clearly more spontaneous, and the food fresher, than on other occasions: "Last Friday I was there in the evening, and a fellow came in wearing rubber boots, and he had two heads of lettuce, and he said, 'This is for you M' ... Things like that. People just come in and support."[96] Besides responding to a basic need, food provision, often in conjunction with the "open house," became a useful strategy to gather the flock and enlist shepherds:

> I volunteered to coordinate the food. It was very soon apparent that food was one way people could show their support and build community. There has been a steady and impressive supply of cooked dishes and provisions coming into the sanctuary kitchen without any urging or pressure.[97]

> We bring in members of the community, the church community, and the [city] area to visit with them, to share a meal with them.[98]

Reference to food was prominent in sanctuary discourse and part and parcel of the intimacy of pastoral power:

> My children would have sleepovers in the church, and ... they'd get there and sleep over on the weekends ... or we'd go and have meals ... and we'd go down and cook a meal with them.[99]

Sanctuary involved, in a separate incident, impromptu dining with the migrants in the church:

> [For] most meal times, not breakfast but lunch and supper, there are often about twenty people that gather. People bring in food, and it just ends up being potluck meals because people drop in to see how they're doing and end up staying for the meal. So it's been quite a gathering of the community and different people all the time trying to help and check up on them.[100]

In other occurrences, previously unannounced visits were sometimes justified through the promise of food. A provider noted that there were women

> who are regularly there at the church, two or three ladies especially who will just drop in unannounced to visit because they so enjoy being there. They realize that their being there is an uplifting thing for M, but they just head out to go for a walk, or they head out to go downtown, and invariably they'll find themselves over at the church visiting with M. They'll phone her up and say: "M I'm going to bring over some sandwiches for lunch and so don't make yourself any lunch." They'll show up, and they'll have sandwiches and some soup or whatever with M for lunch.[101]

In another incident:

> Usually in the afternoon there's different groups of people who – and some-
> times people from the Serbian community here – drop in to spend time
> with her so she can talk her own language ... So they come in to visit.
> Usually at suppertime somebody comes to have supper with her. Either
> people she knows or this one fellow ... [who] said, "A friend and I are com-
> ing to have dinner with M. We're bringing the dinner." And so they turned
> up with the bags full of spinach salad and all this stuff for dinner.[102]

As mundane as it may appear, food provision was significant in that it
served as a common point of reference for providers and migrants in sanctuary. It was not only an end in itself, but also a subtle means of pastoral
governance that facilitated and justified visiting and talk between shepherds and sheep.

In some incidents, especially those of longer duration, support groups,
such as the Friends of the Chileans, the Friends of Mauricio, and the Maria
Committee, comprising one or more members from the local parish or congregation and many from the broader community, formed to organize sanctuary. As suggested by the use of the term "friends" and the migrant's first
name (i.e., Mauricio and Maria) to identify some sanctuary groups, relations with migrants were assumed to be intimate. One such group was comprised of three subgroups: one to strategize, one to maintain a trust fund,
and one to negotiate a private-sponsorship agreement with immigration
authorities.[103] The private-sponsorship application in this case read: "Various church members as well as others from the neighbourhood have already established close personal relationships with the family which will
continue to be nurtured."[104]

Also consistent with the intimacy of some sanctuary visits, after a time
relations with migrants adopted a familial form:

> They were a Catholic couple not connected to the church that this family
> had originally been connected to [and they were] ... good hard working
> people that really just cared and wanted to do ... the right kind of thing. But
> they sort of became like surrogate grandparents to the family ... like for the
> weekend and Friday night ... they sort of played that role in the sense [that]
> they'd get movies and chips or whatever and go to the church or bring in a
> pizza.[105]

This was consonant with the fact that a slight majority of the incidents
involved migrant families, many with children, and that providers were
typically middle-aged adults, who likely had raised children of their own.

In another incident, a provider noted that the migrant "kids ... had many dads, and they had many moms besides M. And I was the parent."[106] In a distinct incident:

My wife and I have almost accepted her as a daughter, and the children ... we just loved them because we just felt sorry for them ... And so they and the congregation feel exactly the same way because they look at these [migrant] children, these are *our children*.[107]

Indeed, another provider noted that a migrant *family*, as opposed to a single male migrant, was a factor in the support that was generated:

If it was just him ... "Okay you're a big boy ... look after yourself" ... but when you see little children and a woman that through no fault of her own ... [is] in a foreign country with no way of getting back, no way of communicating ... The congregation ... had a great deal of empathy for them which they may not have had for just M had he been single.[108]

Another provider remarked that her weekend became the migrants' weekend:

We hung out together ... If you're going to the liquor store ... you might go and buy a six pack and a bottle of wine for the weekend. Well you might multiply it by two and figure well if it's our weekend, it's their weekend, and so ... we kind of felt funny dragging all this booze into the church [laughs]. But ... it was a necessity ... We'd go down there with a case of beer sometimes. We'd have little parties down there ... The year that they were in the church ... they had a great big surprise party for me down there on my birthday, and all the Friends of the M's came, and it was a great big bash. It's really nice, so we celebrated all those days, regular things that happened in people's lives. It's just that we sort of moved it down to the church.[109]

In an incident in which a migrant died of cancer after a lengthy stay in sanctuary, a provider noted that toward the end,

I used to go and visit her in her home with her family. I had meals with them ... because we did get ... to know them very well. I mean the grandkids were here. As I say, we even had a child born in that time [of sanctuary], and they were very ... appreciative of what the congregation and the staff had done for them and were doing for them. So there was a relationship there that was built up. I was very privileged to be part of the family grieving after she had died and to be there with the family and participate in some of their rituals of death ... but they were very welcoming to have us there sharing in their grief.[110]

It is pastoral power's intimacy that is particularly striking in the sanctuary context. Whether manifested as prayer, or sharing meals, or weekend leisure, or rituals of birth and death, this is a mundane but profoundly intensive and personal power.

Lack of Privacy

Because sanctuary was watched, migrants were frequently visited, and intimate knowledge was correspondingly gathered, privacy was imagined to be reduced accordingly:

> Quite a few people from the church ... were with them, and so they were always with somebody. And that's kind of what was difficult for them as a family because they didn't have any privacy.[111]

> They were at everyone's beck and call, and people didn't normally call up and say, "Can I come around to see you?" It was almost like the revolving door... People [just] showed up.[112]

As discussed earlier, providers sought to expose migrants' predicament by writing letters to political authorities and others on their behalf. Form letters sent by the minister of immigration in response to three different sanctuary providers' efforts from one incident read:

> While I appreciate your interest in this case, Canada's Privacy Act prevents me from releasing information on a specific case without the written consent of the person concerned. This legislation was enacted to protect a person's right to privacy when dealing with Canadian government institutions.[113]

One provider noted: "They are not criminals, but they are confined. Their rights as human beings have been suspended."[114] Such "suspension" meant migrants in several incidents literally gave up their privacy by subsequently giving providers written consent to access private information held by immigration authorities.

This lack of privacy has been recognized elsewhere in sanctuary discourse. As one provider noted: "They forget that you have a life of your own. You become a public figure, and you don't have privacy anymore."[115] In a different incident, a provider likened the migrant's situation to living in a "fish bowl."[116] In another occurrence: "Because life carried on for the church, they lacked privacy and freedom."[117] With the intimacy of pastoral power came a concomitant loss of privacy and freedom of choice, elements central to liberal government:

> The fact that these people are confined benignly in a loving community doesn't in any way cancel out the fact that their freedoms have been taken away. [There is a] loss of autonomy, loss of decision-making power in their lives, the inability to make even the daily decisions about whether I'll go to the grocery store and what I will buy.[118]

This dilemma was not simply occasioned by need provision within a few sanctuary incidents. Rather, it appears in other forms as *the* problem within the coupling of liberal and pastoral rationalities. The loss of individual privacy and autonomy is precisely what is unruly within what has been called "liberal welfarism."[119] This vital point of disagreement between governing through need and governing through freedom, between the individual as a living entity with needs that cannot be fulfilled as an individual and the citizen with rights and freedoms, is clearly evinced in the sanctuary context.

Pastoral Education and Guidance

> Volunteers, including teenagers, visit the M family, bring small
> gifts, and sometimes offer schooling lessons.
> – "B.C. Christians Support Family in Church Haven,"
> *Catholic New Times*, 17 March 1996

In addition to fulfilling material needs, sanctuary involved guidance that was meant to improve migrants in diverse ways, partly in an attempt to increase their likelihood of receiving a favourable decision from the Department of Immigration or the Immigration and Refugee Board (IRB) but more broadly in an attempt to continue to "make" them into liberal citizens.[120] The Unitarian Church's sanctuary guidelines note that providers should include "ways to keep occupied, skills training, exercise opportunities, language instruction if needed."[121]

In about two-thirds of the incidents, children accompanied adults into sanctuary, which meant that these children could not attend public school outside. In one such incident, considerable effort was expended to overcome this barrier:

> So we developed a school committee because the kids had to go to school ...
> We had an in-house school, and we had people come in and volunteer to
> teach the curriculum, and we were able to get their school records to find
> out where they were in previous schools.[122]

In another incident:

> The kids needed some education ... so that we had contact with their previous school teachers, [and] we had some volunteers who are really good with kids that came in and worked with them around their workbooks and assignments.[123]

The latter strategy was used in several other sanctuary incidents, with volunteer teachers and tutors from the churches and community teaching or "home-schooling" the migrant children.[124] In one incident, providers appealed to provincial law in order to force the state to supply a tutor:[125]

> We realized that the kids were not going to be able to attend school, so we went [to the provincial government] and said: "Well listen ... under the Education Act the children should be in school. These children can't go to school, so what are you going to do about it? So we want them educated like everybody else." So anyway we were assigned a tutor. We got a bilingual tutor. We got her into the church, and she came in for ... three or four hours a day ... She literally went and got the curriculum, got the textbooks ... and she worked with both children so that they could continue their schooling.[126]

Adult migrants' education was also targeted.[127] In one incident, a migrant woman was taught art and computer skills.[128] Most prominent across the incidents, however, were efforts to teach English to adults (and to those few migrant children thought to require it).[129] This took a number of forms. In one incident:

> People have brought in videos. They've been trying to find Spanish ones, and then somebody said, "Well ... they're trying to learn English and French here so let's bring them other things." So people have brought in videos and then sat and watched with them and talked about what the movie was about to make sure that they were understanding.[130]

About half the incidents involved adult migrants with limited or no knowledge of either English or French. From the perspective of providers who did not know the migrants' language(s), this fit with the governance of these migrants as pastoral objects incapable of exercising choice. An additional element of pastoral care specific to incidents of longer duration was therefore providing migrants with relevant language instruction. In one instance, a person from the community was drawn into the incident on this basis: "So I decided to go mostly because I've been involved in ... teaching English as a second language over the years. And I thought, well, if these people need help, maybe language training is one of the ways that they need help."[131]

If sanctuary was of sufficient duration, pastoral guidance, of which English-language instruction was an integral component, was expected to lead eventually to transformation of the migrants from fearful, passive, and obedient objects into active and self-regulating subjects. The security of sanctuary permitted the alleviation of fear. One provider noted that "the greatest change [is evident in] these children. When they came [into sanctuary] ... they were scared to death, and now they roam around the place as comfortably as can be."[132] Yet something more than quelling fear was imagined going on inside sanctuary's walls. For example, a provider remarked about the migrant to whom she had administered care and guidance for more than a year:

> We made sure M had some routines. And that's what we felt she needed – routines. And she needed consistency... So I think ... M was getting her voice. She was starting to speak out for herself. With all the support she had, she started to speak out for herself. And it was just brilliant and wonderful to see her be able to do that. I was thrilled to pieces that M could be so articulate. But she had to come to that place where she could *break free and become M*.[133]

"That place" was at once the pastoral space of sanctuary and a site in the protected migrant's soul; "becoming M" was tantamount to becoming a "free," self-regulating liberal subject. Despite the ultimate failure of the sanctuary effort to secure legal status for M, "something else" was achieved:

> No, we didn't win the case. It would have been great to have won the case. We didn't win the case, but guess what? We won something else. M knows that she is loved. That she has a place in this world. That she has values. Those kids have never known such a circle of love and support and care. This will always be with them.[134]

Toward the end of another incident, the minutes of a sanctuary group's meeting read:

> With reduced stress and improved medical management, N's strength is returning. He now has a lesson in English as a second language five days per week and he is reportedly doing very well. He has stopped smoking. His sense of humour is surfacing. He is [now] a man *with a life ahead of him*.[135]

Through sanctuary, this migrant was thought to have become stronger and more communicative. Through pastoral power, "bare life" in a bleak present was seen to have become morally uplifted life with a future. Consequently, in sanctuary it was imagined not only that alternatives to the impending threat of deportation would be revisited and negotiated, or at least postponed, but also that a migrant's capacities would gradually be altered in the direction of liberal subjectivity as needs were identified and fulfilled. Sanctuary is a time and a space for such a metamorphosis to occur. When it does transpire, conflict between pastoral and liberal rationalities can only subside. There is a sense, therefore, in which sanctuary mediated not only between immigration authorities and migrants, but also between pastoral and liberal powers.

Shepherds

Pastoral power constitutes authority in the figure of a shepherd.[136] The United Church of Canada's guidelines note that "sanctuary imposes obligations on the protectors. In addition to providing the refugee with food and shelter, they must give assurance to the refugee in a situation of great uncertainty ... Attempting to overcome the refugee's insecurity is a challenge to and an obligation of the sanctuary giver."[137] Sanctuary givers are quintessential pastoral shepherds. A variety of persons were enlisted as shepherds in the incidents, ranging from clergy and congregation or parish members to persons with no obvious religious conviction or connection. Support was broad-based and rarely limited to members of the specific church in which the sanctuary recipient was protected. Often strangers "rose to the surface":

> And very quickly there came about those folks that sort of rose to the surface that you could see had a real keen interest in being a part of the family, and ... they became the key support team.[138]

Another provider similarly noted during an incident:

> I did not know them prior to them going into sanctuary... My husband heard ... on the CBC [Canadian Broadcasting Corporation] about their story right after they had gone into sanctuary. He came home and said to me: "I just have a feeling that these are people that we should get to know." He said, "We know that what they are saying is true, we know how [nation] works, we understand what they are saying, and we could probably empathize with their situation. You ought to follow up and see if there is anything that we could do to help these people." So I did. I called the church.[139]

Typical in this respect was the supporter who recounted in a letter to the editor of a major daily newspaper: "My wife and I went to the Unitarian Church where he is receiving sanctuary after we read the stories in the paper. We were impressed by M and his concerned mother."[140] Significantly, sanctuary's sovereign spectacles generated the potential for pastoral care of the migrants in sanctuary, thus marking one of several links between sovereign and pastoral power. Consistent with such power, spectacles aided the recruitment of shepherds from the community:

> The media attention has galvanized ... widespread public support so that I can't even go into the grocery store without people asking, "How are the refugees? Are they still there? What can we do to help?"[141]

> And we did get a fair amount of people stopping by and saying, "Hey, heard you on the news [and thought you] might need some of this, so here you go" ... There was some community response to it saying, "How can I help? Oh we've probably got some stuff kicking around the house that we don't need."[142]

In generating spectacle, the relation between sovereign and pastoral power is not so much about one power giving rise to the other as it is about overlap and occasional mutual constitution.

During one incident, a middle-aged shepherd, while attending a public consultation meeting for other purposes, recounted rushing to physically block the immigration minister from exiting the meeting room until the minister had first listened to her queries about the status of the migrants in sanctuary:[143]

> We actually went to this press conference that she [the minister of immigration] was having. We had tried to set up a meeting with her ... but somehow those arrangements fell through, and following the press conference everybody was moving around ... [The minister] appeared to be leaving the room with her followers, and I said to the bishop, "We're going to lose her. She's going to close the door. We have to do something. Let's go over there and stand by the door." So what happened was we walked over towards the door, and we stood in the doorway ... I would have never believed I could do such a thing. Afterwards, the bishop said, "We were both acting a bit out of character, weren't we?" I guess so. But anyway she came towards us, and she couldn't get out the door, and so the bishop introduced himself and sort of turned it over to me, and she said, "Well I don't have time, I have a plane to catch" ... I sort of fired the questions at her and got her answers, which were certainly not what I wanted to hear ... What I was asking was that the children be allowed to attend school without fear of being apprehended. And her reaction was, "No I can't ... No I couldn't do that." [So I said,] "Well do you have any advice for us?" [She said,] "Well church sanctuary is not a solution to your problem." She was definitely very much opposed to church sanctuary. She said, "You have lawyers, and there are ways to come into

Canada and talk to your lawyers and go back and reapply through other channels." Well she knew quite well I'm sure that the M's wouldn't qualify under the system that existed then ... [which required] the seventy points.[144] They didn't have it ... So it was insulting really that she would shout that out to us as a solution. It wasn't a solution. It wouldn't have worked because they don't have the education requirements.[145]

While this excerpt reveals what might otherwise be a classic church-state confrontation, more interesting is this provider's claims that she was acting a bit "out of character" and that "I would have never believed I could do such a thing." Pastoral power enlists persons "to do something," even if it means uncharacteristically engaging in a form of physical sacrifice by blocking the immigration minister on behalf of a threatened member of the flock. This same provider recounted that sanctuary

was in a way sort of a life-changing experience ... I made new friends. I was involved with people in the community that I had not known before or had not known well. There was a lot of personal feedback for me because I was ... in control of the [sanctuary] group.[146]

Gaining intimate knowledge of migrants was part and parcel of becoming a protective shepherd:

There was one particular member who really expressed some doubts about this [i.e., the sanctuary situation], and one day he was looking out of the window there and said, "Come and look ... we've got to do something about that ... M is smoking out there ... There's that gate down there on Y Avenue ... These people are out there supposedly with this arrest warrant, and they could rush in here and grab him on his smoke break, and he'd be gone." And I laughed and I said, "You had great doubts as to whether we should have M here, and now you're protective. He said, "Yes ... now that I've got to *know* him."[147]

In a separate incident, a provider explained:

I'm sure that if something were to happen again, and it may very well because he's still not out of the woods ... [or] were he to be arrested at this time ... there would be a real hue and cry over it because people have got to *know the family that well. They've gotten to know and love the kids.*[148]

Other than legal professionals, who tended to play a central role in defining sanctuary's legality and in negotiating with immigration authorities, experts only occasionally entered sanctuary to offer advice or to provide care.

When they did so, it was often not as experts per se. In a few instances, professionals – such as dentists, physicians, and psychiatrists – were deemed necessary to attend to migrants' special needs, once these had been identified, but their involvement tended to be immediate, unofficial, and not linked to a professional fee:

> M got sick, and we had to take her to a doctor, so I arranged for her to see a doctor who ... was a part of Doctors Without Borders ... He just saw this as a mission in his life, and so we secretly took her to have some dental surgery. [It was] all free because we didn't have any money to pay for that.[149]

In another incident:

> We had a medical doctor who ... belonged to the Anglican Church as well, but if we had anything medical, Dr. R dealt with the family and dealt with their medical needs. He came into the church and brought them whatever they needed.[150]

Similarly, in one incident, a psychiatrist treated a mentally ill migrant "free of charge."[151] In these relatively rare moments, the experts of liberalism moved toward becoming the shepherds of pastoral power, as with lawyers who did *pro bono* work for migrants. In contrast to liberal government's reliance on expertise,[152] in pastoral governance expert knowledge typically remained on the periphery. In its place was the volunteering amateur, the sacrificing shepherd who intimately provided the best care that could be cobbled together under the circumstances.

Sheep

> They're going to have to stay there until something happens. If they go back, their life is on the line. They'll be like lambs led to the slaughter.
> – "Sitting Bull," *Telegraph Journal*, 15 June 1998, A1

The objects of pastoral power are to be obedient, passive and (not unlike aimless sheep) deficient in their capacity to exercise autonomy and choice, and to lack inward moral direction. As a consequence, sheep are in need of immediate protection as well as education and direct guidance from shepherds. In one incident involving a large group of migrants, a rule was laid down, consistent with pastoral power, stipulating that providers would be given direct access to the migrant families while they inhabited sanctuary rather than having to deal with migrants' intermediaries:

We wanted to deal with the family, and the coterie kept insisting that they were doing the talking for the refugee claimants. And so you were talking to some of the coterie that was with them, [and] all of the sudden you'd find yourself talking to a different person. And then there were people who were sort of skulking around in the back, obviously talking and having meetings, who had never presented themselves and shown their faces, who were the sort of ... older people. They were people in their forties and fifties, sort of old radicals, who were sort of Rasputin-like, hanging around behind all of this directing. So we didn't know who was directing this or who was involved in this. So eventually we made three rules with them. We made the first rule ... that we would deal with the families.[153]

These particular migrants were later cast out of sanctuary, partly for not being as obedient as required. Another church formed a "covenant" with the sanctuary recipients, again painting a passive picture of migrants whose foremost virtue was obedience rather than a desire to be understood:

It means not leaving the church grounds and complying with any request by myself or the board. Even if they didn't understand the request, we asked that they comply with it because it would only be made on behalf of their safety.[154]

Migrants in sanctuary were referred to in moral terms. Such characterizations were arrived at through the production of intimate knowledge that ostensibly rendered migrants worthy of sanctuary provision:

I knew from talking with R [a close friend] ... that ... she had been an interpreter for the United Nations. It seems to me that was enough to tell me she was a *decent* sort of person ... If I didn't know that I would have wanted to know more about her, but that was enough credentials for me.[155]

They escaped to the States and ... made [a] refugee claim and came across [the border]. Now they did not at that point really affect me because there's a lot of that going on, but he gave me a letter ... signed by a Reverend R – he's a very personal friend of mine – [and] he's a Canadian. And he was [doing] the [missionary] work in El Salvador. They had a couple of hundred churches in El Salvador. And he was the supervisor and superintendent of the work there ... Well when I seen [sic] his letter, then I knew ... M was a *viable* man.[156]

Consistent with imaginings of migrants as "decent" and "viable," they were also frequently deemed to be entities who were gentle, deserving, and good. A provider noted: "He's a really nice man. He's quiet and very gentle ... He doesn't ask for anything."[157] Another remarked that the migrant in sanctuary "appears to me to be a quiet, genuinely sincere and gentle person, who is highly thought of by all the members of our church."[158] In another instance, a provider observed:

> She loves kids. And so the kids from the daycare come over in little groups. And a friend of hers runs a toy company, so he got some toys one day, and they had a little exchange. So the community has ... [embraced] her. She's a very sincere [person], and people see that, and so they say, "What's the matter with the government? Why can't they see that she's a good person?"[159]

In a distinct occurrence, a provider said: "We all really want to help these people. They are good, kind and loving. It is so easy to be supportive of them."[160]

Not inconsistent with these conceptions, migrants in sanctuary were typically not imagined to be authors of their predicament: "Here are two people who are caught up in a situation not of their own making."[161] Partially because of their language "deficiency," but also consonant with such imaginings, migrants granted sanctuary were only rarely included in decision making.[162] Reflective of this is the fact that migrants' utterances are almost entirely absent from the minutes of sanctuary-group meetings. As a provider remarked, migrants "were more the bystanders whom decisions were being made for rather than participants in the decision making."[163] With some exceptions, sanctuary practices tended to occur without securing migrants' input into matters that ostensibly directly affected their lives and that in a sense made their lives possible. It is hardly necessary to note that such practices are unimaginable where active liberal subjects thought to be capable of exercising choice are concerned.[164]

When liberalism confronts subjects assumed to lack a capacity for *proper* autonomy, coercive measures are typically relied upon.[165] Such measures include deportation and forcible physical removal from liberal spaces as well as threatened or actual punishments associated with the criminal-justice apparatus (e.g., arrest, detention, fines, etc.). Consistent with this, in response to a letter from a provider asking for support for a migrant in sanctuary, the immigration critic for the official opposition simply wrote: "An order for removal to the United States was issued and at that time Ms. M made a decision to evade the removal order by seeking sanctuary."[166] This presumes that sanctuary resulted from the migrant's improper choice to avoid a removal order. The mere fact of the order's issuance renders its appropriateness self-evident, and consequently no support from this political authority was to be forthcoming. In a similar instance, the Federal Court's rationale for denying a visa waiver asserted that the migrant family had received substantially more from the community than they have offered ... The applicants state they have a desperate fear of the [nationality] mafia; however, they willingly informed the media of their whereabouts and situation in Canada. The applicants provided little evidence of association with Y church prior to resorting to the church for sanctuary. They state they have lots to offer, however, they have not provided sufficient evidence ... Instead, they provided substantial evidence of the church's support of them.[167]

Here the exposure stemming from the sanctuary incident and the support received became part of a rationale for continuing to deny legal status to the migrant family, thus suggesting, first, an active quality on the part of the migrants in that they "willingly informed" the media and, second, that they were not active in the direction of self-support but only in gaining the support of others. In short, the migrants were active but in the wrong directions. An excerpt from a hearing decision rendered by the Appeal Division of the IRB likewise described a migrant in sanctuary:

The respondent was ordered deported following her conviction for Manslaughter. Her appeal was dismissed. She filed a motion to reopen. In the meantime, she took refuge in a church, and clearly did not intend to emerge until her appeal was reopened. The Minister brought an application to postpone ... until the respondent came out of the church and surrendered herself into immigration custody ... The Appeal Division found that by taking refuge in a place where she knew that enforcement authorities would not seek her out, thus preventing the execution of a valid removal order, the respondent had created the prospect of an abuse of the Appeal Division's process.[168]

In this case sanctuary was actively "taken" rather than passively received. Correspondingly, there is an absence of reference to sanctuary providers' efforts or to the possible illegality of their practices. This migrant not only displayed serious criminal tendencies (i.e., having been convicted of manslaughter), but also apparently acted alone in knowingly "abusing" the appeal process by entering sanctuary. Thus she was undeserving of further opportunities for improvement and worthy only of exclusion. This conclusion contrasts sharply with a sanctuary provider's pastoral imaginings of the *same migrant*:

She is a person who, if you meet and talk with her, endears herself to people as just a genuine, very gentle, unassuming sort of person ... I've had long, long conversations with her, [and] I've never heard her say anything bad about the minister of immigration, or the Immigration Department, or anyone despite her treatment ... She spends a lot of time trying to do good for people.[169]

Besides production of an individualizing knowledge through "long, long conversations" with the migrant, which is illustrative of the shepherd-flock relation, this excerpt reveals the imagined object of pastoral power as passive but possessing the potential "to do good."

As suggested earlier, migrants in sanctuary were also imagined to have considerable prospects to become autonomous, self-supporting liberal citizens. On a Christian television talk show, a provider remarked about the "signs" of such potential:

> What we thought about M is that she would be an *outstanding citizen here in Canada* ... We thought that she would be working, and ... she was already doing volunteer work, upgrading her education. These were types of *signs* that we took to be very serious and very good, and so that's why we gave her all the support that we did.[170]

Reminiscent of the classic moralizing distinction between the deserving and undeserving poor, another migrant "deserved a chance":

> We see in him a bright, intelligent human being, full of humour, warmth and compassion, who deserves the chance to make Canada his new home and to be a contributing and valuable asset to Canada's workforce.[171]

These distinctions varied somewhat, as evinced in another occurrence where a provider explained a migrant's potential by invoking the more contemporary psychological concept of personality:

> Most people really believe they're in charge of their lives ... They have a schedule. They know what they're going to do for the day, and so they ... basically think they're in charge of their life, and that's who she's been. You ... go and find a job. You get work. You ... do these things, and all of the sudden you can't do that ... You have to sit and wait ... She is the *kind of personality who wants to be independent and doesn't want to have to rely on other people.*[172]

Sacrifice

> Was I prepared to put this family ahead of myself, wife and
> church? I loved them, but was I prepared to sacrifice myself ahead

> of them? ... Several times in one's lifetime the opportunity is
> given to serve others at great sacrifice of self.
> – Paul Reynolds, *Faith Subdues Kingdoms: A Pastor's
> Challenge to Immigration*

Foucault suggests that a shepherd "acts, he works, he puts himself out, for those he nourishes and who are asleep."[173] Pastoral power must "be prepared to sacrifice itself for the life and salvation of the flock."[174] Foucault goes on to write that this kind of sacrifice distinguishes pastoral from sovereign power, "which demands a sacrifice from its subjects to save the throne."[175] In sanctuary, sacrifice was not a religious ritual. Rather, it was a pragmatic, built-in component of pastoral power. Saturating sanctuary provision is a language of sacrifice. Shepherds are seen to sacrifice to fulfill the needs of sheep. In contrast, conspicuous by their absence in sanctuary discourse are advanced-liberal notions of partnership, enterprise, and efficiency. The following excerpts are reflective of sacrifice from distinct incidents:

We will go to the line where someone's life is at stake.[176]

We will do whatever it takes. These people are staying here.[177]

People are so willing to go out of their way to help in whatever way they're asked.[178]

Cardinal R was very generous, and he really went out on a limb.[179]

We'll do anything we can to support them.[180]

And so I told him, "I will do anything I can to help you."[181]

I think this is really where the rubber meets the road. We meet the needs of the people in our congregation ... when we stick our necks out ... This one's a big neck out.[182]

Providers going "to the line," "out of their way," "out on a limb," doing "whatever it takes," and "sticking their necks out" – this is a language of giving up and foregoing. But, crucially, this is done on behalf of the disadvantaged, deserving stranger; it does not stem from *direct* self-interest. Rather than spectacular, such sacrifice is often mundane. It also adopts myriad forms.

Although sacrifice was of course evident in the risk of illegality that sanctuary practices created, not all sacrifice was made in response to the threat of legal prosecution. One provider drawn from the local community related how providing sanctuary led to sacrifice:

It was an opportunity to ... do something that might have an impact on people and how they live. I had to contextualize it that way and just say, "Wow." You as an individual aren't apt to do something that big very often ... It kind of came out of nowhere ... You either pass it up or you go with it. But it came with *sacrifice*.[183]

In one instance, a migrant in sanctuary was permitted to remain in Canada when the local church formally offered him employment as a lay minister counselling Spanish-speaking members, which exempted him from the requirement of an immigrant visa. However, this meant allocating a salary drawn from limited church resources. The pastor overseeing these resources remarked: "But we felt it was better for us to make the sacrifice, than them making the sacrifice."[184] Sacrifice in another instance entailed "stresses":

Their situation was legitimate enough ... [but] it wasn't done without any ... personal [sacrifices] ... I've been separated for three years. I can't [say] that it's a result of that, but I don't think it helped any ... But you made the commitment [to providing sanctuary], and I'm not one to back off on something I believe in. If you make a commitment and you've taken this big public stand on something, well you've got to see it through ... It wasn't without its stresses. I'll tell you that.[185]

Elsewhere, sacrifice resulted in more "work" for persons directly involved.[186] Similarly, in another occurrence:

It was encouraging to see the number of people who came together to try and support M through this... [The] pastors ... set their own agendas aside to ... try and meet the needs of M and the family, along with doing their normal duties. So it was extra work for them. It was extra work for the numbers of volunteers who got involved.[187]

Shepherds altered their routines to permit themselves regularly to visit, provide care, and generate support for migrants. A provider recounted:

People who were regulars contributing time or meals would have to take a break because they were going away on holidays. Some people cancelled their holidays so that they didn't have to break their support. That's how strongly they felt.[188]

A member of the clergy noted that sanctuary "interrupt[ed] our mid-week Bible study and ... [was a] significant inconvenience."[189]

However, in most instances, sacrifice was more than stress, extra work, or inconvenience. For example, in one instance, the migrants in sanctuary required passports from their nation of origin. After initial contact with foreign-government officials, it became clear that passports would not be forthcoming without incentives. Understood to require the sacrifice of dearly held principles, this illegal act was nevertheless arranged on migrants' behalf.[190] In another instance, providing sanctuary was seen to "take over" providers' lives: "The amount of time and amount of people's lives that were taken over by [sanctuary was] ... not something that you can kind of keep going forever."[191] Sacrifice was elsewhere described in a sympathetic newspaper editorial:

> For those working on the M situation, there is no glory, no personal aggrandizement. People do what they should and get on with the job at hand. Their names won't go up in lights, nor will songs be written about the stand they are making in Y. These are people who spend hours collecting food and even clothes from stores ... Others make items to raffle to raise money; they think about two kids stuck in two [church] rooms in soaring temperatures and they go out and buy a toddler's swimming pool. Then there are those who spend hours talking on the telephones, writing letters and dealing with a civil service ... The hours are long. The pay is nil. There are rarely results.[192]

The constant need to keep the sanctuary situation visible was also an integral opportunity for pastoral sacrifice and thus a point of overlap or complementarity linking sovereign and pastoral powers. One provider described how, in addition to providing care for the migrants for more than a year, she held press conferences during her lunch on their behalf outside her workplace and risked termination as a result:

> I couldn't tell you how many hundreds of interviews [I did]. Like I would get up in the morning ... at six, do a ten after six piece on CBC Radio live, then get dressed and go to school, and then if something's breaking, I mean on several occasions I had like news crews that just decided on their own volition to come down to [city], and they'd call me and say, "We're halfway down. Can we meet you at lunch time at the side of the school?" And ... so that was kind of icky, too, in the sense that I probably could have been fired ... You're not supposed to be dealing with the media and holding little mini press conferences on your lunch hour.[193]

In another incident, a provider remarked about the sheer volume of telephone calls that her group received:

> So calling that press conference meant an *enormous output of energy* by the committee, and it meant that instead of the one phone that we had in the one desk in the church, we probably could have used ten phones and ten

desks and ten people at them answering all the calls. So ... *it's raised the level of activity in this congregation exponentially.*[194]

A provider from another occurrence related:

It was such an intense effort because some of the people were of course working full time, but at the same time they have to do this at night or through their work days, and ... the media was always after you ... always, constantly ... They were in the newspapers every day.[195]

In one instance, after several months, migrants left sanctuary to enter the US, where they applied for and awaited immigration status. A provider related:

It was the whole family, so the expense component was great. They were there [waiting in the US], so they needed to pay rent and stuff. So at the end of the experience, between fees for immigration, lawyers, flights, everyday [expenses] ... [for] the three months they were there, we figure it was about $35,000.[196]

Following some sanctuary incidents, providers even accompanied migrants to nations such as the US, Mexico, and Peru when the deportation threat that led to sanctuary promised to be rescinded if migrants agreed to exit Canada voluntarily and then reapply for status through Canadian embassies, consulates, or by "flag-polling."[197] When one shepherd escorted migrants to reapply for immigrant status at a Canadian consulate in Peru, she was held up for six months in a slum in Lima. Her mother, also a provider during the incident, related:

And meanwhile, back here I was putting the pressure on the government. I got all my vaccinations and everything else, and I'm an elderly woman with health problems. I would have went if I hadn't been [ill]. I would never let my daughter go. So that was a terrible thing for her father and I to have her down in a Third World country. It was so scary. We thought, not only are we supporting this [migrant] family, but we're *sacrificing* one of our kids ... There was no way I was going to let my daughter be down there [in Peru] at Christmas time ... I was going [to go] down there.[198]

In the same incident, a provider faced considerable ridicule for setting up a visible ramshackle booth in the city square to expose a migrant family's sanctuary situation occurring in a nearby church. Singularly staffing the booth ten hours a day for ten weeks, she collected some 13,000 signatures for a petition on the migrants' behalf. Consistent with both pastoral sacrifice and sovereign spectacle, a large sign next to the booth read: "I'll Come In [from the elements], When They Get Out [of the church with legal status]."[199] This provider reported:

> I'm here until they find a safe solution for the family. I promised them that. If that means going into the cold weather, well we'll cross that bridge when we come to it. But I'm hanging in to the end.[200]

In other incidents, the dominance of sacrifice as risk taking is evident:

> And we were hoping not to get into a situation like that, but we knew that there were risks all the way through this thing. And Christianity is, in part, about risk taking and so we felt that this was one risk that we had to take.[201]

> But that's what churches are about, right? They take chances.[202]

> Thousands of dollars had been spent by a church that really could not afford it. Several weeks of my already crowded schedule was given. This in turn affected my wife and home.[203]

> If you're asking, "Do I put my life between theirs and a [forced] return to [nation]?" I do.[204]

A member of the Southern Ontario Sanctuary Coalition (SOSC) noted:

> We started because of specific people. We stayed faithful to them, which ... is the strength of our group ... If we had just been lawyers or consultants – nobody stays with something for eight years unless it's because of a real personal commitment.[205]

In a different case, the support group that had met virtually every week during a sanctuary incident continued to do so two years afterward to ensure that the migrants' needs were fulfilled.[206] Another provider recalled securing medical care for a migrant in need:

> They were very pale, and N, the oldest boy, when we carried them out, he was having muscle spasms. When we brought him out, we had to lay him in the grass. He couldn't stand up. At one time we did his x-rays, and we got the x-ray machine and pulled the x-ray machine right up to the door. Somebody [had] put it on the truck from the hospital and brought it, and put it in the doorway of the church to do all their x-rays for the immigration papers. Major, major favours were pulled in.[207]

As any governmentalized state knows, to properly satisfy a population's needs, revenue has to be generated. While financial donations by visitors formed a portion of the necessary income, more was typically required. Fulfilling migrants' needs therefore required fundraising. The extent of this effort was remarkable and, again, reflective of sacrifice. One sanctuary group's documents reveal that twenty different fundraisers were held, including a doll raffle, prize raffle, craft raffle, pot luck and yard sale at providers' homes, church pot luck, car wash, bottle drive, yard sale at a hall, benefit supper, benefit concert, tea house, ethnic-food sale at a concert, barbeque at a parade, pie sale, dance, and a 50-50 draw.[208] In another incident:

> We had donations coming in from people that we didn't know ... We had a story appear in the *Observer*. So people would read about the family, and then they'd call me. They'd ask questions, and then they would decide to make the donation to help support the family ... Every time that we went out it created the opportunity for somebody to respond. So we sort of kept it going that way. We had all kinds of incredible fundraising events ... We raised probably close to $2,000 with a full turkey dinner ... If things got really desperate, we'd do a dinner, or we'd sell pies, or there's a hall fair. It's like every season we did stuff all along the way and just kind of kept it going, but ... we had to come up with groceries.[209]

In another occurrence, when a migrant family failed to receive legal status after a lengthy stay in sanctuary, the providers continued to offer the family support in the nation to which they had been forcibly deported. They

> realized that housing was going to be the biggest issue ... We thought that we would raise the money to buy a house for M, which sounds bizarre, because it was going to cost about $31,000! So ... could we actually do this? And we agreed that we could. So between August and November we raised that $31,000 and bought M a house ... and that was in four months ... So she had a place to live, which was the biggest gift that we could give to her and the children.[210]

Neither fulfilling migrants' needs nor the costs of doing so ceased when migrants exited a church. One sanctuary group's files show that following a lengthy incident, the migrant family exited sanctuary to wait in the US for permission to return to Canada as immigrants. In doing so, in addition to housing costs, they incurred medical-insurance costs of $804, application fees of $1,000, landing fees of $1,740, and children's fees of $200, totalling $3,744.[211] Weekly, they also required a $200 allowance and $50 for meat, milk, and incidentals.[212]

Sometimes fundraising was not enough. In at least two incidents, individual supporters signed loans and financial undertakings on behalf of migrants in order to secure private immigrant-sponsorship arrangements. In one case, a letter to the immigration minister asking for acceptance of the sponsorship application is suggestive of a high level of providers' sacrifice:

> We understand and are committed to supporting the family financially and socially through providing housing, health care, education, ESL [English second-language] classes ... and all other aspects of care essential for the family's well-being. We will also ensure that M is provided with job skills training to equip her in supporting her family following the sponsorship period. We estimate the costs of a two-year sponsorship to be approximately $50,000.[213]

Pastoral Spaces

Sanctuary is a set of discourses and practices, but it is also a space. As with liberal government, which demands a private-public spatial split,[214] pastoral power entails certain spatial imaginings. Generating intimate knowledge of pastoral objects and ensuring their wellbeing by providing care and guidance on a continual basis was to be facilitated through sanctuary's spaces. Spatial arrangements provide physical security and also facilitate the constant monitoring of pastoral objects' wellbeing as well as the provision of their less immediate needs. In sanctuary, migrants' spatial location was fixed, often for months on end, which made possible the role of shepherds discussed earlier since members of the community could easily locate and familiarize themselves with these continuously corralled sheep. In sanctuary's spaces, migrants were to be rendered more visible, less mobile, less abstract, and more real. As discussed in Chapter 4, sovereign territory tends to overlap with, but is not equivalent to, this pastoral space.

Church buildings and their spaces are not themselves sanctuaries. Rather, their spaces become sanctuaries through the exercise of power. These spaces are not exclusively religious or sacred. Indeed, it is remarkable upon closer inspection to see how secular and fluid the spaces of churches have become, particularly over the past several decades as regular church attendance and the corresponding revenues derived from it have continued to decline in Canada. Undoubtedly due to their ideal size for small group meetings, their traditional placement in the geographical centre of communities, and their relatively low rental costs, the spaces of churches have become integral to the deployment of all manner of community-based programs. Such programs range from Guides and Cubs, which attempt to instill discipline in youth, to Alcoholics Anonymous and related formats aimed at adults living with addictions of one kind or another.[215] Virtually all the churches that became sanctuaries in the incidents were also used for decidedly nonreligious purposes.[216] That these spaces were integral to these varied community-based programs created problems for the management of the pastoral space of sanctuary. In one instance, the division between user groups' space and sanctuary had to be temporarily reestablished as a consequence:

> The family had to work in connection with the other user groups that would be in the basement. Usually, in the evenings we would have a karate group, Boy Scouts. Sometimes there'd be a church gathering in the basement, and this, of course, created quite a challenge for M and the kids because during those times, they had to be in their cubbyholes, their little ... bedrooms. And then ... there was a Meals on Wheels program that was operating out of the basement as well. So it really was frustrating for them, and in some ways it was difficult for the user groups as well because they wanted to respect the needs of the family, but they also wanted to be able to, like say the Boy Scouts, rough and tumble and run about and play and shoot their floor-hockey pucks [while] ... there was a family hiding behind the doors.[217]

Of course, the family in this case was not so much "hiding" from these groups as attempting to stay out of their way. The creation of pastoral space from spaces in the church was also a sacrifice (on the part of the archdiocese rather than the local parish) in another occurrence since regular revenue was dependent on the commodification of church space:

> Finally, an agreement was hammered out with the parish administrators such that the people would not be in the sanctuary [of the] church but would come downstairs and occupy a particular part of the basement that was not being used as much. Now the important thing to keep in mind is that the parish administration tended to rent out these spaces. It was a very important way of covering some of the ongoing expenses [of the church]. So it involved commitment from the archdiocese to make up the difference. And in the ... agreement with the representative of the migrants, it was [made] clear that there would be a limited number of people who would be able to stay there.[218]

The simple fact that sanctuary occurred in the summer served as a way around this barrier in another incident:

> The library is open. We have a daycare in the basement, too. There was a big basement that they could run around in. It's somewhat segmented. Because it happened in the summer time, that also made it easier because we didn't have to use this space as the Sunday-school room. That made it easier, [and] we only had to [relinquish] this space for Sunday School play, but we juggled it.[219]

Typically, church buildings are ill-equipped for the care of human inhabitants over a long term. A provider noted: "Our building is not designed to have permanent residents and perhaps naively most of those involved didn't anticipate this lasting for so many months."[220] In another incident, a provider stated: "Churches aren't necessarily made to accommodate somebody in that situation unless you happen to have a caretaker's suite, ... and some churches do, but most don't."[221] Sanctuary therefore required spatial rearrangements. When migrants stayed longer than a few days, the internal space of the church was rearranged: furniture was moved, kitchens activated, showers built, and curtains hung to create divisions:

> By the time they arrived ... one room of our church had already been transformed into sort of ... a hotel suite. They got a couple of those blow up beds that you see advertised on TV where they're full of air and the legs pop down. They ... moved the other furniture out of the room.[222]

The rearrangement of space was part of a sanctuary program rather than a spontaneous occurrence. Consistent with pastoral power, the ideal sanctuary space was one that at a minimum provided for fulfillment of vital physical needs, such as eating, sleeping, and maintaining physical hygiene. In one incident:

> The family just went into the area that had previously been discussed with the minister because it's really large. If the family must go into sanctuary, this was probably an ideal set up. The lounge area was very nice, and it had kitchen facilities, and there was a separate room across the hall, which had been a nursery, which became their bedroom area, and at the same level there were bathroom facilities.[223]

A local church was chosen in another case in part because

> it was a large church ... They had another kitchen upstairs so that it wasn't even monopolizing the main church hall in the sense that they could still have church dinners and church functions and whatever because there was an upstairs to that hall which didn't affect the family downstairs. So the church was able to continue and function in its normal way.[224]

Similarly, another provider related:

> The physical plan is important ... for something like this. It's not a very big church, but ... there's a hall where most of the Sunday services are held, and then there's a fairly large hall where they have other events, and attached

to this hall at one end is a fairly large kitchen. They had stoves and coffee makers and dishes ... and the Friends of M's met in this hall where the kitchen was and food was brought to the kitchen for M and his family and for other people who were staying at the time ... Downstairs in the basement, aside from some small classrooms that they had mostly for kids, there were rooms that could be converted into bedrooms sort of where M slept and where his mother slept ... And so it was a fairly good physical set up for us.[225]

There was clearly overlap between pastoral space and sovereign territory in one occurrence in that sanctuary included windows permitting surveillance of the church parking lot (the territorial border) in case immigration authorities suddenly arrived to make arrests:

We knew that that church has like a downstairs area. It has a kitchen. It has a little living room... There were bathrooms downstairs at that level. There were windows ... You could see like the parking lot. So it was actually a pretty good set up for us physically for the family.[226]

In sanctuary, the potential for a lack of hygiene became a spatial concern:

There was a very real concern about ... how the church, the sanctuary, was being used. Furthermore, there was [sic] some real problems in terms of hygiene. There was one lavatory, but there were several families involved ... So there was a big issue.[227]

Corresponding with this, a dominant area of spatial improvisation was the need to arrange migrants' access to shower facilities, which was handled differently in each incident:

This morning, part of the meeting is to discuss how to put a shower in the church because these people are now on day twelve and haven't had a shower, and you can only wash your hair under the sink for so long.[228]

And because the parsonage is next door, we've solved the issue of no shower in the church by letting them use the bathroom in the parsonage.[229]

We had to build a shower for M, so we took one of the washrooms downstairs and ... put a shower in there, and so ... people put that together. And it was a nice community-building exercise.[230]

In sanctuary discourse, there is a definite preoccupation with migrants' hygiene and how it is to be maintained:

She cleans herself in a large basin. Mr. R offered to smuggle her to his house after dark, saying that she could spend the whole night in the shower if she wanted.[231]

And we didn't have a shower facility in this washroom in the nursery. One of the couples that have a boat on Lake Ontario said, "Wait a second. We've got a boat shower that'll work perfectly in there." And they came and got it all set up, so M has a place to shower.[232]

There was no shower. So that was a real challenge, but anyway my aunt, who happened to come and visit, provided the solution to that – camping showers ... We went out, and Zellers actually gave us the shower that the family used ... just a plastic container, and we hung it on the stall in the bathroom, and you could stand in there and run your water and have your little shower and put down the bath mat and whatever.[233]

On the path to liberal citizenship, migrants have often been regarded as needing better physical hygiene.[234] Mariana Valverde, writing of sexual purity and immigration policy in early-twentieth-century Canada, for example, notes the importance of "sanitation" among church missionaries working with new immigrants: "The term 'sanitation' referred primarily to physical hygiene, but since in the minds of social reformers soap and water were spiritual as well as physical cleansers, sex hygiene and moral uplift were also intended. The degree of impurity affecting immigrants, however, was a hotly debated point. Some reformers thought immigrants were basically healthy and only needed some training in the English language, self-control, and self-government to become good Canadians, while others saw 'foreign' immigrants as inherently degenerate in body and spirit."[235] This link between ensuring physical hygiene and "moral uplift" was undoubtedly present in sanctuary as well. In their assumptions about migrants, sanctuary providers from churches in particular were similar – indeed, remarkably so in their attention to English-language instruction and the encouragement of self-control – to these early reformers. Although one risks making too much of the preoccupation with physical hygiene in sanctuary discourse if one sees it as more than providers' concern to fulfill migrants' physical needs in pastoral spaces, it does appear that sanctuary was imagined as a purified space in a broader sense. This is evident when it is recognized that nowhere in sanctuary discourse – not in guidelines, meeting minutes, secondary accounts, or providers' talk – were sexual activity or relations explicitly recognized as an adult migrant's need. Consequently, sexual hygiene was never considered.

Consistent with pastoral power, some sacrifice was also required in making spatial adjustments and rearrangements:

The only place where we could give him somewhere to live was to take a church school classroom. So she had to rearrange how we did things downstairs in the church school in order for that to happen.[236]

The staff had to make some adjustment as to what meetings that we could have and a lot of the meetings are community-type meetings, so it wasn't just a staff meeting; it was a tribunal that was going to be happening here. We have to shift everything around and move our space around. And while meals were being prepared, etc., it was the staff that was making the adjustments, making sure that the family had some place to cook and share their space.[237]

After this [sanctuary situation] was over, we realized ... how difficult it was for this space and the five hundred other people who use this space – how that affected us. And so we knew that having to juggle our space ... took its toll on everybody that was involved as far as having to readjust.[238]

Sometimes, however, sacrifice pertaining to space was decidedly more minor: "The quilters were a little put out. We had to move their quilting."[239]

As noted earlier, with pastoral power's increased intimacy emerged concomitant reductions in privacy and freedom. This, too, had a definite spatial aspect:

The whole problem [is that] the church basement was not a place that you could just say, "Well this is your room and don't worry" ... The church was used. You can go down there right now, and there's going to be people in the basement of that church where the family was staying ... Thirty or forty people in the congregation have keys to the basement ... It's not like sticking someone in this room and saying, "Okay stay in this room. Go out to the bathroom and stuff when you want to, but Joe Blow may walk in while you're down the hall in the bathroom, and you're no longer in your little place."[240]

To be sure, in some instances, migrants' privacy was recognized, but it was then deemed a *need* rather than a *right*. Its fulfillment was at the whim of knowing shepherds rather than a result of migrants' demands or entitlement:

We decided that this classroom is their living space, and we will respect the privacy as though it were a home within a home. So the religious education activities take place elsewhere. There is a social hall on the same level. While the service is going on, any religious-education activity takes place, instead of in that classroom, in the social hall, where we would normally have coffee ... And what was interesting about the congregation is that they were quite willing to make that their living space [and] that they realized the *need* for these two people ... to maintain a certain level of dignity and privacy.[241]

In another incident, a provider explained:

We just sort of picked that section of the church, and there happened to be a little room across the hall ... there was a self-contained ... kitchen ... and then there was the ... church nursery that was carpeted ... and had no windows or anything, so that became sort of the bedroom. And so we put in double beds and colour TV and VCR. It was nice because it was dark and it was private and it was away from the windows ... If they *needed* to have that sort of sense of security, it was there. And then they had the bathroom, too, just down the hallway ... So ... basically they marked out space, and this is where the family is, and this is where everybody else was.[242]

Consistent with an imagined obedient, passive object, pastoral places presume a lack of freedom. Regarding the migrants in sanctuary, a provider noted:

They may get up on their own time in the morning. There might be someone at the door because there's a meeting to be held at the church ... *Their time is not their own.* They live in a religious-education classroom converted to living space. There is a sink in the room. There is a couch in the room, and then there is an area that we've converted to a bed for her, and there is a bookshelf and a table.[243]

In another incident:

The daily routine was that they were basically in the room that we had set aside. We adjusted. We do a lot of food preparation here for people in the Downtown Eastside, so we adjusted all our facilities so that ... first thing in the morning they could use our kitchens to prepare the meal for the morning and then take it in to her. And then they would ... bring cooked food in for her at lunch time ... She had basically ... the one small room. She did have one of our bathroom facilities [that] we put off limits [to others] for her. It was ... a separate washroom that she had access to, and then there is a shower here in the building, and in the evening she would shower when she wanted to. But basically she was in that room because during the day we have so many people in this building. We have five to seven hundred people through these doors between eight-thirty and four, so *she did not have freedom to wander around.* It was just too difficult.[244]

Occasionally, some free space opened up: "With our building being a 'no smoking' zone he has braved some cold days to walk in our enclosed garden to indulge in one of the few pleasures he has the freedom to enjoy."[245] In another occurrence, a provider stated:

> Now once at four o'clock, once we were closed, then she had the freedom to wander around our building ... They used to cook up an evening meal, but it was family that came and had dinner with her ... as a family and set up a table and had a family meal. But basically she was in that one room that had a small television set for her and a radio.[246]

In a separate incident, a provider likewise noted: "On Saturday night we do programs, but during Saturday rarely would there be programs, so she'd have much more freedom. The whole building would be hers."[247]

The pastoral space of sanctuary went well beyond the walls of the church when migrants were temporarily smuggled out to fulfill their needs:

> My family's role initially with the M's had been, we have a home in the country, and we had them out there a couple of times, even while they were in sanctuary. We kind of smuggled them out, got them out for a day or two just to get away, let the kids run on the acreage, chase the goats and ride the horses.[248]

> We had a fire, and we had to literally, bodily take her out of here and hide her somewhere else. Her family ... got in the car and took her for a ride around the block until we were able to make sure that the fire that had started was not spreading anywhere in the building, and it got put out very quickly.[249]

> From time to time, we would make special arrangements where she would spend an evening or a day or an overnight with some of her family, but we pretty well were careful about how she was escorted out.[250]

> There were some times when some people in the church would take the kids out to go get ice cream. They would just sneak them out and do kids' stuff, like going to play in the park.[251]

For the most part, however, migrants in sanctuary had few of the spatial or other freedoms usually associated with liberal subjectivity. In sanctuary, such freedoms were thought to be experienced only momentarily in an adjoining garden space or fenced enclosure, between church programs, after hours, or when and where migrants were smuggled out.

In another instance, the need to keep migrants "busy," noted earlier, was inseparable from the spatial "logistics of sanctuary":

> He is ... now confined to a very small place. We've had to really expand what we think [about] ... the logistics of sanctuary to allow him to do some grounds work on the church in the church property. He does grounds work on both the church and the parsonage just to keep busy.[252]

In sanctuary's spaces, migrants were confined, kept busy, and had limited privacy and freedom. But this does not mean that pastoral spaces were tantamount to Foucault's disciplinary prison.[253] As Mitchell Dean writes: "The character of the enclosed institution cannot be viewed as an exemplar of a 'disciplinary type.' Its spatial and temporal organization, and its use of the instruments of discipline, will vary according to its functioning as a therapeutic space, an educational space, a punitive space, a productive space, and so on, and the way in which these diverse spaces are mapped onto one another."[254]

Resistance

Resistance to sanctuary as pastoral power was evident. Community-church alliances, mentioned throughout this book as forming sanctuary efforts, were not without their obstacles. Resistance stemmed from other aligned congregations:

> Well the Anglican congregation had more trouble with it [i.e., sanctuary], and their priest ... would say, "Just ignore them, they'll come and complain about everything." And part of their complaining came from the fact that the building ... was their old building, which we had completely gutted and renovated. They also didn't like the smells that came from the kitchen and didn't think that M knew how to cook.[255]

The parishioners in another incident

> were feeling somehow that they were being requested and expected to comply and cooperate, and many of them felt that essentially they were being held hostage by this group of hunger strikers. There were also some local politicians who were feeling that the archdiocese and the local parish administration was not using an appropriate strategy to apply the law, that somehow they were putting up with this hostage incident and ... [setting a] precedent ... The wind was turning against the cause.[256]

Regarding a separate instance, a provider noted:

There were some people within the community and within that church who really didn't want them there, and it did create friction ... It was awkward. I mean there's no two ways about it. You can't force people to believe in something you believe.[257]

One church encountered extreme resistance from an unknown source in the community:

December was a tense, difficult few weeks while we sort of made up sanctuary as we went along ... Our church building became the focal point for many people, some who were not supportive. We even had to deal with the effects of a telephoned bomb threat.[258]

In another incident, the sanctuary group supporting a migrant entered a formal, financial agreement with the church. Consistent with the organization of sanctuary provision in many incidents, it was often more the sanctuary group that sacrificed than the local church. In this specific situation, the church board charged the community support group for use of church space at rates of $22 per diem and $676 per month (later reduced to $500 per month) to cover utility bills and loss of rental revenue due to displacement of outside user groups.[259] Here the church board merely served as landlord, an arrangement that became a source of conflict within the sanctuary group and, indeed, that led to a member of the group's resignation:

I wish to tender my resignation from the strategy committee, effective immediately ... It has been demeaning for the M family to realize that they are not truly welcome as a guest and not receiving sanctuary in a Christian or humanitarian sense ... I would like to remark that any attempt by ... board members of the church to join or have *observer status* would be unconscionable. The board has a stated position of not being politically involved. They have proven this by their actions as "landlords." They are not acting as advocates for social justice in this matter and have absolutely no stake in M, other than financial gain ... This is not an attack on the many good people of the church, just stating correctly, the non-political position of the [church] board.[260]

At a meeting of the sanctuary support group several months into the incident, this church board suggested that "sanctuary does interfere with the normal business and plans of the church (e.g., the on-going selection process for a new minister). If it is estimated to be long term, different living arrangements ... may be necessary." The church board "wondered whether or not transfer to another congregational sanctuary ... might not be timely."[261]

Pastoral education likewise had barriers to overcome. In one instance, due to the large number of teachers involved with the migrants, "it was difficult to keep track of books, paper and art supplies and one never knows from one day to the next whether the materials you were working on one day, would be there the next."[262] In another case, a problem clearly stemmed from the fact that educators were volunteers rather than paid professionals or experts. A member of the sanctuary support committee noted that as sanctuary dragged on,

> the volunteer teaching has kind of fallen apart ... the ... teacher still comes, of course, and so does [*sic*] R and the volunteers who teach M English, but ... there are no other volunteers coming to work with the girls on homework or reading ... There's no consistency anymore.[263]

Keeping an around-the-clock watch in sanctuary while encouraging visits was also difficult. After two months, one watch schedule was "experiencing holes,"[264] and despite some screening, "open houses" still led to unwanted visits:

> We had one incident ... the lawyer who screwed us up in the beginning turned up here even though he knew that she had a new lawyer. And I mean that's totally unethical on his part ... I didn't know who he was [when he arrived at the church] ... and he presented himself as a friend of M's. So he came in [to visit], and then M said afterwards [makes shrieking noise]."[265]

Resistance to the imagining of the migrants as obedient, needful sheep was also seen in the incidents. As noted in Chapter 4, some migrants engaged in hunger strikes,[266] refusing to obediently accept material needs provided by sanctuary providers, and some of these were consequently expelled:

> They wanted to occupy the church itself and stay in the sanctuary. And they did so for almost two weeks, but we made it clear at that point that we weren't going to tolerate it and that we're going to be very firm that it was just an unhealthy situation, and that's why. Certainly, we had done our part in good faith. And that somehow there was an expectation that they would respect the parish community that had hosted them and understand that they were no longer willing to be held hostage and that this kind of blackmail was going to be unacceptable. So eventually they understood that ... The new group that came into power was much more radical, less conciliatory, and politically much more savvy – anyways, much more militant, much more difficult to work with.[267]

As noted above, migrants exited sanctuary's spaces from time to time. Leaving sanctuary was not itself resistance or a source of concern, especially if the migrant was smuggled out to fulfill identified needs and in such a way as not to spoil the ongoing spectacle:

> There were some family celebrations, and she would just discretely slip back home. I don't know how often that happened, and we almost didn't want to know ... So a number of occasions she slipped out, and it was all ... hush, hush and low key.[268]

But temporarily exiting was a problem when it was of migrants' own accord or unbeknownst to some providers beforehand. This, too, was plainly resistance to the ideal pastoral object: the obedient, needful sheep. Diverging from this ideal had the potential to "upset" supporters:

> There were a couple of times when he went out at night, and this was very upsetting for some of the members of the committee. I was more inclined to be relaxed about it, feeling it was his responsibility ... But it was a difficult role for him ... from May until July to be locked up in a church building and not be able to get out ... He is a young man in his twenties. That is difficult for him.[269]

Remarking about a migrant who had decided on her own to permanently leave sanctuary unannounced and go underground, a provider similarly noted:

> I felt a little ripped off. I could understand that she was getting frustrated and impatient and scared about what might happen, but I really felt like we had stuck out our necks. We were preparing to have them here for [the] long term until we would sort of work out some sort of situation where we could afford to figure out another solution. We were prepared to do that ... I don't know what she was thinking. She decided that no, I don't want to do that, I don't want to wait, let's get out of here ... There was a little disappointment that it turned out the way that it did.[270]

Other resistance was more mundane, such as when a migrant was secretly consuming alcohol while residing in sanctuary:

> At one point I found some beer-bottle caps [in the church] ... I had to kind of lay down the law on that ... It's not a personal issue, but in terms of the politics of the church, it wasn't a smart thing to do because there's still that kind of prohibition sentiment ... in the church ... that would've given a real

wedge for anybody who had any kind of reservations about M to become very vocal.[271]

In another case, migrants made too many international long-distance telephone calls that were billed to the church:

> They were using the phone quite often ... to Mexico, to [the United] States, everywhere, just long distance, two hours on the phone. Bills [were] high, so we told them to stop. [We told them] maybe call your mom once every two months, but not every week. Their mom was working ... [in] Belize.[272]

Pastoral Power and Advanced Liberalism

Chapter 3 briefly explained advanced liberalism as a rationality of rule in the refugee and immigration domains. Although sanctuary exemplifies pastoral power, there remains the question of how this form of power relates to liberal rationalities.[273] In the existing governmentality literature, sanctuary likely would be understood as resistance that led to refinements in programs or to altogether new programs that are consistent with liberalism. The powers and narratives that made it possible – indeed, the very notion that sanctuary was constituted by powers beyond liberalism – undoubtedly would be ignored. Yet pastoral governance is not simply contained within the framework of a totalizing advanced liberalism. Pastoral power has its own relations, which lie outside of the advanced-liberal discourses of partnership and efficiency. It is not the partner but the pastoral shepherd who is to actively take risks and to sacrifice. This is to be accomplished neither through dialogue nor to yield *immediate* individual gain. Rather, in sanctuary, sacrifice is to be enacted on behalf of the key target of pastoral power, the flock, needy members of which are imagined to passively and silently accept the direct benefit. As the welfare state has continued to be appreciably "rolled back," pastoral power has not simply expired and been entirely replaced by an advanced-liberal configuration entailing localization and responsibilization. Instead, pastoral power can be seen in specific domains that include private refugee resettlement, as discussed above (and more infamously in early philanthropy and later social work targeting "the poor").[274] Pastoral power is a rationality that operates alongside liberalism in domains where the care and wellbeing of the marginalized and "needy" is sought. Although not usually cited as a body of work (i.e., no one study refers to another), previous studies have elaborated pastoral power targeting entities as varied as student youth, colonized Aboriginal peoples, and alcoholics.[275] Like the migrants in sanctuary, these people are imagined in prevailing governmental discourses to be obedient entities requiring care rather than ready-made, self-regulating liberal citizens. Pastoral power and its techniques can also be found in the alternative institutions and practices that new social movements establish for their members in the face of inadequate or insensitive need provision by welfare-state arrangements or by the newer advanced-liberal mechanisms intent on replacing them.

There is nothing inherent in the logic of liberalism that requires care of passive, needy persons such as the migrants in sanctuary. Rather, liberalism tends to defer to other logics, including pastoral power, as a means of rendering capable those currently incapable of self-regulation and, in this instance, to indirectly rely on care of such entities. Yet in this reliance, somewhere in this intricate intersection, lies a potential source of temporary conflict between liberal and pastoral rationalities, a point at which one logic can resist the other. This can take the discursive form of severe disagreements about particular migrants' worth, in the case of sanctuary, as well as broader conflict between governing through need and governing through freedom. This is also the point at which competing sovereign powers can appear. As seen in Chapter 4, in this realm one sovereign power potentially manifests itself as the grantor of exceptional church-community sanctuary and the other as the grantor of an exceptional minister's permit or other official reprieve.[276] Yet sovereign power is not simply an effect of this conflict. In this particular context, pastoral power and sovereign power can be seen to overlap and complement one another at certain points.

Conclusion

Across sanctuary incidents, but especially in those of longer duration, there was a perceived shift in church and community attitudes from ambivalence about the plight of unfamiliar, distant failed refugee claimants to deep, affective concern for individual migrants in sanctuary, whose stories had been heard through mass media and later during intimate visits. It was the close confines and the generation of individualizing knowledge in sanctuary that transformed visiting church and community members into shepherds and migrants into needful sheep. The following encapsulates the integral elements of pastoral power: its continuous intimacy, asymmetry, needful targets, and sacrificing agents:

> It became a *very close friendship. We spent a lot of time with them. We spent holidays with them.* They are going to be here for the family-day weekend. We talk on the phones fairly often. It's become a real close friendship ... [but] this is like becoming friends with someone who's very, very sick. When you become friends with them, there is the delight of their personality and the joy of knowing them, but you are worried about them. You don't have the years of having fairly easy times together and all the memories that you might have built up to then kind of carry you through this rough patch

that you've hit. We came together, and they were in their rough patch, and they have *needed a lot of support,* and there are times *where that has really, really taken it out of me.*[277]

Such pastoral sacrifice is also evident in relation to law and, specifically, in the diverse legal narratives found in sanctuary discourse, which are the focus of the next chapter.

6
Sanctuary and Law

Sanctuary is traditionally thought to be beyond the reach of law. Sanctuary discourse assumes that law will likely remain outside the door and pursuing agents be kept at bay. From inside sanctuary, law is oppressive. It waits threateningly outside for those beyond its grasp. Yet, upon close inspection of sanctuary discourse, law can also be seen to authorize sanctuary, majestically propping up its walls in full view of on-lookers. In still other moments, law gracelessly huddles with providers in a corner, taking advantage of the fleeting, uncertain protection that sanctuary provides in order to plot how its recipients might pass through immigration authorities' arms to freedom. Law is known to play an integral role in liberal government. But sanctuary suggests that it can also be vital within and in relation to subordinate powers – in this instance, a pastoral power and a nonstate sovereign power. The relation between law and sanctuary is therefore more diverse than it first appears, all the more when powers beyond liberalism are acknowledged.

Working from within the tradition of critical legal studies, Patricia Ewick and Susan Silbey offer a groundbreaking account of legal consciousness constructed from interviews with "common" people about law in their everyday lives.[1] Identified are three stories of law: "up against the law," "before the law," and "(playing) with the law." In the first narrative, "up against the law," law is deemed arbitrary, oppressive, and to require resistance; it is a powerful force that cannot be confronted directly. Law is to be coped with via avoidance, tricks, and ruses. Ewick and Silbey write: "Foot-dragging, omissions, ploys, small deceits, humor, and making scenes are typical forms of resistance for those up against the law."[2] In its avoidance of immigration law, at first glance, one would expect sanctuary to most immediately fit this narrative. In the second story, "before the law," law is viewed as majestic, authoritative, and external. Law operates "by known rules in carefully delimited spheres."[3] Here law stands outside and above social life. The third

narrative, "with the law," is consistent with the notion that "law is concrete, partial, flawed, and changing." It is "an arena of competitive tactical
maneuvering where the pursuit of self-interest is expected."[4] Law is a game
open to all but is played best by legal professionals, upon whom there is
considerable reliance.[5] These stories are not thought to neatly match specific persons or personalities, with some persons "up against," others "before," and still others "with" the law. Indeed, these narratives are occasionally
evident within a single utterance or textual segment.[6] One way that the
narratives can be distinguished is in terms of their differing conceptions of
time.[7] Time is a key dimension of each legal narrative and is variously seen
as having to be reacted to as capricious; as conspicuously absent (i.e., timeless), which is consistent with a sanctuary tradition; and as a commodity to
be purchased for pragmatic purpose. Assumptions about time within the
three broader legal narratives instantiated in sanctuary discourse are instances of the powers that shape and make sanctuary possible.

However, rather than uncritically applying this tripartite narrative scheme
to sanctuary, this chapter deploys the scheme in order to aid thinking about
how law relates to and constitutes sanctuary and about relations among
law and two nonliberal powers. Legal narratives and corresponding
subjectivities are – in this specific case – imbricated in a pastoral power and
a nonstate sovereign power that together constitute sanctuary.[8] In some
instances of sanctuary discourse, perhaps as expected, law is imagined as
arbitrary, capricious, and unpredictable. Here law renders pastoral power
possible by serving as an integral element of a condition ripe for "shepherd's"
intervening sacrifice on behalf of "sheep." In other instances, however, forms
of "higher" law authorize sanctuary, which is consistent with the exercise
of a sovereign power that flows from church and community. Yet this narrative and the corresponding authorization that it provides for sanctuary is
rarely complete enough to eliminate the potential for sacrifice or risk that
such practices entail. Finally, in sanctuary discourse, law also appears as a
broader game in which lawyers are called upon to define sanctuary's legality and where sanctuary subsequently becomes merely a tactic deployed in
order to "win." Because migrants have to defer to legal professionals for
strategic advice and in negotiations with immigration authorities (a requirement created by the gradual juridification of refugee determination over
the past two decades) and because migrants are presumed to lack the knowledge and resources necessary to secure such legal assistance, here too law
creates opportunities for providers' sacrifice. Yet, consistent with this narrative, such deference is not enough to ensure that migrants "win." Legal
assistance is just that, and, consistent with the (partially) authorized exercise of a nonstate sovereign power, sanctuary discourse also presumes a need
to create spectacles in order to ultimately fulfill migrants' needs by securing
their legal status. The analysis of sanctuary at once reveals relations among

law and neglected nonliberal powers and raises questions about Ewick and Silbey's tripartite narrative scheme.

Sanctuary up against the Law

Of the three narratives, "up against the law" is the most anticipated within sanctuary discourse. Here law is arbitrary and oppressive and as a consequence is to be avoided. A sanctuary provider said:

> We were helping this [migrant] family ... but the government was trying to break them apart and using all kinds of pressure and tactics to threaten them. It was not a very pleasant situation ... They had decided the stand they'd take. They were not going to allow this family to stay in Canada, and it didn't matter what anybody ever did ... It was the heavy hand of government.[9]

In its symbolic and spatial avoidance of immigration law, sanctuary is seen to immediately fit this narrative. In another incident, a provider explained: "We want to make sure that the weaker party is not crushed by the power of the state, crushed by mechanisms ... free to steamroll over citizens and individuals."[10]

This exercise of state sovereign power that takes the form of law "as command" has a distinct temporal quality.[11] A sanctuary provider noted:

> And I remember saying [to immigration authorities]: "Are you going to take any direct action?" In other words implying, "Are you going to send the troopers in?" They said, *"No, not at this time,"* which was a lovely, tantalizing "not now." And I don't know whether that meant not today, maybe tomorrow.[12]

The timing of enforcement was seen as arbitrary and consistent with oppression:

> It's not an easy thing to go through, especially having to deal with government authorities and with people who *at any time* might come into the church.[13]

In a separate occurence, on behalf of the migrants, providers had filed an application on humanitarian and compassionate grounds:

> So ... for a few minutes you get all your hopes on this and keep saying, "this will do it, this will do it," and so you work and work, and ... when the big day comes, you're waiting for your answer. It normally takes two days for an answer to come back from this board ... and they left them hanging for a week before they would give an answer ... You ask anyone what the

normal process is, [and it's] two days from this little group that decides, and they were left [waiting] a whole week ... So yet again you're thinking, okay they didn't answer today but tomorrow for sure because it's normally two days. And then tomorrow it wouldn't come. And then you knew it was Friday, so no way you're getting an answer until Monday.[14]

Such timing was deemed to be strategic stalling: "Normally it only took two days for an answer, [but] we never got an answer in the normal time, never. Not once for anything. That was directed at us volunteers who were helping."[15] In another incident, a provider stated: "I had saw [sic] how long this took, which I'm sure is part of the [Immigration Department's] strategy to keep us discouraged ... It's a way to wear you down."[16]

Immigration authorities were also imagined to be inconsistent. This was seen in talk regarding decisions about humanitarian and compassionate applications on behalf of the migrants in sanctuary.[17] A provider noted:

The answers to the questions were never the same. *Like you could ask a question one day, and the next day would be a different immigration officer on duty, and you'd get a different answer to the same question.* And so it was hard to figure out where we stood and what was the right answer ... Like there's a 1-800 ... immigration number where you can get information and talk to people if you want to, and the answers are different. *Call one week and ask a question and call the next week for follow up to that previous answer, and the answer is different.*[18]

Although legal provisions that placed migrants in their predicament were defined in immigration law and thought to be oppressive, in some moments of sanctuary discourse, other laws not usually associated with the coercive powers of the state became imagined so. As sanctuary incidents dragged on, providers unexpectedly found themselves "up against" these other laws. As noted in Chapter 5, one sanctuary provider set up a visible booth in her city's square to draw attention to immigration authorities' oppressive treatment of a migrant family and to the fact that they had consequently been forced into sanctuary in a nearby church. Following a legal order from city inspectors to remove the booth, which was said to be in conflict with a local ordinance, the coercion of the migrants and of the woman who erected the shelter on their behalf became one. A sanctuary supporter stated:

The same bureaucratic mentality which is holding up their [i.e., the migrants'] case in Ottawa seems to have pervaded the thinking of our civic administrators and those who advise them: rules are rules, whether good or bad, is the thinking ... This play-by-the-book decision not to allow ... [the]

booth in the square is as out of touch as the blind bureaucracy in Ottawa, which insists that terrified refugee claimants must go through a flawed [legal] ritual.[19]

Another sanctuary effort came up against local fire regulations. Consonant with the arbitrary timing noted above, a pastor remarked that two days after granting sanctuary:

> *All of a sudden,* the city fire inspectors were here and inspecting our [church] facilities where we hadn't had an inspection for years ... They were doing their job, and there were some things we had to do in order to make it safer for them [i.e., the migrants in the church]. That was fine, we did that. They were very supportive. It wasn't like they came in heavy-handed. I just found it interesting, some of the *timing of these things.*[20]

In enforcing the law, the fire inspectors were "doing their job," but the term "just" in the last utterance marks a transition to an "up against the law" narrative, a shift from the legitimate exercise of law as governance to a coercive act, as signalled by its unexpected timing – that is, immediately after sanctuary had commenced. The decision to conduct a fire inspection was plainly suspected to be an effort to coerce sanctuary providers and recipients.

In sanctuary discourse, normally mundane tax laws pertaining to churches' charitable status also became threatening:

> Revenue Canada ... had sent at least one piece of correspondence ... questioning their [i.e., the church's] charitable status and taking issue with it by pointing out the inconsistency between that and this political activity ... of giving sanctuary to a family that was subject to deportation. It could be a case of the left hand not knowing what the right hand was doing, *but* it's the federal government, on the one hand, wanting these people deported and maintaining a position, and [on] the other hand, ... putting pressure on the body giving sanctuary.[21]

In this excerpt, the use of "but" fuses immigration authorities' intention to deport migrants with Revenue Canada's efforts at tax-law enforcement to create a unified power "pressuring" providers and migrants. Consistent with this narrative, however, sanctuary discourse also includes talk of avoidance when such mundane laws became potentially oppressive. In a distinct incident:

> Revenue Canada can come in and say, "Hey you are using church funds for purposes [i.e., helping the migrants] that you can't get receipts for" ... And

we were very careful that any of the funds that were used for this purpose were not received through the church.[22]

Although sanctuary discourse is itself about avoiding oppressive immigration law, upon closer inspection, it can be seen to comprise a range of avoidance strategies. For example, the potentially heavy-handed reaction of immigration authorities to sanctuary was deemed an advantage to providers and migrants. It was thought that if the authorities stormed the church, this would resemble the illiberal persecution that migrants claimed to have fled and would then become an ironic spectacle of oppression as a result. Once set in motion, the Immigration Department's legal power would not be confronted but sidestepped, effectively generating a politically dangerous spectacle that would be fully illuminated by sanctuary's ongoing spectacle, which stemmed from the exercise of a nonstate sovereign power. Typically, this potential for political spectacle was assumed to help keep immigration agents at bay:

> When the immigration people called, the tone went up a bit. Here's officialdom at least that's made a contact. What's going to happen? And then a rumour started to go around that they were going to storm the church. Okay, [but] I didn't give any credence to that at all. I said, "Are you kidding, the PR value of some police force storming a church? No."[23]

Therefore, a related avoidance technique closely associated with clergy and church boards was to keep church doors unlocked. This was assumed to render it difficult for authorities to arrest and charge providers with aiding and abetting migrants in the event that sanctuary was stormed:[24]

> The decision was made right from the outset that this church would never be locked so the authorities could never say that they were stopped from coming into the church. And we went on public record ... that the church was always open and we were not going to stand in the way of the law.[25]

About the same incident, a provider noted:

> We called the immigration people and said, "If you want to come in at any time, we will show you around. We will show you anything you want to see. We want to make sure that you don't think we are some kind of Waco group. There are no guns here, there's not anything." If Immigration's decided that they wanted to come pick her up, they [can] just tell us. We'll hold the door ... We aren't going to stand in the way of an actual apprehension, but we are also going to grant her sanctuary.[26]

Another imagined way to avoid law's reach was to establish separation between sanctuary providers from the community and the church board and clergy,[27] thereby ensuring that although church buildings could be used for sanctuary, moral and financial support of migrants, including fundraising for legal and application fees,[28] would become the responsibility of community supporters. In an instance mentioned in Chapter 5, church authorities charged a community-based sanctuary support group rent for the migrant's use of church space, the relation between the two entities thus being transformed into a landlord-tenant contract.[29]

Following appearance of several sanctuary incidents in the early 1990s, the Inter-Church Committee for Refugees (ICCR) sought to organize a national sanctuary-like network as an alternative to the "physical" sanctuary discussed above. The ICCR programmatic text describing this alternative avoidance strategy reads:

> Congregations/parishes have been actively considering ... granting "sanctuary in their church building." There are many problems with this practice ... It is an all or nothing proposition. Either the case will be resolved positively, or arrest and deportation are virtually assured. Not only can the individuals be heavily fined and penalized, but technically, the church building could be seized by the state! ... This is what has led us to seek an alternative to physical "sanctuary" which ICCR can recommend to the church constituency and which would keep the pressure on for a positive resolution to exceptional cases.[30]

Consistent with the exercise of sovereign power, this program foresaw making the exception for some migrants – but in a novel way. The location and identity of the migrants faced with imminent deportation was to remain unknown to the local church agreeing to offer support, thereby protecting church buildings from legal liability and migrants and providers from arrest. Congregations and other supporters would pledge support for migrants but would know neither their location nor their identity.[31] No migrants actually received sanctuary in this way in the years that followed.[32] The program's failure undoubtedly stemmed from the fact that sanctuary support tends to come from a broader local community as well as from church congregations; to adequately translate into pastoral power, such a scheme must offer providers the opportunity to know the migrants intimately. Absent in this scheme was occasion and space for shepherds to emerge as they sought to gain personal, individualizing knowledge of individual sheep and to guide their futures and provide for their needs accordingly. Nevertheless, consistent with an "up against the law" narrative, these examples reveal that when law was deemed oppressive, providers sought to avoid it.

This narrative also appeared more subtly in sanctuary discourse, such as in attempts at humour. A provider recounted:

It's a very large [church] parking lot. And the [patrolling] police officers on a regular basis ... will pull in here and have their donuts ... [and] they park their cars side by side, and they talk to each other, and they share donuts, right? So anyway that happened at precisely the moment that a whole bunch of the press were here [filming interviews with the migrants]. They were in the [church] building, and two police cars pulled in, so you could imagine what happened ... Everybody runs down the stairs to our parking lot. The [church] door flies open, and the [media] guys come out with their cameras on their shoulders filming see? Well it turns out that the two police officers are so baffled by this [laughs], and they [the media] said [to the police], "Are you here to arrest the spy?" [i.e., the migrant in sanctuary] And the response was, "What spy?" They just wanted donuts. So that was quite hilarious ... For a moment I said, "Wow, they've finally come with the law."[33]

Here legal agents were imagined as both lazy (they sit in parked patrol vehicles consuming donuts) and inept (despite considerable media coverage of sanctuary's spectacle, these agents had no knowledge of the migrant, a former Canadian Security Intelligence Service spy, illegally residing in a church a few steps away). Sanctuary providers could not stop the law if it were to "finally come" to the church door, but they could deride its agents in the process.

Despite avoidance strategies of various kinds, however, uncertainty about immigration authorities' next course of action prevailed across the incidents. In an interview, one provider was asked about this:

RL: How comfortable were you that they weren't going to come in during that entire period?
Provider: You never knew. I mean the lid could have blown off this. We had a couple scares.[34]

This uncertainty stemming from immigration authorities' inconsistency was echoed in a separate incident:

It was quite stressful for me. I didn't know what was going to happen to him. And other people were worried about what was going to happen to them ... because they saw themselves as violating the law or something. But I don't remember when ... it became clear that the government was going to come to an understanding that was acceptable, but it wasn't very early ... The [immigration] minister and bureaucrats in Ottawa were inconsistent or totally cruel, and you didn't know where they were or what they were going to do. A couple of times they essentially said, "We're going to arrest this guy and deport him," which didn't bode well for any kind of negotiations.[35]

A provider observed in relation to another incident:

Are they going to do this or not? I'd never like to think that in this country that someone would storm a church and take someone, but I would never think this country would have done what they did to put them in the church in the first place.[36]

Sacrifice as Avoidance and Risk Taking

Consistent with this "up against the law" narrative, the pressure of immigration (and other) law, and the accompanying inconsistency and arbitrary timing of its exercise, was a key possibility for sacrifice by pastoral shepherds on behalf of needful sheep. Avoidance was not enough to fully eliminate uncertainty or risk to providers: the potential for more significant sacrifice beyond avoidance remained. This is plainly evinced in several occurrences:

It was clear that we could be hauled off to jail with him, and there's nothing we could have done about it. And that was what we were putting on the line ... And we were hoping not to get into a situation like that, but we knew that there were risks all the way through this thing ... This was one risk that we had to take.[37]

We ... could be guilty of breaking the immigration law, and we would be guilty also of conspiring to break the law. So they are two serious federal charges. We had to take these into account ... So we knew there was a risk involved.[38]

We would rather risk offending the law than risk a life.[39]

We are prepared to risk fines, even imprisonment, in order to protect human life and freedom.[40]

The intimidation ... [that] was coming was thick – jail, the $10,000 fine, all of these things – but I believe that there are times in a man's life that he has got to do what's right regardless and put everything on the line.[41]

If they were to be removed from the church, the cathedral clergy would have to be arrested first ... and we would be prepared for that. You have to walk the talk ... There is a time in life when you have to take a risk.[42]

The Anglicans ... were concerned about breaking the law. The United Church people ... were concerned about breaking the law ... the congregation took a big risk.[43]

In providing "opportunity" to take risks while avoiding oppressive law on behalf of needful migrants, the "up against the law" narrative made the exercise of pastoral power possible. Providers sacrificed themselves through avoidance and *potentially* illegal acts in the face of immigration authorities' oppressive threats to the lives and wellbeing of marginalized members of providers' churches and communities.

Sanctuary before the "Higher" Law
In contrast to the "up against the law" narrative, a recent Southern Ontario Sanctuary Coalition (SOSC) mission statement reads:

> We are a *law-abiding group and are firmly committed to seeing that Canada uphold its national and international commitment to refugees.* We believe the Government of Canada is not consistently honouring *its legal responsibilities* to properly review refugee claims and that, as Canadian citizens, we cannot abandon refugees.[44]

While sanctuary discourse reveals that occasionally higher moral or religious principles provide license to providers, it is law that is more prominent in authorizing sanctuary. An SOSC member, for example, noted that in the face of unjust immigration and refugee law bearing down on migrants, "I will obey a higher law."[45] The second legal narrative embedded in sanctuary discourse is "before the law." To be sure, at times during sanctuary incidents, there was clear conformity to immigration law, but at others, sanctuary providers stood before "higher" legal forms of authorization to act. For instance, on several occasions, as above, there were suggestions of an effort to render Canadian immigration and refugee law consistent with international law:[46]

> There is [sic] *two levels of law*. Canada ... is very active in the United Nations [and] has signed a number of declarations, which means Canada should follow those declarations ... In all cases, Canada has not made them part of our domestic legislation. The Immigration Act does not say we don't deport people to a country where they are likely to be tortured or killed, [but] we signed that at the United Nations.[47]

Another provider noted:

We are explicit in our opening sanctuary declaration that we are affirming Canada's international obligations ... Canada wouldn't like to be seen as offending international human rights, even though it's happening more and more frequently ... But nonetheless, the Canadian government likes to be seen as clean in this respect. So we see that as an important element in our repertoire. So everything we do we see as consistent with what has been affirmed in Canada's previous [legal] agreements and obligations.[48]

In another instance, a letter from sanctuary providers to the immigration minister reads: "Canada is a signatory to both the U.N. Convention on Refugees and the U.N. Convention on the Rights of the Child (Articles 2 and 22). Both these conventions apply in the case of Ms. M and Canada needs to honour them."[49] The immigration minister responded: "The convention makes it clear the deportation order should not affect the rights of the children."[50] Note, however, that there is no reference in the minister's response to the situation of the migrant parents, who, ostensibly, continued to be threatened by the order.

Invocation of this higher law went beyond UN Conventions. Another way in which providers stood before a higher law was to appeal to law's "spirit":

I don't avow civil disobedience, but in this case we really believed that the law was being unjust, especially in light of the discretion that was apparently available ... [to] the officer that was in charge. I'm sure he was doing his job, but ... he was following the letter of the law ... I'm not sure it was in the *spirit of the law*.[51]

Law's spirit became a plane higher than written law, one that was easier for a provider to stand before. Similarly, a different provider observed, "Sanctuary is an unwritten law."[52] And in a distinct incident, a provider referred to "social contracts that are unwritten. This [i.e., sanctuary] was one of them, and it panned out."[53] Embedded in these excerpts is a questioning of the necessity of textuality for legal authority, which is usually associated with a "before the law" narrative,[54] thereby creating space in which to authorize sanctuary.

God's law, of course, was also present in sanctuary discourse. In one occurrence, a priest noted: "By being here, she's [i.e., the migrant] following the law, which allows sanctuary."[55] In another incident: "These people are committed to God and to the Bible and are ... appealing in a sense to a *higher* law."[56] A pastor's speech after granting sanctuary to a migrant family referred to a "greater law":

God wants us to pray and intercede for kings and all those in authority. But we are also told God's law is greater than any man made laws, that when authorities go contrary to God's will, we are right to disobey them.[57]

Consistent with the complex blend of church and community efforts that comprise sanctuary efforts, a corresponding mix of higher laws was typically present in sanctuary discourse: "By taking in M, the elders of Y Church are not placing themselves above the law. Rather, they are placing themselves squarely within Roman Law, ecclesiastical and canon law, and English common law, all of which recognize and uphold the right of sanctuary."[58] A provider from a separate incident remarked:

> We talked with several lawyers and ... the unanimous comment we received was that there was no basis in Canadian law for granting of sanctuary, but there was the long-standing precedent in common law for the granting of sanctuary. And so based on common law throughout history, and of course our understanding of the Old Testament, the Biblical law of sanctuary for the Jewish people in Old Testament times, we would go ahead and grant sanctuary. But it was on that basis that we were not going to break the law.[59]

This specific claim to a higher law, it should be noted, is nevertheless dependent on lawyers' advice, an aspect consistent with a third "with the law" narrative, to be discussed below.

Dominant and intimately tethered to the notion of a higher law in sanctuary discourse was a sanctuary tradition, which is to say that some laws were deemed higher due to their tradition:

> We didn't know what legal standing there was. We were honestly concerned that we were actually breaking the law and that I, as an executive member, who chose to do this, could in some way be prosecuted. I guess technically we were in breach of the law, but *the tradition of sanctuary allowed us some leeway*.[60]

In another occurrence, a provider explained:

> We're never quite sure about the boundaries between the religious and the secular world. And so there's this sense in which we're challenging that to define how much respect for that *tradition of sanctuary* there is in this culture of modern-day Quebec. But this congregation and this denomination in general have a strong history of social justice ... Saints in our tradition are the heretics in other traditions. So they always have tended to be those most outspoken for humanitarian causes and most active in reform move-

ments ... We'll probably always need sanctuary ... If we were going to act out our tradition, we needed to take a stand on this issue.[61]

Tradition rendered sanctuary consistent with a "timeless and transcendent"[62] higher law. A sanctuary provider observed:

> The ancient tradition of giving sanctuary ... has been going on for years. This has been going on in times even before the birth of Christ – people were giving sanctuary to people who were in harm's way. This has been going on for generations and generations. We're just a part of that historical moment in history.[63]

In contrast, contemporary constitutional-rights claims rarely appeared in sanctuary discourse. Their relative absence is remarkable given the widespread assumption of an emerging "rights consciousness"[64] in Canada in the two decades following entrenchment of Canada's Charter of Rights and Freedoms in 1982,[65] virtually the same period during which the thirty-six sanctuary incidents occurred. This dearth of constitutional-rights claims was not simply a result of a sober recognition of the failed use of religious freedom as a legal defence in the US sanctuary trials that ultimately resulted in convictions of eight providers during the height of sanctuary activism in that context.[66] Acknowledgement of the existence (or outcomes) of these widely publicized trials in sanctuary discourse in Canada was almost completely absent. Sanctuary in Canada was tied less to a perceived contemporary *right* to religious freedom than it was in the US context, and more to a variety of older authorizing forms of higher law. To be sure, US sanctuary providers on occasion also distinguished "common" and "customary" law, on the one hand, from "statutory" law, on the other.[67] In those moments, US and Canadian sanctuary mirrored one another. But overall, perhaps due to the simple facts that Canada's Charter is in its infancy, and still lacks a tradition, and that sanctuary in Canada was not exclusively or even primarily a religious effort, other forms of higher law tended to be implicated in granting sanctuary.

For Max Weber, modern law originated in "a value-rational belief in higher law."[68] However, Weber argued that legal rationality freed persons from the "eternal yesterday" of custom, from the deadening intimacy of traditional "community."[69] In sanctuary discourse, the eternal yesterday and traditional community return to provide for the emancipation of migrants from legal rationality, or at least from that version that judges migrants in distant legal hearings on the basis of formal abstract knowledge and then seeks to remove those found wanting to dangerous spaces to face imprisonment, economic deprivation, or death. Across sanctuary incidents, it was variously international law, God's law, unwritten law, and common law that authorized sanctuary. This was consistent with a form of church and community sovereign power that protected migrants from deportation and providers from prosecution, but it was nevertheless law. Here higher *law*, more so than higher moral or religious *principle*, returned from the past to erect sanctuary's walls.

Sanctuary with the Law

The third story of law evident in sanctuary discourse is one of playing "with the law." Here law is a game. Despite being intimately involved himself, a sanctuary provider noted that a lawyer

> was the main spokesperson for the media ... You have to have a quarterback, somebody who's going to be calling the plays. My role? I saw myself as a liaison and playing a support role for what the lawyer was doing. I felt that it was not my *game*. Ultimately, the family has to make the decisions with their lawyer.[70]

Sanctuary was not transcendent here. Rather, it was merely among the last plays to buy time in a drawn-out game that the migrants were losing. A provider remarked: "We tried everything we could just to try and *get some time there to do something. We tried to play all the cards that we had to buy ourselves time.*"[71] Another noted: "The only way we could see to *buy time* was to get him into sanctuary."[72] In a separate instance, a provider observed:

> Had we not provided him [through sanctuary] *the time* ... to talk to the media and ... to proceed with the legal process, ... they [would] have grabbed him, and he would have been on an airplane.[73]

Note that the legal process was "proceeded with" rather than avoided or replaced. In a different incident, providers granted "sanctuary in a hope to try and *buy time* to find a solution where this family can stay together."[74] During another situation, a provider said: "We realized in hearing about the case ... that there probably were mistakes in the process and that what we were offering was *time* for those mistakes to be corrected if possible."[75] Here sanctuary provided time to permit the flawed legal system to work in due course. Time is a precious commodity purchased with sanctuary and with shepherds' corresponding sacrifice to "win" the legal game. Correspondingly, sanctuary was a "cooling off" period and place rather than permanent salvation in a sovereign territory. Sanctuary was, as a provider noted, "a temporary demand [that] ... won't continue forever."[76] It was a "time out" to regroup and strategize before returning to the game to potentially snatch victory from what seemed in some moments like certain defeat. Here law was neither of an external and oppressive nor a majestic character. Rather, law was eventually and pragmatically to yield solutions.

Sacrifice for Adequate Legal Representation

Chapter 3 argues that law had fully entered the refugee determination realm in Canada by 1989. A consequence of this shift was that legal assistance became one more need among migrants who managed to arrive on Canadian soil to make refugee claims. Due to the significant reduction in legal aid programs for low-income persons in several provinces during the 1990s,[77] this was a condition that became increasingly ripe for sacrifice. A provider noted that sanctuary support comprised "a group of people ... raising funds for lawyers because there's no legal aid in [the province of] New Brunswick."[78] Nearing the resolution of another incident, a priest noted: "The family has left the church building, but will be in need of prayers and hopefully the legal help."[79] Conceivably, prayers could be easily said on behalf of migrants; legal help came at a greater and more profane price. That providing such legal aid and related administrative fees was deemed a sacrifice is plainly evident in sanctuary discourse. Consider the following two incidents:

> The lawyer told us we would need to budget about $5,000 depending on what level of appeals we have to get to. The meeting that he had with the federal judge cost several thousand dollars. Opening their file cost $1,000. If we have an humanitarian and compassionate appeal, I believe it is $550 per person. So we have three adults that we're dealing with. *And those are just the legal costs on top of all the expenses of having them in the church.*[80]

> We formed a community to help those [migrant] families. We explored ... legal representation, how to help them, how to connect them with lawyers who would know how to deal with the situation ... We started with local lawyers ... and for a whole variety of reasons ended up going to R, who we sort of had heard of through his reputation. But then in the end we called him. We hired him to help those two families, and then we had to look at the whole financial implications of that, and *that was a great big commitment, to put it mildly.*[81]

In the "with the law" narrative, sanctuary is necessary because law is not so much oppressive as fraught with errors. Through sanctuary, it was assumed that the legal system would in time fix itself: "This [sanctuary] option protects the individual at risk in that it allows [time for] the [legal] system to respond, to self correct."[82] Significantly, such errors were often thought to stem from inadequate legal representation: "They had had a lawyer who really messed up in my opinion, who had let them down and who just had not done what needed to be done."[83] In another incident, a lawyer had "initially screwed up" and was "way too placid."[84] In a different case:

> The [migrant's] employer was a lawyer, and so he kind of volunteered to represent M at the first immigration hearing. And ... when the immigration officer said she had to leave [Canada], the lawyer then decided that he should hire another lawyer for her. So there was another lawyer that was hired. He belonged to the same law firm. Unfortunately, the lawyer wasn't really interested in representing M. I think he was more interested in covering the butt of his friend, the employer. And so during the hearing, he didn't ask M what she wanted. He basically just said, "We accept the decision. M is voluntarily leaving the country!"[85]

In another incident, a provider remarked: "Some [migrants] have got terrible lawyers, and a lot of people lose their cases because of bad legal advice."[86] This "bad" advice was often deemed to stem directly from migrants' lack of financial resources for proper legal representation:

> One of the sad things about this story was that there had been a number of immigration lawyers, or so called, and I think partially because the family [in sanctuary] didn't have a lot of money, they got poor lawyers and they got poor advice.[87]

In other instances, poor legal representation was deemed the problem leading to the sanctuary incident and good representation the key to its resolution. In one incident:

> A lawyer that was representing M at that point did not do a very good job in terms of representing her ... If there had been a different presentation, with different documentation, the outcome might have been quite different. And so we felt that again she got blacklisted because she didn't have good legal representation and again because she was marginalized. She didn't speak English very well, couldn't represent herself very well, so would have to be totally dependent on whoever was representing her to do a good job for her. So that's why we ended up looking at another lawyer. Those lawyers ... don't get paid what they deserve to be paid to do that kind of work because the people they're representing don't have the money to pay them.[88]

In another instance, a provider explained:

> We had them in the basement for a number of weeks, and we realized that they were going to be there for a long time because the legal situation was

not going to proceed. In fact the lawyer, R, missed an important date with the federal government and tried to cover it up ... so R was useless, totally useless, so we fired her as M's lawyer within weeks and did some searching out to find some other lawyers ... And finally we found somebody who was willing to take it, and he did ... a very good piece of work for us.[89]

Chapter 2 noted how the SOSC eventually shifted away from providing "physical" sanctuary to migrants (although the SOSC has also more recently threatened to return to sanctuary). In an SOSC response to the long wait to secure status for migrants granted sanctuary in 1993, lawyers' mistakes were thought to have led to the need for sanctuary, while other lawyers were deemed integral to a more efficient, alternative strategy:

We discovered that if a person had entered, say through Buffalo or Detroit ... and they just took the deportation order [and left], within three months they could make another application. It was called the "back door," and so at a certain point, I said, "This is the fastest way." Even if you go to the Federal Court, it'll be three years before you even get your [status]. So we used that [tactic] a lot. And most of the cases were accepted on the second [refugee] hearing because the first ones had been *messed up, usually because of the lawyer*. That's the truth. So for several years I just found that, although it's painful and tragic, especially where there's kids involved, it's not as bad as waiting [in Canada] four years, five years, six years with no resolution. So that's how we dealt with a lot of them ... We would drive them down [to the border] and make sure they were with the people and then when they got back [to Canada], they called, and we *set them up with a good lawyer*. We saw it through. But that was the best way.[90]

Therefore, because of a recognition of inadequate legal representation due to limited state-funded legal assistance provided to migrants in the refugee-determination process and its aftermath, a first step after sanctuary commenced (and occasionally in the harried days immediately preceding it) was to seek a better lawyer to look after the migrant's case:

Immediately, we looked for a lawyer who would review the case and represent it at this humanitarian and compassionate appeal point. And ... the lawyer that we found is experienced in immigration issues, and he comes highly recommended from the francophone community, and he is doing this as his own social action, indicating in our first meeting with him that he preferred to be paid but that was not the determining factor in whether he would handle the case. So of course ... the congregation would prefer to pay him ... reasonably, and that means that we've had to do a fundraising effort.[91]

Another provider recounted:

> So [we] were able to get M to take the case, [but] ... you had to fly [him in]
> every time we needed him. We had to buy the ticket ... We hadn't worked
> with him before, but we had heard that he had experience with refugee
> cases, not so much with sanctuary, but with refugee cases.[92]

As noted, the possible illegality of sanctuary was a form of cost and sacrifice
on behalf of providers and in this way consistent with the "up against the
law" narrative. But sacrifice was also seen when migrants' lack of access to
adequate legal representation led providers to acquire discerning knowledge of the quality of immigration lawyers and, once identified, to secure
resources to cover migrants' legal fees in order to proceed "with the law."
Early on in many incidents, sanctuary providers began organizing fundraisers
to cover the costs of pending legal expenses,[93] themselves a form of sacrifice. Although the "pursuit of self-interest is expected" within this narrative,[94] in the sanctuary context, this effort pertained more to migrants'
immediate interests and needs than to those of providers.

The following provides a further sense of the high costs of good legal
assistance as well as the sacrifice required to secure it in the absence of
adequate levels of state-funded legal assistance. A prominent immigration
law firm originally approached by the sanctuary providers offered three
options, the first two requiring a $2,000 retainer "with no estimate as to
final costs." The third option was to

> petition the provincial Supreme Court that M be allowed to reside in Canada
> because it would be in their best interests to have their mother stay with
> them ... Our firm has taken such cases forward and at the preliminary stage,
> in several instances Immigration Canada has held off from removing the
> parent. We would be willing to work on this option on a flat fee basis for
> $5000 plus disbursements plus taxes. For the fee quoted we would file *only*
> a petition before the court along with supporting material and argue for a
> stay of her removal from Canada. If the court accepted our arguments, there
> would eventually need to be a full hearing on the merits, such a full hearing
> could *cost thousands of dollars more and we provide no estimate as to final costs.*[95]

In another occurrence, the sanctuary group "took a loan at the Royal Bank
in order to enable them to pay their immigration fees, which were hefty,
and their legal fees, which were also pretty hefty."[96]

In a few incidents, once located by providers or otherwise drawn to a
sanctuary incident, lawyers worked to fulfill migrants' legal needs *pro bono*.[97]
In his brassy, popular account of providing sanctuary, a pastor recounted:

They were there to do business for people they had never met ... and WITH-OUT CHARGE! Have you ever heard of that before? – *Lawyers working on their honeymoon? – Lawyers working for nothing? – Lawyers reaching out to strangers?* THE UNBELIEVABLE WAS HAPPENING![98]

In these cases, lawyers moved closer to becoming pastoral shepherds by putting themselves out on migrants' behalf. However, when this *pro bono* basis was absent, as it often was, potential for providers' sacrifice remained.

Consonant with this "with the law" narrative,[99] and as noted earlier, once adequate lawyers were secured, they were often given the thorny tasks of determining sanctuary's legal status[100] and identifying any lingering remains of the legal prospects of a migrant's case.[101] Several lawyers went beyond this to join in visible rallies and protests.[102] One provider noted: "The lawyer tried to do his best to mobilize people from the church."[103] It was also obvious that in some instances, the idea of seeking sanctuary came directly from lawyers. A provider remarked in one case that the lawyer

said it's [i.e., sanctuary] not something we want to do, and hopefully we won't have to do it, but you need to be prepared and you need to be very well organized before it comes to that date. He actually came out and met with the whole congregation the week before ... and he kept saying if they come and bang on your door that morning, this is what you need to be expecting.[104]

In these instances, the uncertainty of sanctuary's legality was such that lawyers had something to sacrifice beyond their fees. In one incident's genesis, there

was a lawyer who had just seen it [i.e., the migrant's predicament] in the newspaper and sensed a gross injustice here and wanted something done about it. And that lawyer has yet to be identified because a lawyer has more to lose ... if they violate [a law] or participate in a crime. They can – they may not go to jail or anything – ... lose their ability to make a living as a lawyer.[105]

One SOSC member noted how lawyers would "cover themselves" in light of this:[106]

Well the lawyers ... can't counsel somebody to do something illegal ... What they will do is if somebody's in sanctuary, they will ... make the applications to the minister [of immigration and use] ... all the various means of appeal. They will do that. And generously and effectively – but they can't counsel people to go into sanctuary or to go into hiding or stay illegally. What they do is they say: "Now go and see M and just tell her I said you should go." They just send them over, and ... then I say, "Well why did they send you?" [And they say,] "Well I'm getting deported." I mean they [i.e., lawyers] have to ... cover themselves, but they send them [i.e., migrants] over.[107]

Deference to Lawyers

In many incidents, lawyers also became centrally involved in direct negotiations with immigration authorities. There was significant deference to lawyers operating in this capacity. In one instance, a provider remarked:

I know nothing about immigration and refugee law ... When we started ... the chances that I would put my foot in my mouth ... [and] say something that was completely stupid were pretty good. So we just agreed that nobody would deal with them [i.e., immigration authorities] except for R [the lawyer], and it's because he had had a longstanding relationship with them.[108]

In another occurrence, a provider explained:

I had some discussions with immigration, and it was one of those situations where R, the family's [the migrants'] lawyer, was the one who was primarily doing the talking. We [i.e., the sanctuary support group] tried to avoid talking as much as possible because he knew what he was doing there, and we didn't want to muddy the waters.[109]

In terms of the resolution of one migrant's predicament, again the lawyer was in control:

The only change that came about was that we obtained a guarantee that the M's could leave the church and immediately leave the country without being apprehended. That was ... what we were working towards ... for a long, long time ... This was a very risky venture that they could leave the church and go to the third country, stay for ninety days, come back in, and seek refugee status again. There was nothing certain about seeking refugee status ... *We just got the word through the lawyer that we could do this.*[110]

Toward the end of another incident, information about developments in negotiations was carefully managed by the lawyer. For example, press releases first "had to be cleared with the lawyer."[111] And in another case:

Once the initial blitz happened, things started to slow down, and there was not anything to feed the media at that point. We just sort of had to wait. I think there was a release of some sort about once a week, but that was being done by the lawyer ... so a lot of that stuff was out of my hands.[112]

Other lawyers sought and secured special legal agreements and handled various undertakings on migrants' behalf.[113] In one incident, after a lengthy dialogue, finally

> a deal was cut, ... and the minister [of immigration] said, "What we can give you is a re-hearing" ... They were put back into the [refugee-determination] system ... There are so many ways that judges can put their fingers on the scale of justice to satisfy their own sense of right and wrong. Their own value system is really what's being reflected in the judgment. They basically come up with ... some really cheesy ways to distinguish this judgment from a different judgment, this case from that case, and say, "This is a different case now" by looking at some really small aspect. It's judicial slight of hand. My sense was that the first [negative refugee-status] judgment was perfectly credible. I'm grateful for the second [positive status] judgment, also credible.[114]

Here law appears concrete and flawed, a lawyer's negotiations making possible a second "credible" judgment of the same migrant family's claim, one that was diametrically opposed to the first.

At a turning point in an extended sanctuary incident, minutes of a special meeting reveal how a private-sponsorship agreement between sanctuary providers and immigration authorities that promised to permit a migrant to leave sanctuary and eventually receive landed-immigrant status was written and presented to immigration authorities as a potential resolution:

> [The lawyer] explained ... his dealings with Immigration Canada in an attempt to improve the original offer. He is very hopeful that something acceptable will be forthcoming within a few weeks and sanctuary will not be necessary over the summer ... He stressed the situation is delicate, Immigration officials sensitive, and that *there must not be any further publicity in this case*. It was agreed that any requests for media interviews would be directly to R [i.e., the lawyer] and *only to him*.[115]

When the lawyer suggested that an article in a local newspaper was "rather unfair to the government's position and particularly that of the local manager of Immigration," a member of the support committee suggested writing a letter to the newspaper "stating 'that discussions are proceeding cooperatively' (and run it by R [i.e., the lawyer])."[116] Such deference to lawyers in how to play the legal game was dominant, but it was not devoid of resistance. Here, for example, the lawyer's move to quell publicity conflicted with sanctuary as sovereign power and the related "before the higher law" narrative, discussed above, which entailed exposure efforts to ensure that the case maintained constant visibility and that those spectacles were regularly produced. In one incident, this resulted in major conflict within the sanctuary group.[117] And in the above incident, in which a prominent lawyer became involved after the migrant was in sanctuary (a common situation), a member of the sanctuary group remarked in his resignation letter:

> The original direction of the [sanctuary] group to be a strong advocacy organization for social justice appears to have become co-opted by the lawyer's influence. Legal advice and opinion was just that, and doesn't have to be followed but only incorporated within the group's existing purpose should the committee deem it necessary.[118]

Conclusion

During the height of US sanctuary activities in the 1980s, an observer commented: "I am struck by the irony of sanctuary legalism. A self-consciously religious and moral movement finds its preferred style of argument in law. Even the substance of its arguments comes mostly from law (if not from a unified legal system)."[119] Yet, in the context studied, law was not only a rhetorical device deployed by sanctuary providers. Nor was it unified. Nor can sanctuary be conceived merely as conflict between conscience and state law.[120] Rather, law was constitutive of sanctuary in diverse ways. Sanctuary at first glance is about avoidance of law, but upon closer inspection the relation between sanctuary and law is revealed to be more complex, being at different moments before, against, and with the law. Consistent with the exercise of a nonstate sovereign power, law authorizes sanctuary. Law is also oppressive and a game that makes pastoral sacrifice possible in various ways. The "before the higher law" narrative provides just enough authorization to grant sanctuary but, consistent with the "up against the law" narrative, never enough – uncertainty remains – to erase the risk and therefore the potential for sacrifice stemming from pastoral power. This kind of authorization has an affinity for spectacle. Both narratives depend, in turn, on a third "with the law" narrative, which imagines deference to legal professionals where sanctuary's legality is defined as uncertain and temporary.

In sanctuary, the "with the law" narrative does not stem from a breakdown of community. Nor is it an obvious attempt to escape a morally stifling community through creation of autonomy and privacy,[121] which would be consistent with liberalism. Rather, in sanctuary discourse, the "with the law" narrative, like the "up against the law" impetus, serves as an opportunity for sacrifice by more entitled members of churches and communities on behalf of those who are barely legally entitled.[122] This is consistent with pastoral power. Playing "with the law" creates needs that provide potential for shepherds' sacrifice. Yet it is sometimes recognized that playing this game is not enough to ensure the wellbeing of the migrants without the public attention created by spectacles associated with a nonstate sovereign power and linked to the "before the higher law" narrative. Time is seen to be a key dimension of the three narratives in the sanctuary context. In sanctuary discourse, no one narrative eclipses the others; they work together, complementing one another in a peculiar way that ultimately makes some migrants' escape from deportation possible.

The foregoing analysis has implications for Ewick and Silbey's tripartite narrative scheme. In the sanctuary context, the three identified narratives are on occasion difficult to distinguish.[123] For example, deference to lawyers as vital players of the legal game, which is consistent with the "with the law" narrative, is not easily separable from standing "before the law," as both entail deference: one to the "flesh and blood" lawyers brought on board the sanctuary effort largely on behalf of migrants rather than for self-interest; and the other to an abstract, distant system of law. At certain points in the sanctuary context, these overlap. In the same way, consistent with the exercise of a nonstate sovereign power, sanctuary providers sometimes stood before a "higher" law. Yet the notion that spectacles are produced through the exercise of this sovereign power is not easily distinguishable from the idea of "making scenes," a mode of conduct that is consistent with the "up against law" narrative.[124] Are providers' publicity campaigns authorized by higher laws or are these (merely) spectacular parodies of state sovereignty that are consistent with an "up against the law" narrative?[125] Ewick and Silbey's otherwise valuable scheme may require some minor refinement in light of this analysis. More broadly, this narrative scheme at times appears somewhat static and as a result could benefit from an engagement with governmentality concepts, such as pastoral power, that are relational and dynamic.[126] For example, in specific contexts, pastoral power and the shepherd-flock relation may well permit a better understanding in of how persons move from one form of legal consciousness to another – in this case through the medium of sacrifice.

In contrast to critical legal studies, in governmentality analyses, subjects' "consciousness is imbricated in the dominant rationalities of government and in the prevailing governance strategies."[127] Despite a clear difference in this respect, the two bodies of work nevertheless share an attention to "the point and places where the human subject gets transformed into a legal subject"[128] and may therefore offer one another fruitful insights for understanding particular domains. Although the point of departure of governmentality studies has been a move from a realist sociology of the state toward the dispersed and diverse forms of power that operate beyond the state, Ewick and Silbey parallel this by shifting away from formal state law and its institutions to a much broader field of "legality."[129] This is also consistent with legal pluralism and work in legal anthropology on folk law. It is also important to recognize, however, that Ewick and Silbey intend their three narratives as cultural and as both a medium and a resource for social action and interpretation.[130] Here these narratives have been deployed in a different register – one consistent with governmentality studies – as the modes of particular constitutive powers at the level of the subject. Perhaps the key difference centres on how agency is understood: the foregoing analysis suggests that agency is less cultural and more a result of a historical configuration of particular powers in specific sites. Therefore, recognition of three legal narratives in sanctuary discourse does not force one to conclude that law is hegemonic. There is more going on here than contradiction that mediates "the incomplete, flawed, practical, and mundane world with the normative legitimacy and consent that all institutions require," more than ideological deception through "the connections between the particular and the general."[131] In this site, the three narratives are revealed to be not so much contradictory forms of ideology as instantiations of sovereign and pastoral powers. Still to be fully explored in governmentality studies are these nonliberal powers and their relations not so much with state law per se as with what Ewick and Silbey more aptly call "legality." Sanctuary is but one of the fragile and fleeting governmental strategies and sovereign territories that such powers and legal narratives make possible.

7
Conclusion

This chapter reviews the main arguments and discusses some of the implications of the foregoing study of sanctuary in Canada. Consistent with the two stated purposes of this book, first, it briefly discusses implications for previous sanctuary research, and second, it considers in more detail the implications of seeing sanctuary as an instance of sovereign and pastoral powers for governmentality studies, including for the four theoretical issues raised in Chapter 1. It concludes with some thoughts about sanctuary as a broader political tactic.

Previous research has depicted sanctuary as a national or regional religious movement positioned against the state. Sanctuary in Canada, in contrast, has occurred in the form of thirty-six incidents, has not expired but is increasing in prevalence, and is as much about local-community efforts as it is about religious efforts. A theme of this book is the sacrifice made on the part of sanctuary providers. It is important to recognize that, although they do not hold a prominent place, there are nevertheless alternative interpretations of sacrifice in previous sanctuary research.[1] Wiltfang and McAdam[2] investigate costs and risks incurred by participants in the US sanctuary effort. Park suggests that sacrifice is of a religious nature: "Members of liberal churches may also adopt sacrifice as a mechanism to signify religious commitment. Future research should examine mainline churches with a historical record of costly and risky activism."[3] As noted in Chapter 2, churches involved in sanctuary have not been limited to those of the liberal variety. More important, sanctuary providers in Canada refer to and incur sacrifices, costs, and risks in part as they pertain to the need to protect and provide for migrants and to the potential illegality of doing so. However, although it is an integral element of sanctuary discourse in Canada, sacrifice cannot be easily reduced to religious aspects. In fact, Wiltfang and McAdam imply that this is the case by treating cost and risk (i.e., sacrifice) in US sanctuary activities as but one instance of the centrality of these elements in social-movement activism generally. This sacrifice is better seen as consistent with a shepherd-flock relation characterizing pastoral power in which "shepherds" are drawn from churches and communities.

The notion of sanctuary's having a local-community character is also of particular importance for previous sanctuary research. Consistent with understanding sanctuary as religious activism exclusively, Cunningham has explored sanctuary to provide insight into transnational political identity.[4] Yet sanctuary discourse in Canada revealed little or no awareness of sanctuary activities in the US or other nations,[5] contrary to what one would expect of such an identity among providers. As well, sanctuary discourse examined here was consistently devoid of "global imagery and rhetoric."[6] Although, consistent with the exercise of a nonstate sovereign power, there were appeals to "higher" law, some of these were invocations of "common law," which is far less than a global, transnational approach to the world. Nor were appeals to "God's law" necessarily commensurate with such a view. Instead, providers saw migrants as needy but ultimately potential contributing members of their *local* rather than a *global* community. It was the worth of particular migrants to this community – however defined – and to a lesser extent the risk of harm that they faced due to deportation to some distant, dangerous place that was consistently asserted, consonant with pastoral power, to be the target of providers' sacrifice. Sanctuary provision was not primarily about the irrelevance of national difference.

Of more relevance to governmentality studies and the theoretical issues raised at the outset of this book is that sanctuary highlights the notions that sovereign power is currently relevant and unrestricted to the nation-state's capacity for ministerial exceptions and exclusion and that it entails the control of territory. As well, such power is seen to have an affinity for the spectacular. In compelling efforts to make sense of coercion in relation to liberalism, coercion is referred to as "despotism"[7] and "authoritarianism"[8] (as well as "unfreedom").[9] There is considerable overlap among these terms and sovereign power to the extent that they refer to a capacity to make the exception – a conception that, although not usually associated with Foucault's *Discipline and Punish,* is nevertheless present therein. However, to the extent that these concepts are meant to refer to coercion, punishment, and the like exclusively, this study of sanctuary suggests that they ought to be distinguished from sovereign power, the latter concept entailing a much stronger linkage to the control of territory and especially to the production of spectacle. Sanctuary suggests that sovereign power is not necessarily about nation-state sovereignty, that other sovereignties may be present in specific contexts.[10]

Sovereign power requires neither obedient pastoral objects nor self-regulating liberal subjects but instead "bare life."[11] But contrary to Agamben's position, the foregoing analysis suggests that refugees, whose plight he equates with "bare life,"[12] begin to cease to be such the moment the sovereign decision results in inclusion and salvation rather than exclusion and coercion[13] or mere inclusion through exclusion. That is to say, the moment of inclusion is the moment at which governmental power – of whatever kind – begins to overlap with and complement sovereign power. Some migrants who make refugee claims, who avoid regular and restrictive national governmental selection streams, and who later face deportation *are* permitted to resettle and to begin to live (again) as needful beings and free liberal citizens. Not all such migrants are deported to extremely insecure economic conditions, left to wither in camps, or "killed but not sacrificed" without exception, as Agamben's account of sovereign power implies. To be sure, compared to the thousands deported annually from Canada, they remain statistically rare and as exceptions perhaps necessarily so. Migrants in sanctuary are also subjected to the varying intensity of an often paternalistic pastoral power and an arbitrary sovereign power along the way. These were the powers that protected but silenced "Raphael" and then used his masked and hooded "bare life" to create a spectacle in a church in Montreal in January 1984. Yet ultimately, "Raphael" and other migrants in sanctuary were *included* in communities and the nation, the theoretical significance of which is that this inclusion was due to the presence of and complex relations among powers and legal narratives that governmentality studies have yet to fully explore.

Although previous research has elaborated sanctuary in the US as emblematic of conflict between perpetual church (or a national religious movement) and state,[14] it is perhaps better seen as a more complex tension among these powers. Pastoral and liberal rationalities have coexisted in regular resettlement programs for migrants for some time. For example, tens of thousands of migrants have been resettled through these arrangements over the past two decades.[15] This coexistence is not one of accommodating principles[16] but of an array of discourses and practices accompanied by the occasional grinding together of their respective elements. That is to say, advanced liberal and pastoral powers can conflict. One of their ill-fitting conjunctions may produce demands for authorities to make exceptions, and when this occurs it is tantamount to a crisis, although relative only to the specific program in question rather than to a broad state of emergency.[17] Although the question of how rationalities relate to sovereign power is not fully resolvable here,[18] sanctuary nevertheless sheds light on this issue by suggesting that rationalities can overlap with sovereign power without obvious contradiction and can create a capacity to make the exception when resistance is encountered. It follows that governmental spaces and sovereign territories can also overlap.[19] For example, nation-states can overlap with the reach of liberal governance.[20] More broadly, both liberal and pastoral rationalities may be dependent on a capacity to make the exception, which at some moments is realized as symbolic salvation and at others as exclusion and coercion. For this reason, governmental programs can continue without declaration of failure, although perhaps not eternally or without some incompleteness.[21] This is not to suggest that governmentality moves toward perfection through deferment to sovereign power to manage programmatic crises, that governmentality is a system "in the process of perfecting itself."[22] On the contrary, sanctuary suggests that sovereign power itself, at least as seen in its spectacle, periodically encounters resistance.[23] Yet sovereign power may not simply overcome such resistance; this power may be constitutive of programs and the laws that enact them "in the first place." If Agamben is right on this point, and further inquiry and debate may bear this out, the sovereign exception not only overcomes resistance, but constitutes the rules (and norms) of specific rationalities and programs and, hence, the lack of an exact fit between them. Agamben writes of this peculiar nonlinear relation: "The exception does not subtract itself from the rule; rather, the rule, suspending itself, gives rise to the exception and, maintaining itself in relation to the exception, first constitutes itself as a rule."[24] In this sense, sovereignty may at once constitute and be constituted by rationalities and conflicts between them. And in this way, sovereign power has to be seen as *outside* and as occasionally *overlapping* with, rather than *within*, advanced-liberal, pastoral, or other governmentalities.

From the perspective of advanced liberalism, pastoral power is complementary only to the extent that it is a form of private or community governance beyond the state.[25] Sanctuary can then be seen as a site where "government at a distance" (in this case, to resettle new migrants more efficiently through private or community means)[26] becomes "too distant."[27] From the perspective of pastoral power, those parts of the refugee and immigration domains shaped by advanced-liberal rationalities are conditions of possibility for the emergence of the pastoral identities of the shepherd and sheep. The demands of advanced liberalism for individual enterprise and autonomy highlight the deficiencies of, and in a sense create, needful sheep for whom shepherds can provide and sacrifice themselves in private refugee-resettlement programs. Provisions in immigration legislation allowing deportation of some migrants and prohibiting citizens from aiding them create the possibility for the illegality of sanctuary, which provides an opportunity for further "sacrifice" and the exercise of a nonstate sovereign power. Juridification of determination has led to a need for adequate legal representation of refugee claimants, which, due in part to inadequate legal-aid programs, also serves as a condition of possibility for "sacrifice."

Most fundamentally, the present study of sanctuary in Canada suggests that governmentality studies should leave open the possibility of a plurality of governmental and sovereign powers beyond those of liberalism and nation-state coercion and violence in particular instances of governance. The latter two, of course, remain important for analyses of our present, but their receipt of almost exclusive attention seems inconsistent with the spirit of a "later Foucault" and neglects the possibility of discovering alternative forms of governance and resistance. Somewhere along the line in governmentality studies, governmentality became synonymous with liberalism. It ought to be seen instead as a generic concept potentially referring to a range of governmental logics that are often complementary and at other times in conflict. The foregoing examination of sanctuary suggests that nonliberal powers ought not to be deemed "merely obstructionist" in governmentality studies. Sanctuary suggests that liberal and pastoral rationalities can be resistant to one another (as well as, in other contexts, to still other rationalities). Sanctuary reveals that the possibilities for what is called resistance in our present are at least as heterogeneous and complex as the varied powers that have made sanctuary possible. Resistance is, then, more than an irrational source of the failure of liberal government or a constituent element of liberal government.

One way to refer to the relation between two (or more) rationalities in governmentality studies has been in terms of hybridity. Although hybridity rightfully recognizes more rationalities (technologies, knowledges, etc.) than might otherwise be acknowledged, it is deficient in avoiding discussion of *how* these rationalities (understood as ideal types) work together or conflict, suggesting instead that they are empirically accessible to the analyst only in a fully formed state (i.e., only *after* being "constituted"). There is therefore a sense in which hybridity closes down investigation by suggesting that in a particular instance of governance, a new form (i.e., a hybrid), albeit comprising elements from the past, has taken shape. In this way, hybridity ignores the possibility of conflict between or among elements at particular intersections, conflict that can be laid bare through empirical research (as this study of sanctuary has sought to show) and that can lead to or at least overlap with the exercise of sovereign power. In short, hybridity permits the issue of how two rationalities reinforce one another, or are in tension, to be set aside rather than explored. Avoiding such research is not unconnected to the preference for state texts to the neglect of talk, as noted in Chapter 1. When such avoidance occurs, invoking hybridity marks the end, rather than the beginning, of analysis. Foucault's oft-cited[28] triangle – sovereignty-discipline-government[29] – has tended to be used in a similar way. While properly suggesting that sovereignty has not been surpassed and coexists with governmentalities, it reveals little about the relations among the identified powers. Biological and geometrical metaphors such as these (i.e., hybrids, triangles, and the like) are ultimately poor replacements for empirical research, which can, potentially at least, uncover the remarkable complexities of governance and sovereignty in our present.

Another consequence of the recognition of other rationalities (and sovereignties) is to cast doubt on the usefulness of the concept of responsibilization deployed in Chapter 3. From the perspective of advanced liberalism, this concept implies a shift in only one direction, from the state to a variety of actors, including communities. But what appears as responsibilization from the totalizing perspective of advanced liberalism is the proper exercise of community authority from the perspective of pastoral and nonstate sovereign powers. In the same way, the imagined enterprising and responsible risk-taking liberal subject in advanced liberalism[30] is a shepherd poised to sacrifice in order to provide for the needs of obedient sheep in pastoralism. The imagined pastoral shepherds, those who "put themselves out" and take risks on behalf of the flock, ostensibly converge on some level with the preferred risk-taking subjects of advanced liberalism,[31] but the former need not be reduced to the latter.

The acceptance of the possibility of the presence of two or more rationalities in a particular context also problematizes the well-known concept of moral regulation.[32] That governance (or regulation) is often moral is not in doubt.[33] As seen in earlier chapters, refugee-resettlement practices and the provision of sanctuary to migrants (with which these practices overlap) are plainly about moral regulation. This is perhaps most evident in how these practices target migrants' subjectivity. Yet it may be more fruitful to seek to determine with what rationalities and commensurate moralities such practices are shaped and made possible. Moral regulation is important, but its study may be subsumed under the investigation of specific historical rationalities of government.

Another implication for governmentality studies concerns the concept of programs. Sanctuary, as discussed in Chapters 4 and 5, was often "made up as we went along" by deploying a mix of traditional and contemporary techniques to render the invisible visible and to respond to migrants' needs, was not always laid out in programmatic texts, occurred at a local level, and was of limited scope. But this does not mean that sanctuary was not a program in the Foucauldian sense. As stated in Chapter 1, consistent with this, sympathetic critics of governmentality studies have noted: "Many programmes exist only in the process of messy implementation."[34] Micro-sanctuary programs were messy, but they were as much programs as the grand determination and resettlement plans discussed in Chapter 3. That is to say, they were an idealized scheme for ordering social life that pronounced knowledge of a particular domain, in this case intimate knowledge of the rearranged spaces and desperate souls of sanctuaries.

The new emphasis on law in refugee determination, as seen in Chapter 3, has served as a condition of possibility for sanctuary incidents and, in particular, for sanctuary providers to sacrifice themselves to ensure that migrants are properly represented by legal professionals, their refugee claims and appeals adequately heard. It was argued that this was consistent with one legal narrative. Yet the inadequacy of determination that leads to immigration authorities' efforts to deport migrants, along with the potential illegality of preventing this from occurring through sanctuary, is consistent with a second narrative. A third narrative implicates different kinds of "higher" law in authorizing sanctuary. The use of these legal narratives and specifically the work of Ewick and Silbey suggest that governmentality studies can benefit from an engagement with the literature on critical legal studies in seeking to understand law as governance at the level of the subject without necessarily invoking the concept of ideology. One element in particular that sanctuary reveals as important where law as governance is concerned – time[35] – requires more attention.

Pastoral power in the sanctuary context appears to be as much community- as faith-based and therefore suggests that this rationality is of potentially much wider relevance. Governing through need is by no means limited to the activities of churches and communities directed toward migrants. With this in mind, and following Foucault's lead in his previously noted claim about the welfare state, one wonders precisely how pastoral power, with its needs discourses, related to liberalism to form "liberal welfarism,"[36] a logic that has received remarkably little empirical attention in governmentality studies given its relation to advanced liberalism as a foil. The two rationalities – liberalism and pastoralism – were (and to some extent still are) mediated by a state bureaucracy,[37] an aspect that is often at the centre of criticism from both the Left and the Right and, indeed, that forms part of the ongoing critique of the welfare state. In sanctuary, the provision of needs mobilized local churches and communities, occurred in a more intimate and direct way, and entailed more immediate sacrifice than need provision through the bureaucratic apparatus of the welfare state. This may be suggestive of an alternative mode of need provision, especially when contrasted with, for example, the explicit coercion of current neoliberal workfare and similar modes,[38] but considerable caution is nevertheless in order. Although the same kind of need provision is seen in private refugee-resettlement efforts, described in Chapter 3, the limits of shepherds' sacrifice – that is, whether such need provision exemplified in sanctuary is sustainable, transferable, or desirable – remains uncertain.

Evident in sanctuary, particularly in how shepherds "rose to the surface" during the incidents, were elements of what Mitchell Dean aptly calls the "ethical cultivation of the desire to give."[39] These aspects have been neglected compared to the attention paid to the state and its fiscal capacities in relation to welfare provision.[40] It is precisely the processes that give rise to these ethical rudiments that cannot be simplistically summarized as responsibilization, as an automatic acceptance of responsibility for those in need by those upon whose shoulders it is dropped. These processes require more scholarly attention but in a way that avoids essentialist assumptions about agents' humanitarianism or propensities to give.[41]

The stark fact also remains that sanctuary provision raises the question that has relevance to today's broader context of welfare-state decline and the rise of advanced liberalism: How can the needs of strangers be provided for in a way that respects their privacy and freedoms? The uncertain coupling of liberal and pastoral rationalities that comprises what has been called "liberal welfarism" raises the problem of governing through need, which requires intimate knowledge, coming up against governing through freedom, which demands privacy, freedom, and decidedly more space in relations with the governed.[42] Pastoral power is not necessarily a progressive logic of government or obviously superior – in this respect – to the current arrangements of rule that imagine removing this power from the state and reassigning it. In some spaces and moments of sanctuary, pastoral power was unambiguously paternalistic. More broadly, relations between shepherds and members of the flock are less than equal, and there exists considerable *potential* for oppression as a result. Indeed, in a chilling passage in *Postmodern Ethics*, Zygmunt Bauman writes of pastoral power as typical of "one of the most insidious of the many shapes of domination, as it blackmails its objects into obedience and lulls its agents into self-righteousness by representing itself as self-sacrifice in the name of 'the life and salvation of the flock.' But on not too infrequent an occasion they supply a welcome excuse for cold and relentless cruelty with which 'the best interests' of the others are pushed through their throats."[43] Yet, contrary to the tenor of Bauman's assertion, it is also necessary to acknowledge the equally stark fact that on this specific "occasion," without sanctuary provision, which was partially shaped by this form of power, 261 migrants would have been all too efficiently deported to face severe economic insecurity, physical harm, imprisonment, or early death.

In Foucault's essay "Omnes et Singulatim: Towards a Criticism of Political Reason," where he elaborates the theme of pastoral power in ancient Christian literature, he points out a particular paradox of pastoral sacrifice as it concerns the shepherd: "But by saving his sheep, he lays himself open to getting lost ... If he does get lost, it is the flock that will incur the greatest danger."[44] If shepherds were jailed for sanctuary activities, or otherwise weakened due to their sacrifices, the flock would be in peril. Who then would be left to look after the needs of the flock? Foucault argues further that in *The Statesman*, Plato examines pastoral power as a central theme and considers whether the head of the city could also adopt the shepherd's role. Foucault paraphrases the practical problem that Plato raises: "How would the politician ever find the time to come and sit by each person, feed him, give him concerts, and care for him when sick?"[45] In the welfare state, such time for need provision has been made possible through a complex system of taxation and revenue generation and through a rationalized state bureaucracy to dispense monetary and moral assistance. But such provision has also been less intimate, less sensitive to particular needs of groups of individuals, and less immediately sacrificial. Partially as a consequence, it has been open to criticism on such grounds.

According to Foucault, although Plato rejected the pastoral role, he argued that the proper role of the king was instead about "binding" in order to ensure "the city's unity."[46] It is this very tension between an individualizing pastoral power and the centralizing power of the state in Western history that represents not so much an alternative mode of need provision as a long-standing challenge in Western governance. Foucault was interested in pastoral power in the past because it provided insight into the present welfare-state problem. It has been assumed throughout this book that the flock in the sanctuary context is the community or a local church congregation and that the binding that went on in this context was local in its scope and rivalled a larger centralizing sovereign power. In describing pastoral government in relation to the medieval church, Foucault notes that those who criticized the church for having failed to meet its obligations chose to "reject its hierarchical structure, [and] look for the more or less spontaneous forms of community in which the flock could find the shepherd it needed."[47] Sanctuary is an exemplar of such an effort, but ironically the rejection here is of the larger centralizing and binding efforts of the nation-state rather than the church. Although temporally and spatially limited, at their peak, sanctuary incidents' reverberations nonetheless resonate with those of modern social movements that have strived to forge their own communities and to find their own shepherds, partially in response to what they perceive as the failings or even the tyrannical insensitivity of the welfare state's universal need provision, especially along the lines of class, gender, race/ethnicity, or sexual orientation.

One final and related point about sanctuary and powers is necessary, one alluded to in the introduction to this book. Sanctuary may not have been deployed only by churches and communities in the direction of migrants over the past twenty years. Sanctuary may well have been a more general political tactic[48] consistent with varying forms of pastoral and sovereign power that, since the decline of the church in the eighteenth century, has been deployed in conjunction with an array of social movements and modern institutions. Regarding the latter, a complete genealogy of sanctuary would undoubtedly be intertwined in complex ways with the development of nineteenth- and twentieth-century state asylums, which is comparatively well researched. Yet if sanctuary can be made possible by a pastoral power and a sovereign power that operate outside the state, a long-term genealogy might seek to include sanctuary-like spaces and practices found in social movements and similar sites. Even in the contemporary period, sanctuary-like discourses and practices can be glimpsed in that arm of the women's movement that targeted violence against women,[49] in the draft-resistance movement during the 1960s and early 1970s in relation to the Vietnam War, and in the gay-rights movement in its fight against HIV/AIDS, which overlaps with the modern hospice movement. With respect to the women's movement, the following bears consideration:

> Refuge provides a crucial material resource for women at a time of crisis. It provides women with a place to recover from injury, overcome isolation, and begin the process of regaining confidence and greater control over their own lives. It provides the physical location for mutual contact between women living and working in their temporary home rather than contact with "clients" in the business office of therapists and counsellors. It provides a source of inspiration and a vision about the problem which extends beyond an individual service to wider issues of changing women's social, economic and political status. It is a living laboratory of social change.[50]

In regard to draft resistance,[51] in the 1960s churches and universities in the US provided sanctuary to those who resisted the draft and the Vietnam War,[52] some of whom were eventually arrested and prosecuted by authorities. Draft resisters were also housed and intimately provided for in private residences in the US and Canada.[53] In a different vein, Patrick Conlon's popular book on Casey House, the first Canadian hospice for people dying of AIDS, is entitled, simply, *Sanctuary*.[54] Establishing such hospices in North America was a tactic and goal, at one juncture,[55] of the gay-rights movement. Indeed, this effort was tethered to the earlier and broader hospice movement of the 1950s and 1960s, which centred on care of the dying.[56]

No doubt there are significant differences among these "sanctuaries," even within the movements above: a women's shelter is not an AIDS hospice is not a safe house for draft resisters. Yet they are all protected, exceptional places, last resorts that provide a temporary caring space for life and the fulfillment of needs ostensibly outside the dominant gaze of the disciplines – that is, the psychological, social-work, and medical professions and interventions, about which Foucault and governmentality scholars have written at length. These places also all entail selection: if everyone were permitted to enter these spaces, they would be neither protected nor exceptional. This is as true for church sanctuaries as for women's shelters. Providers' and scholars' accounts of contemporary sanctuary invoke a "sanctuary tradition" in a manner suggesting that sanctuary had all but disappeared by the 1700s in Europe only to suddenly reappear in the US in the 1980s. Little is said of what might have occurred in between or in less obvious domains. Sanctuary may well possess a decidedly more complex genealogy that has yet to be traced and that need not be limited to the confines of churches and states in our thinking.

Postscript

On 5 March 2004 Quebec City police entered St. Pierre United Church to arrest Mohamed Cherfi. Living in sanctuary since 18 February, Cherfi was an Algerian migrant facing deportation who, like most sanctuary recipients before him, had failed to gain status through the refugee-determination process. He was quickly deported to the US to await a hearing to determine whether he would be further removed to Algeria. The reaction to this "violation" of sanctuary was swift.[1] A wide variety of groups and individuals across Canada publicly and vehemently expressed concern about the illiberal nature of this action. Indeed, the outcry was more widespread than support for any previous sanctuary incident. The fear expressed by sanctuary providers involved in the incidents described in this book, over the possibility that their sanctuaries could be stormed, suddenly seemed fully justified. Although this occurrence was widely assumed to be the first of its kind, what was forgotten or unknown was the previous expulsion of migrants from a church in Montreal in 1998. This expulsion was enforced by local police, who entered a church that they deemed illegitimate in order to make arrests. Nevertheless, perhaps as a consequence of the more recent visible police action, for awhile concurrent sanctuary efforts came closer to forming at least a regional sanctuary movement than ever before, although each incident continues to have local origins. If this action was the reigning federal immigration minister's attempt to forcibly bring an end to sanctuary in Canada once and for all – it remains unclear whether this was strictly a local police action or was orchestrated by the minister or federal-Cabinet colleagues in conjunction with immigration authorities – it did not have the desired effect.

During 2004 migrants continued to enter sanctuary, albeit not at an increased rate. Two new cases appeared in addition to the Cherfi case above. In late January 2004 three Palestinian migrants took sanctuary in Notre-Dame-de-Grace Roman Catholic Church in Montreal.[2] Following the pattern described in this study, in mid-June 2004, after the arrest of Cherfi, the supporters of an Iranian migrant who had failed to obtain status as a refugee phoned several churches in Vancouver and, upon receiving a positive response one and a half hours before he was due at the airport for deportation, finally took sanctuary in St. Michael's Anglican Church.[3]

Partly in response to these incidents, the immigration minister installed after the 2004 federal election, Judy Sgro, made an unusually public and alarmist claim during the summer of 2004 that churches should stop granting sanctuary because they were serving as a backdoor for migrants seeking legal status.[4] By September 2004 a website had been put in place to describe the regional Interfaith Sanctuary Coalition, which had commenced in 2003 and was briefly described in Chapter 1. The website displayed a rationale for sanctuary, details of all ongoing sanctuary incidents, information about upcoming protests, including those on behalf of Cherfi, and news about sanctuary outcomes in Canada. Under this group's banner and with support from a variety of different church and community groups, a Sanctuary Week was subsequently held across Canada with events in Quebec City and at the churches offering sanctuary in Montreal and Ottawa. On 29 September a meeting was held between the minister and mainline Christian churches – Roman Catholic, Presbyterian, Lutheran, Mennonite, Quaker, and United – during which the minister apparently made a secret offer that would see churches regularly putting forward names of exceptional cases for an independent review with a ten-day turnaround time,[5] a process that largely mirrored existing sanctuary practices. In a sense, Immigration was granting more legitimacy than ever before to sanctuary efforts: sanctuary was to be regularized and incorporated into a liberal governmental program in place of the much larger and expensive appeal system that had been promised when the new Immigration Act came into effect in 2002. After word of this offer became public, resulting in extensive criticism of its secret and exclusive nature, on 2 November the minister offered a revised arrangement that would see other nonchurch groups also having this authority. This was followed by a meeting with church representatives on 16 November.[6] The church representatives subsequently refused to become part of such a process. Sanctuary would continue.

Judy Sgro's legitimacy as immigration minister came into grave doubt when it was publicly alleged during the same period, first, that a nonstatus exotic dancer had worked on her federal-election campaign earlier in the year in exchange for special consideration for a visa – on its face an embarrassing situation, which was subsequently dubbed "strippergate" – and, second, that a migrant facing deportation reported that he had been asked to provide pizzas to Sgro's team during the same election campaign in exchange for legal status. These alleged arrangements to grant persons legal status in exchange for the minister's personal and direct gain contrasted sharply with her public denial of status to those living in churches, migrants who had the vocal and widespread support of Canadian churches and communities. By December it was clear this immigration minister was on her way out, her political capital spent. Coupled with other events, there is little doubt that her ill-conceived foray into sanctuary politics during the summer of 2004 marked the beginning of the end of her tenure in the federal Cabinet.

In contrast to the minister's fate, among the thirty-six incidents covered by this study, all four incidents that were still unresolved at the time of writing at the end of 2003 had by February 2005 come to a successful conclusion. Early in June 2004 a migrant in sanctuary in Halifax received a sixty-day suspension of her deportation order.[7] She then left Canada for Mexico to reapply as an immigrant. As with other migrants who had exited Canada to reapply after being in sanctuary, her application was processed quickly, and by the end of February 2005 she had returned to Canada as an immigrant, where she was welcomed by supporters. Shortly after Sanctuary Week and just prior to Immigration Minister Sgro's resignation on 13 December 2004, a Bangladeshi migrant who had been in sanctuary in Ottawa since 2003 was granted a minister's permit to remain,[8] as was an Ethiopian family in sanctuary in Montreal for a similar period. In mid-February a Colombian family that had been in sanctuary in a United Church since 2003 received news that their review on humanitarian and compassionate grounds had been approved, paving the way for them to receive landed-immigrant status in the near future.[9]

Since 1983, elected members of Parliament assigned the position of minister of immigration have had remarkably short political careers. As the prevalance of sanctuary incidents has increased, immigration ministers seem to have changed more frequently. Few have survived to move on to preferred Cabinet positions such as finance or external affairs or to leave the position with their political reputations enhanced. There is little doubt that sanctuary in Canada has played a role in this. As sovereign exceptions, instances of sanctuary will likely remain few in the future in part because they demand such sacrifice among providers, but they and the powers that make them possible will continue to have real effects on the lives of providers, migrants, and immigration ministers.

Appendix: The Interviews

The providers interviewed for this study included clergy, retired persons, small-business owners, and professionals. They were members of churches and of the broader secular communities in which the incidents occurred. As well, one interviewee was an employee of a national church and another of a national ecumenical church body, neither of whom was necessarily directly involved in specific sanctuary incidents. Nevertheless, their positions made them aware of local sanctuary incidents, and they were intimately involved in developing sanctuary guidelines on behalf of local churches after the fact. The forty-six interviewees were initially contacted with a formal letter outlining the research. This was necessary since I had a previous relationship with only one of the interviewees. The letter was usually followed a week or so later by a telephone call to ascertain their interest in participating in the research and to arrange a time and place for a meeting. The interviewees were offered access to information about results of the study in exchange for their participation. Arranging and conducting these interviews was at times arduous (although admittedly at other times enjoyable) due to the wide geographic dispersion of sanctuary incidents and Canada's immense size, which also necessitated extensive travel. The venues of these interviews included a café in Old Montreal, a remote Vancouver Island acreage, a public library on the New Brunswick-Maine border, a church office in Halifax, a sandwich shop in a Winnipeg mall, a mission in Vancouver's infamous Downtown Eastside, a home office in Guelph, a business office in Kingston, and residences in Calgary and Edmonton, among many others. In some instances, interviewees' work, lunch hours, holidays, family gatherings, and other demanding times were interrupted. Despite advance scheduling and travel to the arranged locations, several interviews could not take place in person; a hastily scrawled note pinned to a church or office door relating this or that emergency was encountered instead. Because of this and due to some incidents occurring after travel to a particularly distant locale had taken place, such as some incidents in 2003, several telephone interviews were conducted. All these open-focused interviews commenced by asking providers to recount the sanctuary incident in which they had been involved. From there questions focused on the origins of the incident, organization of sanctuary efforts once commenced, and legal outcomes as well as effects on the local church and community and on the providers themselves.

Notes

Chapter 1: Introduction

1 Throughout this book, "immigration officials," "immigration authorities," and the like refer to those acting on behalf of the federal Department of Citizenship and Immigration or its earlier incarnations: the Department of Manpower and Immigration; and Employment and Immigration Canada. At times, the designation "the Department of Immigration" is also used. Because the department of External Affairs had responsibility for immigrant selection for a brief period after 1983, it is also mentioned in Chapter 3.

2 The first sanctuary incident began 23 December 1983; see Interview 16.

3 R. Block, "Sanctuary and the Defiant Churches," *Maclean's*, 30 January 1984, 43.

4 "Church Officials Offer Sanctuary to Guatemalans," *Winnipeg Free Press*, 21 January 1984, B3.

5 M. Foucault, "Politics and Reason," in *Politics, Philosophy, Culture, Interviews and Other Writings, 1977-1984*, ed. L. Kritzman, 57-85 (New York: Routledge, 1988).

6 Ibid., 67.

7 For example, see H. Cunningham, *God and Caesar at the Rio Grande* (Minneapolis: University of Minnesota Press, 1995), 82-3; C. Davison, "Sanctuary: The Humane Response," *Law Now* 22, 1 (1997): 1-12.

8 Ibid.

9 See C. Cox, *The Sanctuaries and Sanctuary Seekers of Medieval England* (London: George Allen and Sons, 1911); J. Bellamy, *Crime and Public Order in England in the Later Middle Ages* (Toronto: University of Toronto Press, 1973); I. Bau, *This Ground Is Holy: Church Sanctuary and Central American Refugees* (New York: Paulist Press, 1985); C. Stastny, "Sanctuary and the State," *Contemporary Crises* 11 (1987): 279-301; R.J. Macrides, "Killing, Asylum, and the Law in Byzantium," *Speculum* 63 (1988): 509-38. For a concise summary, see Cunningham, *God and Caesar*. An extensive section on sanctuary tradition is not included in this book since such coverage is readily available in the above works, but it is worth noting from these histories that sanctuary has not always entailed religious spaces and practices. For example, in Greek and Roman culture, sanctuary was often secular rather than religious in nature. Similarly, eight cities of refuge were designated in England in 1540 under Henry VIII. The first underground railroad that aided slaves in the US in the mid-nineteenth century involved clergy and congregations or parishes, but significantly these "religious agents did not see the protection they provided as any different from that afforded by the other participants"; see Bau, *This Ground Is Holy*, 160-61. During the Vietnam War, war resisters in the US took refuge in churches and universities; see Bau, *This Ground Is Holy*.

10 Cunningham, *God and Caesar*, 72.

11 Bau, *This Ground Is Holy*, 131.

12 C. Stastny, "Sanctuary and the State."

13 Bau, *This Ground Is Holy*, 156.

14 P. Weller, "Sanctuary and the British Churches," *Modern Churchman* 30 (1989): 12-17; S. Cohen, *From the Jews to the Tamils: Britain's Mistreatment of Refugees* (Manchester: South Manchester Law Centre, 1988).

15 Bau, *This Ground Is Holy*; E. Ferris, "The Churches, Refugees, and Politics," in *Refugee and International Relations*, ed. G. Loescher and L. Monahan, 159-77 (New York: Oxford University Press, 1989), 164; C. Trueheart and A. Swardson, "Thousands Denounce Detention of Migrants," *Ottawa Citizen*, 24 August 1990, A6; L. Gay, "Dutch Government Begins to Crack Down on Influx of Illegal Immigrants," *Montreal Gazette*, 23 December 1991, C10; Y. Sharma, *Religion-Germany: Church, State Clash over Sanctuary for Refugees*, 1998, http://www.oneworld.org/ips2/jul98/03_34_002.html; Sanctuary Network, *Support the East Timorese Refugees*, 2002, http://www.uq.net.au/~zzdkeena/NvT/55/1.html.

16 H. Cunningham, "The Ethnology of Transnational Social Activism: Understanding the Global as Local Practice," *American Ethnologist* 26 (2000): 583-604 at 583.

17 A. Crittenden, *Sanctuary: A Story of American Conscience and the Law in Collision* (New York: Weidenfeld and Nicolson, 1988).

18 C. Gordon, "Afterword," in *Power/Knowledge: Selected Interviews and Other Writings, 1972-1977, by Michel Foucault*, ed. C. Gordon, 229-59 (New York: Pantheon, 1980), 248.

19 N. Rose and P. Miller, "Political Power beyond the State: Problematics of Government," *British Journal of Sociology* 43 (1992): 173-205 at 175.

20 M. Dean, *Critical and Effective Histories: Foucault's Methods and Historical Sociology* (London: Routledge, 1994), 182.

21 P. Miller and N. Rose, "Governing Economic Life," *Economy and Society* 19 (1990): 1-31 at 14.

22 M. Valverde, "'Despotism' and Ethical Liberal Governance," *Economy and Society* 25 (1996): 357-72 at 358.

23 For example, R. Lippert, "Rationalities and Refugee Resettlement," *Economy and Society* 27 (1998): 380-406; R. Lippert, "Sanctuary Practices, Rationalities and Sovereignties," *Alternatives* 29 (2004): 535-55; P. O'Malley, L. Weir, and C. Shearing, "Governmentality, Criticism, Politics," *Economy and Society* 26 (1997): 501-17 at 510.

24 J. Habermas, *Theory of Communicative Action*, vol. 1 (Boston, MA: Beacon, 1983).

25 See Foucault, "Politics and Reason," 59.

26 For example, P. Miller and N. Rose, "Political Rationalities and Technologies of Government," in *Texts, Contexts, Concepts: Studies on Politics and Power in Language*, ed. S. Hanninen and K. Palonen, 166-83 (Helsinki: Finnish Political Science Association, 1990).

27 In a 1998 article in *Economy and Society* (a condensed version of which forms part of Chapter 3), I argue that the concept of advanced liberalism is problematic for this reason; see Lippert, "Rationalities and Refugee Resettlement." See also P. O'Malley, "Genealogy, Systematisation and Resistance in 'Advanced Liberalism,'" in *Rethinking Law, Society and Governance: Foucault's Bequest*, ed. G. Wickham and G. Pavlich, 13-25 (Portland, OR: Hart Publishing, 2001); and B. Frankel, "Confronting Neo-Liberal Regimes: The Post-Marxist Embrace of Populism and Realpolitik," *New Left Review* 226 (1997): 57-92.

28 O'Malley, Weir, and Shearing, "Governmentality, Criticism, Politics," 513.

29 Miller and Rose, "Governing Economic Life," 14.

30 N. Rose, "Government, Authority and Expertise in Advanced Liberalism," *Economy and Society* 22 (1993): 263-300 at 292.

31 Ibid., 290.

32 For example, see Rose, "Government, Authority and Expertise"; M. Dean, *The Constitution of Poverty: Towards a Genealogy of Liberal Governance* (New York: Routledge, 1991); Valverde, "'Despotism' and Ethical Liberal Governance."

33 S. Ashenden, "Reflexive Governance and Child Abuse: Liberal Welfare Rationality and the Cleveland Inquiry," *Economy and Society* 25 (1996): 64-88 at 85n.

34 See C. Gordon, "Governmental Rationality: An Introduction," in *The Foucault Effect: Studies in Governmentality*, ed. G. Burchell, C. Gordon, and P. Miller, 1-51 (Toronto: Harvester Wheatsheaf, 1991).

35 See P. O'Malley and D. Palmer, "Post-Keynesian Policing," *Economy and Society* 25 (1996): 137-55; Rose and Miller, "Political Power," 198-201; Rose, "Government, Authority and Expertise."

36 N. Rose, *Powers of Freedom: Reframing Political Thought* (Cambridge: Cambridge University Press, 1999), 139.
37 The term "post-Keynesian" has also been used; see O'Malley and Palmer, "Post-Keynesian Policing," 152n.
38 Rose, *Powers of Freedom.*
39 For example, G. Burchell, "Liberal Government and Techniques of the Self," *Economy and Society* 22 (1993): 267-81; W. Larner, "'A Means to an End': Neoliberalism and State Processes in New Zealand," *Studies in Political Economy* 52 (1997): 7-38; R. Lippert, "Canadian Refugee Determination and Advanced Liberal Government," *Canadian Journal of Law and Society* 13 (1998): 177-207; R. Lippert, "Policing Property and Moral Risk through Promotions, Anonymization, and Rewards: Revisiting Crime Stoppers," *Social and Legal Studies* 11 (2002): 475-502; R. Lippert, "Governing Refugees: The Relevance of Governmentality to Understanding the International Refugee Regime," *Alternatives* 24 (1999): 295-328; M. Dillon and J. Reid, "Global Governance, Liberal Peace, and Complex Emergency," *Alternatives* 25 (2000): 117-43; Rose, "Government, Authority and Expertise"; Rose and Miller, "Political Power"; Gordon, "Governmental Rationality."
40 Rose, *Powers of Freedom.*
41 N. Rose, "The Death of the Social? Re-Figuring the Territory of Government," *Economy and Society* 25 (1996): 327-56.
42 Foucault, "Politics and Reason," 67, 71.
43 For an exception to this, see I. Hunter, *Rethinking the School: Subjectivity, Bureaucracy, Criticism* (St Leonards, NSW, Australia: Allen and Unwin, 1994). For summaries of Michel Foucault's concept of pastoral power, see M. Dean, *Governmentality: Power and Rule in Modern Society* (Thousand Oaks: Sage, 1999); B. Hindess, *Discourses of Power: From Hobbes to Foucault* (Cambridge, MA: Blackwell, 1996).
44 On needs, see N. Fraser, "Talking about Needs: Interpretive Contests as Political Conflicts in Welfare State Societies," *Ethics* 99 (1989): 150-81; P. Springborg, *The Problem of Human Needs and the Critique of Civilization* (London: Allen and Unwin, 1981). There is a considerable volume of scholarship regarding needs in relation to Marx. See for example, K. Soper, *On Human Needs: Open and Closed Theories in a Marxist Perspective* (Brighton: Harvester, 1981)
45 This is not to suggest that power is a zero-sum game such that if pastoral power leaves the state, it must reappear elsewhere in equal proportion.
46 On this point, see B. Hindess, *Discourses of Power*, 122.
47 In Canada one of these remnants is the continued public character of health-care provision, which has received a recent significant reinvestment by the federal government.
48 For example, J. Torfing, "Towards a Schumpeterian Workfare Post-National Regime: Path-Shaping and Path-Dependency in Danish Welfare State Reform," *Economy and Society* 28 (1999): 369-402; R. Weiss, "Charitable Choice as Neo-liberal Social Welfare Strategy," *Social Justice* 28 (2001): 35-53; L. Mead, *The New Paternalism* (Washington: Brookings, 1997).
49 R. Lippert and D. O'Connor, "Security Assemblages: Airport Security, Flexible Work and Liberal Governance," *Alternatives:* 28 (2003): 331-58.
50 See Hunter, *Rethinking the School*; G. Pavlich, "Mediating Community Disputes: The Regulatory Logic of Government through Pastoral Power" (PhD dissertation, University of British Columbia, 1992).
51 Lippert, "Rationalities and Refugee Resettlement." See also O'Malley, "Genealogy, Systematisation and Resistance."
52 See Lippert, "Sanctuary Practices, Rationalities and Sovereignties"; M. Dean, "Liberal Government and Authoritarianism," *Economy and Society* 31 (2002): 37-61; A. Pratt, "Sovereign Power, Carceral Conditions and Penal Practices," *Studies in Law, Politics, and Society* 23 (2001): 45-78; P. Fitzpatrick, "'These Mad Abandon'd Times,'" *Economy and Society* 30 (2001): 255-70; M. Constable, "Sovereignty and Governmentality in Modern American Immigration Law," *Studies in Law, Politics and Society* 13 (1993): 249-71; K. Stenson, "Crime Control, Governmentality and Sovereignty," in *Governable Places: Readings on Governmentality and Crime Control*, ed. Russell Smandych, 45-73 (Aldershot: Ashgate, 1999).
53 Constable, "Sovereignty and Governmentality"; M. Dillon, "Sovereignty and Governmentality: From the Problematics of the 'New World Order' to the Ethical Problematic of the

World Order," *Alternatives* 20 (1995): 323-68; Stenson, "Crime Control, Governmentality and Sovereignty."

54 For example, N. Rose, *Powers of Freedom: Reframing Political Thought* (Cambridge: Cambridge University Press, 1999), 23; L. Blake, "Pastoral Power, Governmentality and Cultures of Order in Nineteenth-Century British Columbia," *Transactions of the Institute of British Geographers* 24 (1999): 79-93 at 81. A similar point is found in M. Dean, "Powers of Life and Death beyond Governmentality," *Cultural Values* 6 (2002): 119-38 at 123. For an exception to this tendency that involves a distinction between coercion and sovereign instruments, see Dean, "Liberal Government and Authoritarianism," 40.

55 Dillon, "Sovereignty and Governmentality"; Stenson, "Crime Control, Governmentality and Sovereignty."

56 For example, Constable, "Sovereignty and Governmentality." Consistent with the concept of sovereignty, the term "nation-state" is used throughout this book to highlight the territorial aspects of the state.

57 For example, Lippert, "Governing Refugees"; A. Pratt and M. Valverde, "From Deserving Victims to Masters of Confusion: Redefining Refugees in the 1980s," *Canadian Journal of Sociology* 27 (2002): 135-61.

58 See Constable, "Sovereignty and Governmentality"; Dillon, "Sovereignty and Governmentality"; Lippert, "Governing Refugees"; Stenson, "Crime Control, Governmentality and Sovereignty"; Pratt, "Sovereign Power, Carceral Conditions and Penal Practices"; Dean, "Powers of Life and Death beyond Governmentality."

59 For example, A. Hunt and G. Wickham, *Foucault and Law: Toward a Sociology of Law as Governance* (Boulder: Pluto Press, 1994), 59-71.

60 For example, ibid.; N. Rose and M. Valverde, "Governed by Law?" *Social and Legal Studies* 7 (1998): 541-51; Rose, *Powers of Freedom*, 155-56; M. Valverde, *Law's Dream of a Common Knowledge* (Princeton: Princeton University Press, 2003).

61 Rose and Valverde, "Governed by Law?"; M. Foucault, *History of Sexuality,* vol. 1, *An Introduction* (New York: Random House, 1978), 144.

62 B. Curtis, "Taking the State Back Out: Rose and Miller on Political Power," *British Journal of Sociology* 46 (1995): 575-89 at 583; see also 577, 582, and 585-86.

63 See Frankel, "Confronting Neo-Liberal Regimes," 83; D. Garland, "'Governmentality' and the Problem of Crime: Foucault, Criminology, Sociology," *Theoretical Criminology* 1 (1997): 199-201; D. Kerr, "Beheading the King and Enthroning the Market: A Critique of Foucauldian Governmentality," *Science and Society* 63 (1999): 173-202 at 196; O'Malley, Weir, and Shearing, "Governmentality, Criticism, Politics," 504, 509, 512-13; K. Stenson, "Beyond Histories of the Present," *Economy and Society* 27 (1998): 333-52 at 334.

64 N. Rose, "Contesting Power: Some Thoughts on Governmentality," in *New Forms of Governance: Theory, Practice, Research,* ed. M. Valverde, 6-9 (Toronto: Centre of Criminology, University of Toronto, 1997); Rose, *Powers of Freedom,* 16-19, 274-84.

65 Rose, "Contesting Power," 7.

66 For example, K. Kramar, "Review of K. Haggerty, *Making Crime Count,*" *Canadian Journal of Law and Society* 18 (2001): 159-63 at 159.

67 See A. Hunt, *Governing Morals: A Social History of Moral Regulation* (Cambridge: Cambridge University Press, 1999); Hunt and Wickham, *Foucault and Law;* J. Hermer and A. Hunt, "Official Graffiti of the Everyday," *Law and Society Review* 30 (1996): 455-80.

68 O'Malley, Weir, and Shearing, "Governmentality, Criticism, Politics," 510.

69 Ibid. See also P. O'Malley, "Indigenous Governance," *Economy and Society* 25 (1996): 310-26 at 312.

70 O'Malley, Weir, and Shearing, "Governmentality, Criticism, Politics," 509-10.

71 Ibid., 512.

72 See O'Malley, "Indigenous Governance," 312.

73 Stenson, "Crime Control, Governmentality and Sovereignty," 58-59.

74 Hilary Cunningham's acknowledgement of the use of sanctuary in Western Europe in the 1970s is an exception in the sanctuary literature; see Cunningham, *God and Caesar,* 211n.

75 P. Reynolds, *Faith Subdues Kingdoms: A Pastor's Challenge to Immigration* (New Westminster, BC: Conexions Publishing, 1992); M. Leddy, *At the Border Called Hope: Where Refugees Are Neighbours* (Toronto: Harper Collins, 1997).

76 D. Matas, "Canadian Sanctuary," *Refuge* 8, 2 (1988): 14-17; W.G. Plaut, *Asylum: A Moral Dilemma* (Wesport, CT: Praeger, 1995), 129-37. See also D. Matas, *The Sanctuary Trial* (Winnipeg: Legal Research Institute of the University of Manitoba, 1989), 147-51.

77 C. Stastny and G. Tyrnauer, "Sanctuary in Canada," in *The International Refugee Crisis: British and Canadian Responses*, ed. V. Robinson, 175-95 (London: Macmillan, 1993).

78 In suggesting this, these various authors are not alone. An immigration spokesperson noted during a 1992 incident that "it was the first time in Canada that someone facing removal was given sanctuary in a church"; see "Church Helps Salvadorans Try to Re-enter Canada" *Vancouver Sun*, 11 March 1992, B2. As late as 2002 a major Canadian newspaper claimed that sanctuary "has been only used three times"; see "Mexican Family Seeks Sanctuary in Church: Deportation Order Fought," *Calgary Herald*, 23 April 2002, A1.

79 United Church of Canada, *Sanctuary for Refugees? A Guide for Congregations* (Etobicoke, ON: Division of Mission in Canada, United Church of Canada, 1997); Matas, "Canadian Sanctuary."

80 One especially interesting work by a Dutch criminologist mentions contemporary sanctuary granted to refugees but only in passing as part of a larger argument to encourage reintroduction of sanctuary as an alternative to criminal justice; see H. Bianchi, *Justice as Sanctuary: Toward a New System of Crime Control* (Bloomington: Indiana University Press, 1994), 146-47.

81 For example, Crittenden, *Sanctuary*; G. Wiltfang and D. McAdam, "The Costs and Risks of Social Activism: A Study of Sanctuary Movement Activism," *Social Forces* 69 (1991): 987-1010; R. Lorentzen, *Women in the Sanctuary Movement* (Philadelphia: Temple University Press, 1991); S. Coutin, *The Culture of Protest: Religious Activism and the U.S. Sanctuary Movement* (Boulder: Westview Press, 1993); S. Coutin, "Enacting Law through Social Practice," in *Contested States: Law, Hegemony and Resistance*, ed. M. Lazarus-Black and S. Hirsch, 282-303 (New York: Routledge, 1994); Cunningham, "The Ethnology of Transnational Social Activism"; Cunningham, *God and Caesar*; H. Cunningham, "Transnational Social Movements and Sovereignties in Transition: Charting New Interfaces of Power at the U.S.-Mexico Border," *Anthropologica* 44 (2002): 185-96; K. Park, "The Religious Construction of Sanctuary Provisions in Two Congregations," *Sociological Spectrum* 18 (1998): 393-421; K. Park, "The Sacrifice Theory of Value: Explaining Activism in Two Sanctuary Congregations," *Sociological Viewpoints* 12 (1996): 35-50.

82 Weller, "Sanctuary and the British Churches"; Cohen, *From the Jews to the Tamils*.

83 Coutin, *The Culture of Protest*; Cunningham, *God and Caesar*; Cunningham, "Transnational Social Movements"; Park, "The Religious Construction of Sanctuary Provisions"; Park, "The Sacrifice Theory of Value"; Wiltfang and McAdam, "The Costs and Risks of Social Activism."

84 Wiltfang and McAdam, "The Costs and Risks of Social Activism," 1003.

85 Cox, *The Sanctuaries and Sanctuary Seekers*, 17.

86 See D. Lyon, "Introduction," in *Rethinking Church, State, and Modernity: Canada between Europe and America*, ed. D. Lyon and M. van Die, 3-19 (Toronto: University of Toronto Press, 2000).

87 Regarding the US context, see for example, Lorentzen, *Women in the Sanctuary Movement*, 26-7; Bau, *This Ground Is Holy*, 34.

88 See E. Canel, "New Social Movement Theory and Resource Mobilization: The Need for Integration," in *Organizing Dissent: Contemporary Social Movements in Theory and Practice*, ed. W.K. Carroll, 22-51 (Toronto: Garamond Press, 1992).

89 For example, Wiltfang and McAdam, "The Costs and Risks of Social Activism."

90 M. Foucault, "Truth Is in the Future," in *Foucault Live (Interviews, 1961-1984)*, 2nd ed., ed. S. Lotringer, trans. L. Hochroth and J. Johnson, 298-301 (New York: Semiotext(e), 1996), 299.

91 Hunt, *Governing Morals*, 18. See also Canel, "New Social Movement Theory"; A. Hunter, "Post-Marxism and the New Social Movements," *Theory and Society* 17 (1988): 885-900.

92 P. Weller, "Sanctuary as Concealment and Exposure: The Practices of Sanctuary in Britain as Part of the Struggle for Refugee Rights," paper presented at the conference "The Refugee Crisis: British and Canadian Responses," Keble College and Rhodes House, Oxford, England, 4-7 January 1989.

93 For example, C. Stastny, "The Roots of Sanctuary," *Refugee Issues: BRC/QEH Working Papers on Refugees* 2 (1985): 19-39; Cunningham, *God and Caesar*, 584.

94 Interview 31. See also M. Scott, "Minister Offers Church Refuge for Ghanaians," *Montreal Gazette*, 26 March 1988, A3; F. Serre, "Church Intervenes for Refugee," *Canadian Baptist*, July/August 1992, 47-8; Southern Ontario Sanctuary Coalition, "A Declaration: A Civil Initiative to Protect Refugees," press release, Toronto, 7 October 2002.

95 M. Farber, "Saving Refugee Was Bold Act," *Montreal Gazette*, 22 January 1985, A3. This is the only such case encountered during this study. The extent of concealed sanctuary in Canada remains unknown, and this research – despite involving interviews with persons who might have known of such situations and, due to guarantees of confidentiality, might have divulged their existence – revealed nothing to suggest that it exists on a significant scale.

96 See "Refugees Desperate for Safe Haven Get Help from Churches," *Ottawa Citizen*, 7 December 1996, C7; B. Bettson, "Suffering under New System," *United Church Observer* 55 (1992): 17-20 at 18.

97 Interview 17.

98 See W. Cornelius, "Interviewing Undocumented Immigrants: Methodological Reflections Based on Fieldwork in Mexico and the U.S.," *International Migration Review* 16 (1982): 378-411.

99 Reynolds, *Faith Subdues Kingdoms*; Leddy, *At the Border Called Hope*.

100 Migrants granted sanctuary were not interviewed for this study. Ultimately, this decision was made mostly for ethical reasons. These were persons who obviously found themselves in a very precarious legal position, and for some individuals this remained the case even months after they had exited sanctuary. Most of the working-class adult migrants had little or no access to a sustainable income or other financial resources due mostly to the threat of deportation. Formally interviewing them would also possibly have contravened Canada's new Tri-Council Ethical Guidelines, a vital consideration since the research was supported by a grant from the Social Sciences and Humanities Research Council, without which the research could not have been carried out. Deciding not to interview the migrants was also a consequence of considerable language barriers since some migrants involved did not comprehend or speak English (or French) to any extent. Perhaps needless to add, the decision was also due to the stark fact that some migrants had gone underground or had been deported, so their whereabouts were unknown or not easily ascertained. As a consequence, it is difficult to comment on migrants' subjectivity within relevant rationalities and legal narratives.

101 Each of the twelve collections of unpublished documents is referred to as a "case file," and each document has been assigned a number. In what follows, these documents are referred to accordingly (e.g., Case File 4, Document 4).

102 G. Agamben, *Homo Sacer: Sovereign Power and Bare Life* (Stanford: Stanford University Press, 1998).

103 This contrasts with the US context, where migrants tended to enter illegally without having first entered a formal selection process abroad or a determination process at a port of entry.

104 For example, D. Gregory, *Geographical Imaginations* (Cambridge, MA: Blackwell, 1994), 194; Blake, "Pastoral Power, Governmentality and Cultures of Order," 81.

105 See for example, M. Valverde, *Diseases of the Will: Alcohol and the Dilemmas of Freedom* (Cambridge: Cambridge University Press, 1998).

Chapter 2: Features of Canadian Sanctuary Incidents, 1983-2003

1 In addition to the four developments discussed in this chapter, there was a sanctuary meeting in September 1992 at First United Church in Vancouver's Downtown Eastside at which two of the three guest speakers were pastors from two previous, unconnected incidents in the region; see L. Coulter, "Sanctuary: A Brief Update," *The Globe* 19 (1994): 4-6.

2 Cunningham, *God and Caesar*, 65.

3 Coutin, "Enacting Law through Social Practice," 288-89, 291, 302.

4 For example, the term is used in Coutin, *The Culture of Protest*.
5 Canada, Citizenship and Immigration Canada, *Canada and U.S. Negotiators Agree to Final Draft Text of Safe Third Country Agreement*, 2002, http://www.cic.gc.ca/english/policy/safe-third.html.
6 Crittenden, *Sanctuary*, 294; Stastny and Tyrnauer, "Sanctuary in Canada."
7 J. Simon, "Refugees in a Carceral Age: The Rebirth of Immigration Prisons in the United States," *Public Culture* 10 (1998): 577-607 at 579.
8 Pratt, "Sovereign Power, Carceral Conditions and Penal Practices."
9 See A. Macklin, "Refugee Women and the Imperative of Categories," *Human Rights Quarterly* 17 (1995): 213-77.
10 A. Finlayson, "The Underground Railroad to Canada," *Maclean's*, 13 May 1985, 42-44; "Church Groups Guide Refugees to Canada," *Toronto Star*, 17 March 1987, A14.
11 Interview 16.
12 Interview 16.
13 Interview 22; "Salvadorans Seeking Sanctuary Place New Hope in Canada," *Winnipeg Free Press*, 4 February 1985, 15.
14 Interview 16.
15 Interview 10, emphasis added.
16 Interview 37.
17 Leddy, *At the Border Called Hope*, 158.
18 United Church of Canada, *History*, 2003, http://www.united- church.ca/ucc/history/home.shtm.
19 United Church of Canada, 5.
20 United Church of Canada; Interviews 15, 21; Case File 4, Document 59.
21 Case File 4, Document 180.
22 Interview 39.
23 See Leddy, *At the Border Called Hope*.
24 Interview 31.
25 Interview 17.
26 Interviews 17, 30, 31.
27 Interview 17.
28 Interview 17.
29 Interviews 17, 30, 31. Despite repeated promises to do so, immigration officials did not resolve all of these migrants' files until 2002. See also Leddy, *At the Border Called Hope*.
30 Interview 17.
31 Interview 31.
32 Interview 17.
33 Interviews 5, 17, 40; Inter-Church Committee for Refugees (ICCR), *Keeping Faith: A Guide for Church Group Participation in the Pilot Project* (Toronto: ICCR, 1994). An earlier version was issued in June 1993 entitled "Keeping Faith with the Faceless: A Proposal for an ICCR Pilot Project of Alternative Sanctuary"; see Coulter, "Sanctuary: A Brief Update."
34 Anonymization is a key technique of "government at a distance," deployed to avoid the moral risk resulting from close association with illegal activity, but it is precisely this aspect that renders it incommensurate with a pastoral power that seeks intimate knowledge of individuals. On anonymization, see Lippert, "Policing Property and Moral Risk."
35 Interviews 5, 35. For this reason, the ICCR's activities were excluded as one of the incidents. The ICCR ceased to exist in 2001.
36 Interview 38.
37 At best, national churches developed and disseminated guidelines after the fact in response to local churches having granted sanctuary. However, this is not to say that a national movement could not yet develop.
38 The duration of four continuing incidents was calculated only to the end of 2003, consistent with coverage of a twenty-year period.
39 Interview 17.
40 Interview 37.

41 Interview 26.
42 Interview 10, emphasis added.
43 Of course, since there is a long tradition of sanctuary and potentially a very complex gene-
    alogy, the "original" source of the idea of seeking sanctuary lies in the distant past.
44 Interview 13.
45 Reynolds, *Faith Subdues Kingdoms,* 53.
46 Ibid., 54.
47 Interviews 10, 29, 37.
48 Interview 7.
49 Interview 34.
50 Interview 24.
51 Interview 36.
52 It is unclear whether US sanctuary activities were primarily or exclusively religious or merely
    tended to be represented this way in previous research; see for example, Bau, *This Ground Is
    Holy,* 30. Of the 448 sanctuary locations declared in the US by June 1987, 405 (90 percent)
    had been organized by either congregations or seminaries and only 43 (10 percent) by
    nonreligious entities, such as cities and universities; see B. Yarnold, "The Role of Religious
    Organizations in the U.S. Sanctuary Movement," in *The Role of Religious Organizations in
    Social Movements,* ed. Barbara Yarnold, 16-46 (New York: Praeger, 1991), 31. During sanctu-
    ary efforts in Tucson, Arizona, "the Manzo Area Council informed Tucson church groups
    about the arrival of undocumented Salvadorans"; see Coutin, "Enacting Law through So-
    cial Practice," 287.
53 Interview 9.
54 For example, Interviews 4, 10, 33.
55 Interview 6, emphasis added.
56 Interview 10.
57 Interview 36.
58 In another reference to contact with a person involved in the US sanctuary effort, a sanctu-
    ary provider noted that "it was there in a deep memory, and it surfaced when needed ... but
    it wasn't that any of us intended to be in touch or anything"; see Interview 17.
59 Interview 24.
60 "Religious Disobedience," *Light Talk,* television broadcast, 20 July 1999, Winnipeg, Manitoba.
61 Interview 36.
62 Interview 39.
63 Interview 26.
64 Case File 2, Document 57.
65 See Coutin, "Enacting Law through Social Practice," 286; Lorentzen, *Women in the Sanctu-
    ary Movement,* 7.
66 Eighteen were women and nine were men, while information about the gender of three
    others was unavailable; see Case File 4, Document 16.
67 Interview 39.
68 On the gendered division of labour in sanctuary in the US, see Lorentzen, *Women in the
    Sanctuary Movement.*
69 For example, Interviews 2, 15.
70 Interviews 8, 10, 26, 32.
71 Interview 2.
72 Interview 27.
73 Interview 32.
74 Interview 8.
75 Interview 9, emphasis added.
76 For example, Interviews 10, 27.
77 Interview 27.
78 Interview 16.
79 Interview 23.
80 Case File 1, Document 50, emphasis in the original.

81 Interview 11, emphasis added.
82 Interview 24, emphasis added.
83 Wiltfang and McAdam, "The Costs and Risks of Social Activism."
84 Interview 31. See also "Church Groups Ready to Shelter Refugees Facing Deportation," *Catholic New Times*, 13 June 1993, 10.
85 Southern Ontario Sanctuary Coalition, "A Declaration: A Civil Initiative to Protect Refugees," emphasis added.
86 For example, Interview 24.
87 Interviews 4, 6.
88 An interviewee from the SOSC estimated that 65 migrants and their dependents were granted sanctuary by this coalition in connection with 23 cases, many of which involved a claimant and their dependents. On the 23 cases, see Leddy, *At the Border Called Hope*. The figure of 196 additional migrants was established by summing the numbers of migrants quoted in documents and corroborated through interviews for each incident.
89 The small N reflects the unavailability of the age of migrants involved in the three incidents that accounted for 63 percent (166) of the migrants. Yet nothing was unearthed about these incidents in interviews or other sources to suggest that migrants involved were other than young adults often accompanied by their children.
90 For example, Coutin, *The Culture of Protest*.
91 See M. Bossin, "'After a Thorough and Sympathetic Review': The State of Humanitarian Applications in Canada," *Journal of Law and Social Policy* 14 (1999): 107-22.
92 Lyon, "Introduction."
93 Interview 17.
94 Ibid.
95 Case File 2, Document 111.
96 Police entered a "church" lacking a city permit to arrest several Chileans in Montreal in 1998.
97 In contrast to the Canadian context, in the Viraj Mendis incident in Britain, after a long period, British authorities entered a church to arrest the migrant in question; see Weller, "Sanctuary as Concealment and Exposure." Similar actions occurred in Germany and France in the 1990s; see Sharma, *Religion-Germany*; C. Trueheart and A. Swardson, "'Thousands Denounce Detention of Migrants," *Ottawa Citizen*, 24 August 1990, A6. In the US the sanctuary trials that occurred between 1985 and 1986 resulted in the prosecution of eight US sanctuary activists; see Matas, *The Sanctuary Trial*; Crittenden, *Sanctuary*.
98 Interviews 1, 16, 28.
99 Ibid.
100 On sacrifice in US sanctuary activities, see Park, "The Sacrifice Theory of Value"; Wiltfang and McAdam, "The Costs and Risks of Social Activism"; Coutin, "Enacting Law through Social Practice," 295.

Chapter 3: Advanced-Liberal Refugee Determination and Resettlement
1 See Lippert, "Governing Refugees."
2 Rose, "Government, Authority and Expertise."
3 N. Rose, "Governing 'Advanced Liberal' Democracies," in *Foucault and Political Reason: Liberalism, Neo-Liberalism, and Rationalities of Government*, ed. A. Barry, T. Osborne, and N. Rose, 37-64 (London: UCL Press, 1996), 57.
4 Rose, "Government, Authority and Expertise," 295.
5 Ibid.; Rose, "Governing 'Advanced Liberal' Democracies," 54-55.
6 See for example, D. Garland, "The Limits of the Sovereign State: Strategies of Crime Control in Contemporary Society," *British Journal of Criminology* 36 (1996): 455-71 at 452; K. Hannah-Moffat, "Prisons That Empower: Neo-Liberal Governance in Canadian Women's Prisons," *British Journal of Criminology* 40 (2000): 510-31 at 514.
7 O'Malley and Palmer, "Post-Keynesian Policing," 141-42.
8 K. Stenson, "Community Policing as a Governmental Technology," *Economy and Society* 22, (1993): 373-89; O'Malley, "Indigenous Governance," 313.

9 Rose, "The Death of the Social?" 331-37.
10 B. Cruikshank, "Revolutions Within: Self-Government and Self-Esteem," in *Foucault and Political Reason: Liberalism, Neo-Liberalism and Rationalities of Government*, ed. A. Barry, T. Osborne, and N. Rose, 231-51 (London: UCL Press, 1996); Rose, "The Death of the Social?" 336.
11 N. Rose, "Governing the Enterprise Self," in *The Values of the Enterprise Culture: The Moral Debate*, ed. P. Heelas and P. Morris, 141-64 (London: Routledge, 1992).
12 Rose, "Governing 'Advanced Liberal' Democracies," 53-54.
13 Ibid., 53.
14 28 July 1951, 189 U.N.T.S. 137; 31 January 1967, 606 U.N.T.S. 267.
15 G. Dirks, *Canada's Refugee Policy: Indifference or Opportunism?* (Montreal and Kingston: McGill-Queen's University Press, 1977), 230.
16 L. Gilad, *The Northern Route: An Ethnography of Refugee Experience* (St. John's, NF: Institute of Social and Economic Research, 1990), 349.
17 Canada, *The Immigration and Population Study* (Ottawa: Information Canada, 1974), 116.
18 M. Mandel, *The Charter of Rights and the Legalization of Politics in Canada*, rev. ed. (Toronto: Thompson Educational Funding, 1994), 241.
19 A. Nash, *International Refugee Pressures and the Canadian Public Policy Response* (Ottawa: Institute on Research on Public Policy, 1989), 39.
20 Canada, *The Immigration and Population Study*, 116; Nash, *International Refugee Pressures*, 39-43.
21 Canada, *The Immigration and Population Study*, 41.
22 Ibid., 42.
23 Gilad, *The Northern Route*, 320-21.
24 G. Goodwyn-Gil, "Determining Refugee Status in Canada," *Refugees* 27 (1987): 27-28.
25 Nash, *International Refugee Pressures*, 43; H. Adelman, *Canada and the Indochinese Refugees* (Regina: L.A. Weigl Educational Associates, 1982), 41.
26 Canada, Department of Manpower and Immigration, *The Immigration Bill: Explanatory Notes of an Office of Consolidation of the Immigration Bill* (Ottawa: Ministry of Supply and Services, 1976), 29.
27 In 1974 only 89 refugee-status claims were reviewed; see Canada, *The Immigration and Population Study*, 116. By 1979 the figure was 1,165, and by 1987 it was 15,805; see G. Creese, "The Politics of Refugees in Canada," in *Deconstructing a Nation: Immigration, Multiculturalism, and Racism in 90's Canada*, ed. V. Satzewich, 1-20 (Halifax: Fernwood, 1992), 8. By mid-1986 there were also 20,000 claimants in a backlog; see Canada, Ministry of Employment and Immigration, *Refugee Determination in Canada: Proposals for Canada*, by W.G. Plaut (Ottawa: Ministry of Supply and Services, 1985), 42-43.
28 Ashenden, "Reflexive Governance and Child Abuse," 66.
29 A. Simmons and K. Keohane, "Canadian Immigration Policy: State Strategies and the Quest for Legitimacy," *Canadian Review of Sociology and Anthropology* 29 (1992): 421-52 at 432.
30 J. Hathaway, "The Conundrum of Refugee Protection in Canada: From Control to Compliance to Collective Deterrence," *Journal of Policy History* 4 (1992), 71-92 at 84; D. Stoffman, "Open Door Travesty," *Saturday Night*, 1 November 1994, 55.
31 Canada, Employment and Immigration Canada, *Indochinese Refugees: The Canadian Response, 1979 and 1980* (Ottawa: Ministry of Supply and Services, 1982).
32 See for example, S. Hier and J. Greenberg, "Constructing a Discursive Crisis: Risk, Problematization and Illegal Chinese in Canada," *Ethnic and Racial Studies* 25 (2002): 490-513.
33 Nash, *International Refugee Pressures*, 70, 86; Simmons and Keohane, "Canadian Immigration Policy," 423; G. Dirks, *Controversy and Complexity: Canadian Immigration Policy during the 1980's* (Montreal and Kingston: McGill-Queen's University Press, 1995), 83. The resources and processing times of the queue vary considerably, with generally more visa officers and shorter processing times in Western regions; see Canadian Council for Refugees (CCR), *Refugee Family Reunification* (Montreal: CCR, 1995), 30.
34 Nash, *International Refugee Pressures*, 91n. See also W. Walters, "Mapping Schengenland: Denaturalizing the Border," *Environment and Planning D: Society and Space* 20 (2002): 561-80.

35 See Stenson, "Community Policing as a Governmental Technology," 375.
36 Canada, Employment and Immigration Canada, *The Refugee Status Determination Process: A Report of the Task Force on Immigration Practices and Procedures*, by W. Robinson (Ottawa: Ministry of Supply and Services, 1981).
37 Nash, *International Refugee Pressures*, 45.
38 "RSAC to Be Independent of CEIC," *Refuge* 1, 7 (1982): 4.
39 "'Non-status' Refugee Loses Living Allowance from Federal Treasury," *Globe and Mail*, 26 October 1982, 9.
40 "Refugees Protest Lack of Aid," *Winnipeg Free Press*, 22 October 1983, 12.
41 Canada, Ministry of Employment and Immigration, *A New Refugee Status Determination Process for Canada*, by E. Ratushny (Ottawa, Ministry of Supply and Services, 1984), 10, emphasis added.
42 Ibid.
43 Canada, Ministry of Employment and Immigration, *Refugee Determination in Canada*, 60-143.
44 *Singh v. Minister of Employment and Immigration* [1985] 1 S.C.R. 177.
45 Mandel, *The Charter of Rights*, 241.
46 B. Jackman, "Canada's Refugee Crisis: Planned Mismanagement?" in *Human Rights and the Protection of Refugees under International Law*, ed. A. Nash, 321-26 (Halifax: Institute for Research on Public Policy, 1988), 321.
47 Nash, *International Refugee Pressures*, 48.
48 On juridification, see A. Hunt, "Legal Governance and Social Relations: Empowering Agents and the Limits of Law," in *Law, Regulation and Governance*, ed. M. MacNeil, N. Sargent, and P. Swan, 54-77 (Don Mills: Oxford University Press, 2002), 58.
49 Dirks, *Controversy and Complexity*, 88.
50 Creese, "The Politics of Refugees in Canada," 123-43.
51 Ibid.
52 Ibid., 133-34; Jackman, "Canada's Refugee Crisis," 323.
53 Mandel, *The Charter of Rights*, 246; Dirks, *Controversy and Complexity*, 90.
54 See Mandel, *The Charter of Rights*, 248; Creese, "The Politics of Refugees in Canada," 129; "Church Groups Fail to Get Exemption under Refugee Bill," *Ottawa Citizen*, 2 August 1987, A1-2.
55 See Creese, "The Politics of Refugees in Canada," 135; Dirks, *Controversy and Complexity*, 87-8. By the mid-1980s several provinces had begun to provide welfare to claimants while they awaited determination of their claims. Claimants were not granted work permits until May 1986. Work permits to be issued a few months later, in February 1987, and began to be issued again in 1993.
56 See J. Simon, "In the Place of the Parent: Risk Management and the Government of Campus Life," *Social and Legal Studies* 3 (1994): 15-45 at 17; Ashenden, "Reflexive Governance and Child Abuse," 64.
57 Jackman, "Canada's Refugee Crisis," 322.
58 Canada, Citizenship and Immigration Canada, *Refugee and Humanitarian Immigration to Canada, 1947-1995* (Ottawa: Ministry of Supply and Services, 1995), 11.
59 Canada, Refugee Affairs Division Policy and Program Development Branch, *Refugee Perspectives: 1986-1987* (Ottawa: Employment and Immigration Canada, 1986), 50.
60 Ibid., 51.
61 For example, ibid., 50-51.
62 Canada, Refugee Affairs Division Policy and Program Development Branch, *Refugee Perspectives*, 50. This was the standard "magnet effect" argument promulgated by senior immigration officials, who, from the outset, resisted establishing inland refugee determination; see Hathaway, "The Conundrum of Refugee Protection in Canada," 4 (1992): 71-92.
63 Nash, *International Refugee Pressures*, 51.
64 Canada, Employment and Immigration Canada, "Ministers Act to Curb Refugee Claims Abuse," press release, February 1987, 1.
65 Ibid., 1-3.
66 Ibid.

67 Bill C-55, an Act to Amend the Immigration Act, 1976, House of Commons, first reading, 5 May 1987.
68 Dirks, Controversy and Complexity, 95-6; Canada, Citizenship and Immigration Canada, Refugee and Humanitarian Immigration to Canada.
69 In the first stage, eligibility was to be determined. In the second stage, credibility was to be decided following an oral hearing. If rejected at this point, the claimants could then appeal to the Federal Court (but not on the merit of the claim); see Dirks, Controversy and Complexity, 90.
70 Hathaway, "The Conundrum of Refugee Protection in Canada," 82.
71 Although the RSAC had a small research unit, the emphasis on the need for formal knowledge was first highlighted in the Plaut Report. Both the new and old determination processes were, of course, dependent on informal knowledge generated by, and disseminated among, participants. For example, legal professionals share information about which IRB members are likely to prefer certain kinds of evidence, likely to decide in favour of claimants from certain nations over others, and so on.
72 Dirks, Controversy and Complexity, 90.
73 Bill C-84, an Act to Amend the Immigration Act, 1976, House of Commons, first reading, 11 August 1987.
74 Provisions for carrier sanctions were present in the 1976 Immigration Act, but penalties were significantly increased in Bill C-84. In practice, since passage of Bill C-84, several airlines have been fined for transporting persons to Canada who did not have proper documentation; see "Immigration Checks Yield $5.5 Million in Airline Fines," The Vancouver Sun, 21 February 1997, A1.
75 Hathaway, "The Conundrum of Refugee Protection in Canada," 81; Mandel, The Charter of Rights, 254.
76 "March of Defiance," Macleans, 18 April 1988, 12.
77 "Minister Offers Church Refuge for Ghanaians," Montreal Gazette, 26 March 1988, A3.
78 ICCR, "Triennial Assembly of CCC Adopts Court Challenge," ICCR Bulletin, April/May 1988, 2; ICCR, "Churches to Seek Leave to Have Supreme Court Overturn Setback Decision," ICCR Bulletin, March/April 1990, 1.
79 D. Stoffman, Pounding at the Gates (Toronto: Atkinson Charitable Foundation, 1992), 20-3.
80 Mandel, The Charter of Rights, 254.
81 Bill C-86, an Act to Amend the Immigration Act and Other Acts in Consequence Thereof, R.S.C. 1992.
82 Canada, Employment and Immigration Canada, Refugee Affairs Branch, "Canada's Refugee Policy," Dialogue 1 (1992): 1-11 at 1.
83 Ibid.
84 Canada, Department of Citizenship and Immigration, Refugee and Humanitarian Resettlement Program: In Canada (Ottawa: Ministry of Supply and Services, 1997).
85 "Sanctuary for Refugees a Growing Movement," Montreal Gazette, 2 August 2003, A1.
86 See for example, B. Bettson, "Suffering under New System"; ICCR, "Government and Church Lawyers Agree Our Action Would Make Constitutional History," ICCR Bulletin, January/February 1990, 1.
87 See A. Ceyhan and A. Tsoukala, "The Securitization of Migration in Western Societies: Ambivalent Discourses and Policies," Alternatives 27 (2002): 21-39; D. Bigo, "Security and Immigration: Toward a Critique of the Governmentality of Unease," Alternatives 27 (2002): 63-92.
88 H. Adelman "Canadian Borders and Immigration Post 9/11," International Migration Review 36 (2002): 15-28.
89 Southern Ontario Sanctuary Coalition, "A Declaration: A Civil Initiative to Protect Refugees."
90 Hindess, Discourses of Power, 100.
91 Canada, Employment and Immigration Canada, Study of the Impact of the 1979-80 Indochinese Refugee Program on Canada Immigration Centre and Canada Employment Centre Operations (Ottawa: Ministry of Supply and Services, 1981), 9. See also Canada, Citizenship and Immigration Canada, Refugee and Humanitarian Resettlement Program in Canada, operations memorandum (Ottawa: Ministry of Supply and Services, 1997), 10.

92 M. Lanphier and O. Lukomskyj, "Settlement Policy in Australia and Canada," in *Immigration and Refugee Policy: Australia and Canada Compared,* vol. 2., ed. H. Adelman, A. Borowski, M. Burnstein, and L. Foster, 337-71 (Toronto: University of Toronto Press, 1994), 342.
93 Ibid.
94 Ibid.
95 Social-service agencies dealing exclusively with the resettlement of immigrants existed before the 1970s. Toronto's International Institute, created in 1956, is a well-known example of such an organization; see F. Iacovetta, "Making 'New Canadians': Social Workers, Women, and the Reshaping of Families," in *Gender Conflicts: New Essays in Women's History,* ed. F. Iacovetta and M. Valverde, 261-303 (Toronto, University of Toronto Press, 1992), 268. Permanent arrangements for federal funding (e.g., the ISAP) for such nonprofit organizations was new in the 1970s. By 1972 the Department of Immigration had created Immigrant Reception Centres to be run by state agents in five Canadian cities, but as the historian Freda Hawkins writes, at this point, "the funding of voluntary agencies which attempt to provide some vital services to immigrants is still in a confused and undeveloped state"; see F. Hawkins, *Canada and Immigration: Public Policy and Public Concern* (Montreal and Kingston: McGill-Queen's University Press, 1972), 297.
96 R. Heipel, "Refugee Resettlement in a Canadian City: An Overview and Assessment," in *Refugee Policy: Canada and the U.S.,* ed. H. Adelman, 344-55 (Toronto: York Lanes Press, 1991), 348.
97 Canada, Employment and Immigration Canada, *Indochinese Refugees,* 13.
98 Canada, Employment and Immigration Canada, *Study of the Impact of the 1979-80 Indochinese Refugee Program,* 9.
99 D. Indra, "Bureaucratic Constraints, Middlemen and Community Organization: Aspects of the Political Incorporation of Southeast Asians in Canada," in *Uprooting, Loss, and Adaptation: The Resettlement of Refugees in Canada,* ed. K. Chan and D. Indra, 147-77 (Ottawa: Canadian Public Health Association, 1987), 154.
100 Ibid., 152.
101 Canada, *Immigration Settlement Adaptation Program: Handbook for Service Provider Organizations* (Ottawa: Ministry of Supply and Services, 1996), 9. See also Indra, "Bureaucratic Constraints," 152.
102 Canada, *Immigration Settlement Adaptation Program,* 9.
103 Ibid., 8.
104 Rose, "Governing 'Advanced Liberal' Democracies," 55.
105 Ibid., 56.
106 Lippert and O'Connor, "Security Assemblages."
107 For example, community colleges in some regions offer certificate programs in settlement. As well, settlement workers in Canadian provinces are represented by professional associations.
108 The thousands of immigrants admitted to Canada after 1978 from abroad by way of the family-class category were not imagined undergoing screening as rigorous as that required for immigrants selected through the independent class – although the screening of family-class immigrants was still more rigorous than that required for refugee claimants.
109 For example, Canada, Employment and Immigration Canada, *Immigration Levels Planning: The First Decade* (Ottawa: Employment and Immigration Canada, 1988), 2, 24.
110 H. Adelman, *The Indochinese Refugee Movement: The Canadian Experience* (Toronto: Operation Lifeline, 1980), 83.
111 Private refugee sponsorship did not begin in the 1970s following release of the Green Paper. For World Refugee Year in 1959, a program of private sponsorship appeared that envisaged private groups assuming "full and continuing responsibility for the cost of health and welfare services for the refugee families until they could qualify for these services under public auspices"; see "Bringing Refugees to Canada," *Canadian Welfare,* 15 March 1960, 79-80. The point, however, is that their responsibility was imagined to refer only to a small proportion of those selected within this larger program; see Canada, "Canada's Refugee Programmes, 1945-1961," in *Studies and Documents on Immigration and Integration in Canada,* ed. J. Kage, 1-13 (Montreal: Jewish Immigrant Aid Services of Canada, 1962). Of the more than 5,000 refugees resettled during a two-year period beginning in July 1959,

the official start of World Refugee Year, only about 700 were sponsored by private organizations. Czechoslovakians and Chileans also appear to have been mostly state-sponsored; see Canada, *Czechoslovakian Refugee Study: A Report on the Three-Year Study of the Economic and Social Adaptation of Czechoslovakian Refugees to Life in Canada, 1968-69* (Ottawa: Department of Manpower and Immigration, 1975), 39; Canada, Employment and Immigration Canada, *Final Report: Chilean Refugee Households in Canada* (Ottawa: Employment and Immigration Canada, 1976), 6. To the extent that the displaced persons of Europe who began to be selected in 1946 were considered refugees, they appear to have been primarily sponsored by relatives or private employers rather than by the state; see J. Vernant, *The Refugee in the Post-War World* (New Haven, CT: Yale University Press, 1953), 546-53.

112 Nash, *International Refugee Pressures*, 40.
113 D. Indra, "An Analysis of the Canadian Private Sponsorship Program for Southeast Asian Refugees," *Ethnic Groups* 7 (1988): 153-72 at 155. See also Adelman, *The Indochinese Refugee Movement*, 84.
114 Adelman, *The Indochinese Refugee Movement*, 83-84. Perhaps due to a recognition of the connotations of a master-slave relation, master-agreement holders are now called sponsorship-agreement holders.
115 See for example, Canadian Council for Refugees, *Resettlement out of Signatory Countries*, 2000, http://www.web.net/~ccr/signatory.htm.
116 Canada, Employment and Immigration Canada, *Study of the Impact*, 16.
117 Ibid., 14-16.
118 Ibid., 14-15.
119 Ibid.
120 "Friendship Families," *Refuge* 1, 3 (1981): 4-5 at 4.
121 Ibid.
122 Ibid. See also Centre for Research and Education in Human Services, *Refugee Resettlement in Kitchener-Waterloo: A Participatory Evaluation* (Kitchener: Kitchener Centre for Research and Education in Human Services, 1984), 13.
123 "Friendship Families," *Refuge* 1, 3 (1981): 4-5 at 5.
124 Ibid.
125 Ibid.
126 Ibid. See also Centre for Research and Education in Human Services, *Refugee Resettlement*, 14-16.
127 Indra, "An Analysis of the Canadian Private Sponsorship Program," 159.
128 "Friendship Families," *Refuge* 1, 3 (1981): 4-5.
129 M. Lanphier, "Host Groups: Public Meets Private," in *The International Refugee Crisis: British and Canadian Responses*, ed. V. Robinson, 255-73 (London: Macmillan, 1993); H. Adelman, "Refugee Resettlement: A New Policy," *Refuge* 4, 2 (1984): 16-21.
130 Lanphier, "Host Groups," 255.
131 C.M. Lanphier, *Refuge* 7, 4 (1988): 1, 3-6 at 1.
132 Canada, Employment and Immigration Canada, *Host Family Program: Summary Report* (Ottawa: Employment and Immigration Canada, 1987), 2.
133 C.M. Lanphier, *Refuge* 7, 4 (1988): 1, 3-6 at 1.
134 For example, Canada, Department of Citizenship and Immigration, *Not Just Numbers: A Canadian Framework for Future Immigration: Immigration Legislative Review* (Ottawa: Ministry of Public Works and Government Services Canada, 1998), 34.
135 C.M. Lanphier, *Refuge* 7, 4 (1988): 1, 3-6 at 1.
136 For example, Canada, Health Promotion and Programs Branch, *National Health Research and Development Program* (Ottawa: Ministry of Supply and Services, 1996), 1, 9; C.M. Lanphier, *Refuge* 7, 4 (1988): 1, 3-6 at 5-6; "Metro Toronto Host Program," *Refuge* 9, 3 (1990): at 11.
137 Canada, *Annual Report to Parliament: Immigration Plan for 1991-1995* (Ottawa: Employment and Immigration Canada, 1990), 15.
138 Ibid.
139 See for example, D. De Voretz, *Diminishing Returns: The Economics of Canada's Immigration Policy* (Vancouver: C.D. Howe Institute and the Laurier Institution, 1995).

140 See for example, Canada, Citizenship and Immigration Canada, *Be a Host to a Newcomer*, 2003, http://www.cic.gc.ca/english/newcomer/involve/canadian-host.html.

141 Rose and Miller, "Political Power," 175.

142 Ibid., 184.

143 Rose, "Governing 'Advanced Liberal' Democracies," 57; O'Malley and Palmer, "Post-Keynesian Policing."

144 H. Adelman, "Refugee Resettlement: A New Policy," *Refuge* 4, 2 (1984): 16-21 at 21, emphasis added.

145 Canada, Citizenship and Immigration Canada, *Departmental Outlook on Program Expenditures and Priorities, 1996-97 to 1998-99* (Ottawa: Ministry of Supply and Services, 1996), 9, emphasis added.

146 Centre for Refugee Studies, *Centre for Refugee Studies Newsletter* February 1997, 9, emphasis added.

147 See Adelman, *The Indochinese Refugee Movement*, 25-26, emphasis added.

148 W. Giles, "Voice and Empowerment," *Refuge* 14, 7 (1994): 1-2 at 1. In June 1988, for example, such a conference was held regarding refugee women; see "Refugee Women in Canada," *Canadian Woman's Studies* 10 (1989): 5-15.

149 V. Lassailly-Jacob, "Empower the Most Vulnerable: A People-Oriented Planning Workshop," *Refuge* 13, 4 (1993): 21-22 at 21.

150 Canada, Citizenship and Immigration Canada, *The Right of Landing Fee and Immigrant Loans Program* (Ottawa, Citizenship and Immigration Canada, 1995), 3. This particular fee was rescinded for refugees in 2000; the others remain.

151 Ibid.

152 All figures are in Canadian dollars.

153 Canada, Citizenship and Immigration Canada, *Departmental Outlook*, 18. The fee was expected to generate CDN$136 million dollars in revenue, while these programs were estimated to cost a total of CDN$250 million dollars.

154 "News Digest," *Refuge* 5, 2 (1985): 19. A similar emphasis is seen in the Refugee Studies Program at Oxford University and in the *Journal of Refugee Studies* produced there; see C.M. Lanphier and N. Spencer Nimmons, "The Refugee Crisis: British and Canadian Responses," *Refuge* 8, 3 (1989): 10-11 at 10.

155 Indra, "An Analysis of the Canadian Private Sponsorship Program," 169. See also N. Spencer-Nimmons, "A Canadian Concern" *Refuge* 7, 4 (1988): 6-10 at 6.

156 The latter two assessments are most transparent in sanctuary cases in Calgary and Toronto, the former involving a migrant diagnosed with schizophrenia and the latter a migrant family with physically disabled and elderly members.

157 Rose and Miller, "Political Power," 174.

158 B. Hindess, "The Liberal Government of Unfreedom," *Alternatives* 26 (2001): 93-111 at 102.

159 Dean, "Liberal Government and Authoritarianism," 54.

160 P. White, "Send Romero to El Salvador," *Calgary Herald*, 1 February 1994, A6.

161 "Officials Waiting for Romero to Appear," *Calgary Herald*, 6 January 1994, B5, emphasis added.

162 Case File 4, Document 69.

163 Unidentified caller, "Religious Disobedience," *Light Talk*, television broadcast, 20 July 1999, Winnipeg, Manitoba.

164 "There's Still No Room at the Inn for Some," *Calgary Herald*, 30 December 1993, A9, emphasis added.

Chapter 4: Sanctuary as Sovereign Power

1 M. Foucault, *Discipline and Punish: The Birth of the Prison* (New York: Vintage, 1979), 32. For example, P. O'Malley, "Risk, Power and Crime Prevention," *Economy and Society* 21 (1992): 252-75 at 261; B. Hudson, "Punishment and Governance," *Social and Legal Studies* 7 (1998): 553-59 at 558.

2 Foucault, *Discipline and Punish*, 53.

3 For example, Fitzpatrick, "'These Mad Abandon'd Times.'" An issue of importance here, about which Agamben is inconsistent, is the extent to which sovereign power entails

spectacle. This inconsistency centres on his treatment of sacrifice; see N. Hussain and M. Ptacek, "Thresholds: Sovereignty and the Sacred," *Law and Society Review* 34 (2000): 495-515 at 505.

4 C. Schmitt, *Political Theology: Four Chapters on the Concept of Sovereignty* (Cambridge, MA: MIT Press, 1985), 5.

5 D. MacDonald, "Sanctuary Still Last Resort," *Montreal Gazette*, online edition 2 November 2002, 1, http://www.canada.com/montreal/montrealgazette/index.html.

6 Interview 23.

7 Interview 27.

8 Interview 24.

9 Case File 2, Document 89, emphasis added.

10 For a notable and excellent exception, see Coutin, "Enacting Law through Social Practice."

11 See ICCR, *Keeping Faith;* United Church of Canada, *Sanctuary for Refugees?*; Unitarian Church of Calgary, "A Checklist of Practical Considerations When Offering Sanctuary," unpublished information sheet, May 1996.

12 Schmitt, *Political Theology*, 5.

13 For example, Interviews 4, 9, 31, 33, 38; F. Barahona, "Women at Risk," *The Ubyssey* 95 (1995): 1-4; C.-A. Nicholson, "Hurtados Seek Sanctuary," *St. Stephen Courier*, 30 June 1998, A2.

14 "Desperate Family Finds Easter Sanctuary: Rejected Refugees Given Shelter by Parkdale Church," *Toronto Star*, 12 April 1998, A1, emphasis added.

15 "Unitarians Sheltering Refugee Claimants," *Montreal Gazette*, 4 July 2003, A1.

16 M. Macafee, "Canadian Churches Follow Old Testament Tradition," 2003, http://cnews. canoe.ca/CNEWS/Canada/2003/08/10/pf-157964.html.

17 Interview 31.

18 "Refugees Seeking Sanctuary," *United Church Observer* 57 (1993): 28-29 at 28, emphasis added.

19 Case File 2, Document 62, emphasis added.

20 Interview 1, emphasis added.

21 Interview 1.

22 For example, Interview 25.

23 Interview 1.

24 "Religious Disobedience," *Light Talk*, television broadcast, 20 July 1999, Winnipeg, Manitoba, emphasis added.

25 For example, Case File 2, Document 124; Interviews 14, 36.

26 Interview 10.

27 Interviews 1, 3, 4, 9, 12, 13, 18, 20, 23, 40. Following sanctuary incidents, in an attempt to avoid being contacted by such migrants, some churches have sought to develop explicit selection guidelines, albeit not along national (or ethnic/racial, gender, religious, or denominational) lines; see Interviews 1, 5, 10, 21.

28 For example, Interviews 9, 17.

29 Interview 27.

30 "Church Evicts Refugees," *Calgary Herald*, 16 April 1999, A10; U. Vu "Chilean Refugees Appeal to Ottawa: Want Permission to Stay for 5 Years," *Montreal Gazette*, 20 November 1998, A6.

31 Interview 28.

32 In sanctuary discourse, a distinction is rarely made between immigration authorities and the IRB, contrary to the advanced-liberal effort to place determination "at a distance" from both immigration officials and political interference, as described in Chapter 3.

33 Interview 17, emphasis added.

34 Macafee, "Canadian Churches Follow Old Testament Tradition."

35 Interview 39.

36 Agamben, *Homo Sacer,* 83, 94.

37 Ibid., 18.

38 On Canadian immigration detention and sovereign power, see Pratt, "Sovereign Power, Carceral Conditions and Penal Practices," 8.

39 *Bahsous, Olivia Nadim v. M.C.I. Immigration and Refugee Board* (Appeal Division), Sangmuah, Egya, T99-07016, 1 September 2000.
40 Ibid., emphasis added.
41 Interview 32, emphasis added. See also United Church of Canada, *Sanctuary for Refugees?* 16.
42 Case File 2, Document 96, emphasis added.
43 Interview 24.
44 R. Walker, "Community Unites around Lucy Lu: Immigration Minister Still Unresponsive," *Pic Press*, online edition, May 2001, 1, http://www.geocities.com/ThorrasicPark/index.html.
45 C.-A. Nicholson, "Community Pleads for Family's Freedom," *St. Stephen Courier*, 3 November 1998, A1.
46 M. Foucault, "Governmentality," in *The Foucault Effect: Studies in Governmentality*, ed. G. Burchell, C. Gordon, and P. Miller, 84-104 (Toronto: Harvester Wheatsheaf, 1991), 93. For an alternative interpretation of the importance of territory in the writings of de la Pierre, on whom Foucault draws in order to argue that territory becomes of secondary importance with the rise of governmentality, see D. Dupont and F. Pearce, "Foucault Contra Foucault: Rereading the 'Governmentality' Papers," *Theoretical Criminology* 5 (2001): 123-58 at 137-38.
47 Foucault, "Governmentality," 93. See Garland, "The Limits of the Sovereign State," 341; Stenson, "Crime Control, Governmentality and Sovereignty," 66.
48 When a group of migrants in Montreal found themselves about to be deported in 1988, providers contemplated church buildings as well as neighbouring Aboriginal lands straddling the US-Canada border as potential sanctuary sites because they were deemed sovereign; see Interview 29.
49 Interview 20, emphasis added.
50 Interview 26.
51 Interview 8, emphasis added.
52 Interview 27.
53 Case File 4, Document 180.
54 Interview 38.
55 Interview 9, emphasis added.
56 Interview 11.
57 Interview 8.
58 Interview 2.
59 Interview 10.
60 Interview 26, emphasis added.
61 For an insightful analysis of discretionary power as productive, see A. Pratt, "Dunking the Doughnut: Discretionary Power, Law and the Administration of the Canadian Immigration Act," *Social and Legal Studies* 8 (1999): 199-225.
62 See Dean, "Powers of Life and Death beyond Governmentality," 125.
63 There were, for example, more than eight thousand "removals" in the 2000-2001 fiscal year; see Canada, Citizenship and Immigration Canada, *Performance Report*, 2001, http://www.cic.gc.ca/english/pub/dpr2001/dpr%2D02d.html.
64 Pratt, "Sovereign Power, Carceral Conditions and Penal Practices," 51. See also Simon, "Refugees in a Carceral Age," 579.
65 Pratt, "Sovereign Power, Carceral Conditions and Penal Practices," 66-67.
66 Canada, Citizenship and Immigration Canada, *Pre-Removal Risk Assessment*, 2002, http://www.cic.gc.ca/english/refugees/asylum-3.html.
67 Hier and Greenberg, "Constructing a Discursive Crisis." This is evident in other national contexts, including that of the US, which in 1980 placed the "Mariel Immigrants" in mass detention. On the US context, see B. Hufker and G. Cavender, "From Freedom Flotilla to America's Burden: The Social Construction of the Mariel Immigrants," *The Sociological Quarterly* 31 (1990): 321-35; Simon, "Refugees in a Carceral Age." It is also seen in more recent events in Australia; see M. Gee, "None Is Too Many," *Globe and Mail*, 30 August 2001, A13.

68 Foucault, *Discipline and Punish*, 53.
69 Compared to the thousands deported annually, both those granted sanctuary and those permitted to stay on humanitarian and compassionate grounds are statistically rare. Regarding the latter, see Bossin, "'After a Thorough and Sympathetic Review.'"
70 Block, "Sanctuary and the Defiant Churches," *Maclean's*, 30 January 1984, 43.
71 Susan Coutin describes in superb detail the spectacle that surrounded the US sanctuary trials that occurred between 1985 and 1986. Although it was ultimately short-lived, this spectacle nevertheless "publicized the defendants' version of legality to such an extent that it undermined the authority of verdicts"; see S. Coutin, "Smugglers or Samaritans in Tuscon, Arizona: Producing and Contesting Legal Truth," *American Ethnologist* 22 (1995): 549-71 at 561.
72 This ancient aspect of sanctuary is dominant, for example, in most media accounts of specific sanctuary incidents, particularly early in the coverage. For example, I. Hunter, "St. Paul's Cathedral Is Not above the Law Sheltering an Iranian Family," *London Free Press*, 26 August 1998, A11; C. Solyom, "Sanctuary for Refugees a Growing Movement," *Montreal Gazette*, 2 August 2003, A1.
73 C. Enman, "In the Sanctuary of the Church," *Ottawa Citizen*, 24 December 1997, A3.
74 Interview 30.
75 For example, Interview 15.
76 Interview 13.
77 Interview 10.
78 Case File 11, Document 1.
79 "Nigerian Refugees Desperate for Lawyer: Donors Offer Everything but Legal Help," *Calgary Herald*, 3 December 2002, B1.
80 Interview 40.
81 Case File 2, Document 124.
82 Reynolds, *Faith Subdues Kingdoms*, 108.
83 Case File 5, Document 2.
84 Interview 26, emphasis added.
85 Interview 10, emphasis added.
86 Interview 24, emphasis added.
87 Interview 26.
88 Interview 38.
89 Interview 26, emphasis added.
90 Ibid., emphasis added.
91 Ibid., emphasis added.
92 Interview 37.
93 Interview 27, emphasis added.
94 Interview 40, emphasis added.
95 P. Fitzpatrick, "Terminal Legality," *Social and Legal Studies* 7 (1998): 431-36.
96 Foucault, *Discipline and Punish*, 65.
97 Interview 16.
98 Interview 15.
99 "Taking Sanctuary," *Listen Up*, 5 April 2001, http://www.crossroads.ca/listenup/programs/010405sanc.htm.
100 See for example, "Hunger Strikers End Fast," *Calgary Herald*, 10 August 1983, B6; C. Cattaneo, "Hunger Strikes Unite Romanian Families," *Montreal Gazette*, 4 January 1983, A3.
101 Interview 14.
102 Case File 1, Document 50.
103 See Agamben, *Homo Sacer*.
104 Hunt and Wickham, *Foucault and Law*, 85-86.
105 Interview 14, emphasis added.
106 Interview 28, emphasis added.
107 M. Dean, "'Demonic Societies': Liberalism, Biopolitics, and Sovereignty," in *States of Imagination: Ethnographic Explorations of the Postcolonial State*, ed. T. Hansen and T. Stepputat, 41-64 (London: Duke University Press, 2001), 54, emphasis added.

108 A. Akbari, "Immigrant 'Quality' in Canada: More Direct Evidence of Human Capital Content, 1956-1994," *International Migration Review* 33 (1999): 156-75.
109 See M. Dean, "'Demonic Societies'"; Constable, "Sovereignty and Governmentality."
110 Foucault, *Discipline and Punish*, 63.
111 For example, Interviews 1, 6, 7, 8, 14.
112 K. Lunman, "Standing up to Be Heard," *Calgary Herald*, 12 December 1993, B3.
113 Case File 2, Document 96.
114 Dillon, "Sovereignty and Governmentality," 328.
115 Agamben, *Homo Sacer*, 21.
116 Ibid., 18.
117 Ibid., 27.

Chapter 5: Sanctuary as Pastoral Power
 1 M. Foucault, "The Political Technology of Individuals," in *Technologies of the Self: A Seminar with Michel Foucault*, ed. L. Martin, H. Gutman, and P. Hutton, 145-62 (Amherst: University of Massachusetts Press, 1988), 60.
 2 Ibid., 61-62.
 3 Ibid., 63, 68-71.
 4 H. Dreyfus and P. Rabinow, *Michel Foucault: Beyond Structuralism and Hermeneutics* (Chicago: University of Chicago Press, 1983), 214.
 5 Foucault, "Politics and Reason," 79.
 6 Foucault, "The Political Technology of Individuals," 62.
 7 Ibid., 67.
 8 Ibid.
 9 Hindess, *Discourses of Power*, 118-23; Dean, *Governmentality*, 74-83. Mitchell Dean, for example, argues that pastoral power continues to have relevance but takes a nonreligious form today.
10 As quoted in Dreyfus and Rabinow, *Michel Foucault*, 214, emphasis added.
11 See D. Winland, "Christianity and Community: Conversion and Adaptation among Hmong Refugee Women," *Canadian Journal of Sociology* 119 (1994): 21-45 at 38; Y. Woon, "The Mode of Refugee Sponsorship and the Socio-Economic Adaptation of Vietnamese in Victoria: A Three-Year Perspective," in *Uprooting, Loss, and Adaptation: The Resettlement of Refugees in Canada*, ed. K. Chan and D. Indra, 132-46 (Ottawa: Canadian Public Health Association, 1987), 142.
12 Indra, "An Analysis of the Canadian Private Sponsorship Program," 158, emphasis added.
13 See for example, British Columbia Association of Social Workers (BCASW), *Guidelines for Social Work Practice with Refugees and Immigrants* (Vancouver: BCASW, 1980), 19.
14 Woon, "The Mode of Refugee Sponsorship," 139.
15 For example, Interview 8.
16 Interview 9.
17 Interview 24.
18 United Church of Canada, *Sanctuary for Refugees?* 18.
19 Interview 33.
20 Interview 9.
21 "Nigerian Family Gets Flood of Support," *Calgary Herald*, 1 December 2002, A1.
22 Interview 40, emphasis added.
23 Interview 23.
24 "Deportation Delayed," *Halifax Chronicle Herald*, 14 September 1990, C1.
25 D. Barr, "Let Romero Stay in Canada," *Calgary Herald*, 24 December 1993, A6.
26 "Desperate Family Finds Easter Sanctuary: Rejected Refugees Given Shelter by Parkdale Church," *Toronto Star*, 12 April 1998, A1.
27 Interview 38.
28 Interview 24.
29 Interview 3.
30 Interview 11.
31 Interview 40.

32 Interview 34.
33 Interview 32.
34 For example, Blake, "Pastoral Power, Governmentality and Cultures of Order," 81.
35 N. Fraser, *Unruly Practices: Power, Discourse and Gender in Contemporary Social Theory* (Minneapolis: University of Minnesota Press, 1989), 162.
36 Foucault, "The Political Technology of Individuals," 69.
37 For example, "Two Churches Offer Refugee Sanctuary," *Canadian Unitarian* 4 (2003): 3; "The Season of Hope," *Montreal Gazette*, 21 December 2003, C1.
38 Interview 26.
39 Case File 4, Document 109.
40 Interview 26.
41 Interview 39.
42 Rose and Miller, "Political Power."
43 As quoted in Dreyfus and Rabinow, *Michel Foucault*, 214.
44 Foucault, "The Political Technology of Individuals," 69.
45 In her study of US sanctuary activities, Susan Coutin similarly found that such intimate knowledge flowed primarily from migrants to providers rather than from providers to migrants; see Coutin, *The Culture of Protest*, 127.
46 United Church of Canada, *Sanctuary for Refugees?* 13.
47 Interview 27.
48 Interview 38.
49 Interview 25.
50 Interview 11.
51 CBC Radio, transcript of interview with sanctuary providers, Toronto, 23 July 2003.
52 Lippert, "Governing Refugees."
53 Foucault, "The Political Technology of Individuals," 62.
54 Interview 27.
55 Interview 24.
56 Interview 27.
57 For example, Interview 42; M. Clarkson and M. Stewart, "Supporters on Hand around Clock," *Calgary Herald*, 5 December 1993, A4; J. Morrison, "Church Says It Will Stand by Bangledeshi Refugee Claimant," *Ottawa Citizen*, 15 July 2003, C3; "Two Churches Offer Refugee Sanctuary," *Canadian Unitarian* 4 (2003): 3; K. Egan, "Officials to Respect Church Refuge," *Ottawa Citizen*, 25 November 2003, A13.
58 Interview 6.
59 Interview 35.
60 Interview 24.
61 "B.C. Christians Support Family in Church Haven," *Catholic New Times* 17 March 1996, 11.
62 Interview 6.
63 Interview 10.
64 Anglican Church, http://www.nspeidiocese.ca/netnews/2003/04_30_2003.htm.
65 Interview 27.
66 Interview 26.
67 Interview 8.
68 Interview 34, emphasis added.
69 Interview 26.
70 "Daddy, Why Can't We Go Outside?" *Times Globe*, 22 July 1998, A1-2.
71 Interview 40.
72 Interview 11.
73 Interview 38.
74 Interview 14.
75 As quoted in Dreyfus and Rabinow, *Michel Foucault*, 214.
76 Interview 35.
77 Interview 14.
78 Interview 40.

79 Caller named "Darryl," "Religious Disobedience," *Light Talk*, television broadcast, 20 July 1999, Winnipeg, Manitoba.
80 Case File 4, Document 29.
81 Interview 39.
82 Ibid.
83 Interview 38.
84 Ibid.
85 Interview 35.
86 Interview 38.
87 Interview 39, emphasis added.
88 Interview 40.
89 C.-A. Nicholson, "Hurtados Will Leave Canada ... If They Can Return," *St. Stephen Courier*, 12 January 1999, A2
90 A. Marshall "Churches Asked for Help," *Calgary Herald*, 13 January 1994, B5.
91 Interview 26.
92 Interview 35.
93 Interview 36.
94 Ibid.
95 Interview 42.
96 Participant, "Religious Disobedience," *Light Talk*, television broadcast, 20 July 1999, Winnipeg, Manitoba.
97 Case File 5, Document 9.
98 CBC Radio, transcript of interview with sanctuary providers, Toronto, 23 July 2003.
99 Interview 26.
100 Interview 39.
101 Interview 6.
102 Interview 40.
103 Case File 2, Document 68.
104 Case File 4, Document 144.
105 Interview 26.
106 Interview 8.
107 Interview 14, emphasis added.
108 Interview 14.
109 Interview 26.
110 Interview 3.
111 Interview 23.
112 Interview 27.
113 Case File 4, Documents 37, 40, 41.
114 Interview 38.
115 Interview 24.
116 Case File 2, Document 161.
117 For example, Case File 4, Document 180.
118 Interview 38.
119 See for example, Ashenden, "Reflexive Governance and Child Abuse," 85n. See also the discussion of liberal welfarism in Chapter 1.
120 For example, Unitarian Church of Calgary, "A Checklist of Practical Considerations."
121 Ibid.
122 Interview 8.
123 Interview 9.
124 Interview 36; Case File 4, Document 126, 170; S. Knapp, "An Appeal for Safety, and Place to Call Home," *Calgary Herald*, 10 August 2002, B1.
125 The arrangement of appealing to another level of the state despite the illegality under federal law was evident in the State of California in recent years, whereby a referendum on whether "illegal" immigrants should be permitted to attend public schools was held.
126 Interview 26.

127   For discussions of pastoral education in other contexts, see A. Howley and R. Hartnett, "Pastoral Power and the Contemporary University: A Foucauldian Analysis," *Educational Theory* 42 (1992): 271-83; I. Hunter, "Assembling the School," in *Foucault and Political Reason: Liberalism, Neoliberalism and Rationalities of Government,* ed. A. Barry, T. Osborne, and N. Rose, 143-65 (London: UCC Press, 1996).

128   "Taking Sanctuary," *Listen Up,* 5 April 2001, http://www.crossroads.ca/listenup/programs/010405sanc.htm.

129   For example, Interviews 10, 36.

130   Interview 39.

131   Interview 27. See also "Two Churches Offer Refugee Sanctuary," *Canadian Unitarian* 4 (2003): 3.

132   Interview 14.

133   Interview 8, emphasis added.

134   Ibid.

135   Case File 2, Document 126, emphasis added.

136   Foucault, "The Political Technology of Individuals."

137   United Church of Canada, *Sanctuary for Refugees?* 18.

138   Interview 9.

139   Interview 36.

140   G. Melnyk, "Government Attitude Smacks of Discrimination," *Calgary Herald,* 19 December 1993, 7.

141   Interview 38.

142   Interview 34.

143   Interview 27.

144   This refers to the number of points required to be selected as an immigrant (as opposed to being granted refugee status) through the immigrant point system in place since 1967.

145   Interview 27.

146   Ibid.

147   Interview 11, emphasis added.

148   Interview 14, emphasis added.

149   Interview 8.

150   Interview 26.

151   K. Lunman, "Refugee Spending Christmas in Hiding," *Calgary Herald,* 24 December 1993, B1.

152   Hindess, "The Liberal Government of Unfreedom."

153   Interview 28.

154   Interview 38.

155   Interview 40, emphasis added.

156   Interview 13, emphasis added.

157   J. Morrison, "Bangladeshi Seeks Refuge in Church," *Ottawa Citizen,* 10 July 2003, F1, 10.

158   "Killer Seeks Sanctuary in Church," *Windsor Star,* 24 November 2000, B1.

159   Interview 40.

160   S. Knapp, "An Appeal for Safety, and Place to Call Home" *Calgary Herald,* 10 August 2002, B1.

161   Interview 38.

162   To be sure, a few migrants were involved but often in a reduced capacity; see for example, Interview 40.

163   Interview 36.

164   Rose, "Governing the Enterprise Self"; Hindess, *Discourses of Power,* 100.

165   Dean, "Liberal Government and Authoritarianism," 48. See also Stenson, "Community Policing as a Governmental Technology."

166   Case File 4, Document 22.

167   Federal Court of Canada, Trial Division, *Jesus Manuel Elizondo Gonzalez et al. v. M.C.I.,* 12 March 2003, Docket No. IMM-4255-02.

168   *Zhao, Kuei Kuan v. M.C.I. Immigration and Refugee Board* (Appeal Division), Toronto, Ontario, T90-04793, Aterman, Paul, 1 February 2001.

169   Interview 6.

170 Deacon of a Winnipeg church, "Religious Disobedience," *Light Talk*, television broadcast, 20 July 1999, Winnipeg, Manitoba, emphasis added.
171 Case File 2, Document 126.
172 Interview 40, emphasis added.
173 Foucault, "The Political Technology of Individuals," 62.
174 As quoted in Dreyfus and Rabinow, *Michel Foucault*, 214.
175 Ibid.
176 "Desperate Family Finds Easter Sanctuary: Rejected Refugees Given Shelter by Parkdale Church," *Toronto Star*, 12 April 1998, A1.
177 "Stateless Family Clings to Canada Day Dream," *Toronto Star*, 2 July 1998, B5.
178 Interview 6.
179 Interview 1.
180 CBC Radio, transcript of interview with sanctuary providers, Toronto, 23 July 2003.
181 Interview 13.
182 Deacon of Winnipeg Baptist Church, "Religious Disobedience," *Light Talk*, television broadcast, 20 July 1999, Winnipeg, Manitoba.
183 Interview 26, emphasis added.
184 K. Bolan, "Church Helps Salvadorans Try to Re-enter Canada," *Vancouver Sun*, 11 March 1992, B2.
185 Interview 26.
186 Interview 11.
187 Unidentified caller, "Religious Disobedience," *Light Talk*, television broadcast, 20 July 1999, Winnipeg, Manitoba.
188 Interview 6.
189 Interview 2.
190 Interview 33.
191 Interview 26.
192 C.A. Nicholson, "The Human Spirit Survives and Soars," *Saint Croix Courier*, 29 June 1999, A5.
193 Interview 26.
194 Interview 38, emphasis added.
195 Interview 23.
196 Ibid.
197 For example, Case File 4, Document 180; Interview 10; K. Bolan, "Church Helps Salvadorans Try to Re-enter Canada," *Vancouver Sun*, 11 March 1992, B2. "Flag-polling" refers to entering the US at a border-crossing with the sole aim of circling the flagpole erected on the US side, and then immediately re-entering Canadian territory to satisfy technical immigration requirements to apply for status from outside Canada.
198 Interview 24, emphasis added.
199 Ibid.; "Guatemalans Must Go Home," *Times Globe*, 28 May 1998, A1.
200 "Sitting Bull," *Telegraph Journal*, 15 June 1998, A1, A8.
201 Interview 4.
202 Interview 15.
203 Reynolds, *Faith Subdues Kingdoms*, 63.
204 "Canadian UUs Give Sanctuary to 3," *UUWorld* 17, 6 (November/December 2003): 55, http://www.uuworld.org/2003/06/news.html.
205 Interview 17.
206 Case File 2, Document 85.
207 Interview 24.
208 Case File 5, Document 3.
209 Interview 26.
210 Interview 9.
211 Case File 5, Document 8.
212 Case File 5, Document 9.
213 Case File 4, Document 139.

214 See Valverde, "'Despotism' and Ethical Liberal Governance"; Rose and Valverde, "Governed by Law?"
215 For a superb governmentality-inspired analysis of Alcoholics Anonymous programs, see Valverde, *Diseases of the Will*.
216 Several are no longer used as churches. One has become an art gallery.
217 Interview 9.
218 Interview 1.
219 Interview 34.
220 Case File 2, Document 124.
221 Interview 8.
222 Interview 39.
223 Interview 27.
224 Interview 26.
225 Interview 10.
226 Interview 26.
227 Interview 1.
228 Interview 39.
229 Interview 38.
230 Interview 8.
231 O. Moore, "Woman's Church a Refuge and a Prison," *Globe and Mail*, 22 November 2001, A17.
232 Interview 6.
233 Interview 26.
234 See for example, G. Fine and L. Christoforides, "Dirty Birds, Filthy Immigrants, and the English Sparrow War: Metaphorical Linkage in Constructing Social Problems," *Symbolic Interaction* 14 (1991): 375-93.
235 M. Valverde, *The Age of Light, Soap, and Water: Moral Reform in English Canada, 1885-1925* (Toronto: McClelland and Stewart, 1991), 116.
236 Interview 11.
237 Interview 3.
238 Ibid.
239 Interview 26.
240 Interview 24.
241 Interview 38, emphasis added.
242 Interview 26, emphasis added.
243 Interview 38, emphasis added.
244 Interview 3, emphasis added.
245 Case File 2, Document 161.
246 Interview 3.
247 Interview 2.
248 Interview 36.
249 Interview 3.
250 Interview 9.
251 Interview 34.
252 Interview 38.
253 Foucault, *Discipline and Punish*. Nor should pastoral power be reduced to disciplinary power. For an explication of some differences, see Hindess, *Discourses of Power*, 96-136.
254 Dean, *Critical and Effective Histories*, 182.
255 Interview 8.
256 Interview 1.
257 Interview 26.
258 Case File 2, Document 124.
259 Case File 2, Document 83.
260 Case File 2, Document 80, emphasis in the original.
261 Case File 2, Document 69.
262 Case File 4, Document 170.

263 Case File 4, Document 169.
264 Case File 2, Documents 68, 73.
265 Interview 40.
266 Interview 28.
267 Interview 1.
268 Interview 2.
269 Interview 20.
270 Interview 34.
271 Interview 20.
272 Interview 25.
273 On liberal rationalities, see Dean, "Liberal Government and Authoritarianism."
274 See for example, D. Andrew, *Philanthropy and Police: London Charity in the Eighteenth Century* (Princeton: Princeton University Press, 1989); Valverde, *The Age of Light, Soap, and Water*, 122; K. Stenson, "Social Work Discourse and the Social Work Interview," *Economy and Society* 22 (1993): 42-76.
275 Hunter, *Rethinking the School*; Valverde, *Diseases of the Will*; Blake, "Pastoral Power, Governmentality and Cultures of Order," 81.
276 Of course, migrants and citizens are subjects/objects of advanced liberalism, pastoralism, sovereignty, and other forms of power, and they resist and otherwise defy how they are imagined in myriad ways.
277 Interview 36, emphasis added.

Chapter 6: Sanctuary and Law
1 P. Ewick and S. Silbey, *Common Place of Law: Stories from Everyday Life* (Chicago: University of Chicago Press, 1998); P. Ewick and S. Silbey, "Common Knowledge and Ideological Critique: The Significance of Knowing That the 'Haves' Come Out Ahead," *Law and Society Review* 33 (1999): 1025-41.
2 Ewick and Silbey, *Common Place of Law*, 47.
3 Ibid.
4 Ibid., 48.
5 Ibid., 152-53.
6 Ibid., 50-51.
7 Ibid., 82.
8 Although not the only narratives present in sanctuary discourse, legal narratives nevertheless dominate.
9 Interview 19.
10 Interview 1.
11 For example, Foucault, *Discipline and Punish*, 53.
12 Interview 15, emphasis added.
13 Ibid., emphasis added.
14 Interview 24.
15 Ibid.
16 Interview 17.
17 For example, Interview 27.
18 Interview 27, emphasis added.
19 "Council's Playing by the Rules Is Unimaginative," *Times Globe*, 10 July 1998, B1.
20 Interview 33, emphasis added.
21 Interview 32, emphasis added.
22 Interview 33.
23 Interview 15.
24 Sanctuary is illegal under Canada's Immigration Act and Criminal Code because it involves aiding and abetting as well as conspiracy. Since at least 1976, the Immigration Act has prohibited aiding and abetting migrants subjected to deportation orders and has stipulated fines of up to CDN$5,000 and two years imprisonment. See Block, "Sanctuary and the Defiant Churches," *Maclean's*, 30 January 1984, 43; United Church of Canada, *Sanctuary for Refugees?* 12.

25 Interview 11.
26 Interview 34.
27 Interviews 8, 10, 26, 27.
28 Such as those fees described in Chapter 3. For example, Interviews 10, 32, 33.
29 Case File 2, Document 81.
30 Interviews 5, 17, 40; ICCR, *Keeping Faith.*
31 Anonymization such as this is a key technique in "government at a distance" deployed to avoid risk to property and moral risk resulting from close association with illegal activity; see Lippert, "Policing Property and Moral Risk." It is precisely this aspect and the fact that it reduces opportunities for sacrifice accordingly that renders anonymity incommensurate with a pastoral power that seeks intimate knowledge of individuals.
32 Interviews 5, 35. For this reason, it was excluded as one of the thirty-six incidents. The ICCR ceased to exist in 2001.
33 Interview 14.
34 Interview 26.
35 Interview 10.
36 Interview 24.
37 Interview 4.
38 Interview 31.
39 Block, "Sanctuary and the Defiant Churches," 43.
40 Southern Ontario Sanctuary Coalition, "A Declaration: A Civil Initiative to Protect Refugees."
41 Interview 13.
42 "Family Staying in Basement until Immigration Case Won," *London Free Press,* 15 August 1998, A12.
43 Interview 8.
44 Southern Ontario Sanctuary Coalition, "Mission Statement of the Ontario Sanctuary Coalition," press release, Toronto, November 1998, emphasis added.
45 Interview 30.
46 For example, Leddy, *At the Border Called Hope,* 158; Stastny and Tyrnauer, "Sanctuary in Canada," 188-89; Case File 2, Document 80.
47 Interview 30, emphasis added.
48 Interview 31.
49 Case File 4, Document 45. Letters from other supporters referred to the UN Convention on the Rights of the Child exclusively; see Case File 4, Documents 19, 46, 49.
50 D. Gawthrop "Trying to Solve a Problem Like Maria's," *HEU Guardian,* November/December 1996, 12. The same convention was handwritten on a large placard carried during a spectacular protest; see C.A. Nicholson "Community Pleads for Family's Freedom," *St. Stephen Courier,* 3 November 1998, A1.
51 Interview 33, emphasis added.
52 Interview 3. On unwritten law and its association with vigilantism, see J. Phillips and R. Gartner, *Murdering Holiness: The Trials of Franz Creffield and George Mitchell* (Vancouver: UBC Press, 2003).
53 Interview 32.
54 Ewick and Silbey, *Common Place of Law,* 99.
55 "Pastor Defends Right to Offer Sanctuary," *Western Catholic Reporter,* 21 February 2000, http://wcr.ab.ca/news2000/0221/nannysanctuary022100.shtml.
56 "Religious Disobedience," *Light Talk,* television broadcast, 20 July 1999, Winnipeg, Manitoba.
57 Case File 9, Document 5.
58 "Taking Sanctuary," *Listen Up,* 5 April 2001, http://www.crossroads.ca/listenup/programs/010405sanc.htm.
59 Interview 6.
60 Interview 34, emphasis added.
61 Interview 38, emphasis added.
62 Ewick and Silbey, *Common Place of Law,* 95.

63 Interview 8. Elsewhere a provider referred to "the historic right of sanctuary"; see Case File 4, Document 108.
64 A. Hunt, "Rights and Social Movements," *Journal of Law and Society* 17 (1990): 309-28; M. Ignatieff, *The Rights Revolution* (Toronto: House of Anansi Press, 2000); C. Boucock, *In the Grip of Freedom: Law and Modernity in Max Weber* (Toronto: University of Toronto Press, 2000); Ewick and Silbey, *Common Place of Law*, 224.
65 Boucock, *In the Grip of Freedom*.
66 Matas, *The Sanctuary Trial;* K. Greenawalt, "Should Religious Convictions about Injustice Figure in Criminal Trials?" *Journal of Church and State* 40 (1998): 541-51 at 541.
67 Coutin, "Enacting Law through Social Practice," 300n.
68 Boucock, *In the Grip of Freedom*, 11.
69 Ibid., 10.
70 Interview 32, emphasis added.
71 Interview 26, emphasis added.
72 Interview 10, emphasis added.
73 Interview 15, emphasis added.
74 Interview 33, emphasis added.
75 Interview 38, emphasis added.
76 Ibid.
77 Canada, Statistics Canada, *The Daily: Legal Aid 2000/01*, 2002, http://www.statcan.ca/Daily/English/020524/d020524c.htm.
78 Interview 23.
79 B. Schute, "Dec. 15 2002: 3rd Sunday in Advent," http://members.shaw.ca/stceciliacalgary/message021215.html.
80 Interview 39, emphasis added.
81 Interview 26, emphasis added.
82 United Church of Canada, *Sanctuary for Refugees?* 4.
83 Interview 26.
84 Interview 41.
85 Interview 7.
86 Interview 28.
87 Interview 11.
88 Interview 9.
89 Interview 8.
90 Interview 17, emphasis added.
91 Interview 38.
92 Interview 23.
93 For example, Interview 38; B. Power "Church Offers Woman Safe Haven," *Halifax Herald*, 9 April 2003, 1.
94 Ewick and Silbey, *Common Place of Law*, 48.
95 Case File 4, Document 150, emphasis added.
96 Interview 27.
97 For example, Interviews 1, 24.
98 Reynolds, *Faith Subdues Kingdoms*, 83, emphasis in the original.
99 Ewick and Silbey, *Common Place of Law*, 155.
100 For example, Interview 12.
101 This dependence was seen in the US context as well. See Coutin, "Enacting Law through Social Practice," 288; J. Corbett, *Borders and Crossings*, vol. 1, *Some Sanctuary Papers, 1981-86* (Tucson: Tucson Refugee Support Group, 1986), 64.
102 "Vigil at UU Church of North Hatley," 7 July 2003, http://ccs.ubishops.ca/ljensen/uucnh/vigil.html.
103 Interview 35.
104 Interview 39.
105 Interview 10.
106 For example, Interview 37; Stastny and Tyrnauer, "Sanctuary in Canada," 190.

107 Interview 17.
108 Interview 40.
109 Interview 33.
110 Interview 27, emphasis added.
111 Case File 5, Document 7.
112 Interview 34.
113 For example, Interview 31.
114 Interview 32.
115 Case File 2, Document 78, emphasis in the original.
116 Case File 2, Document 77.
117 Interview 36.
118 Case File 2, Document 80.
119 T. Gerety, "Sanctuary: A Comment on the Ironic Relation between Law and Morality," in *The New Asylum Seekers: Refugee Law in the 1980's*, ed. David Martin, 159-80 (London: Martinus Nijhoff, 1988), 174.
120 For example, Crittenden, *Sanctuary*.
121 See S. Merry, *Getting Justice and Getting Even: Legal Consciousness among Working-Class Americans* (Chicago: University of Chicago Press, 1990).
122 For example, in Canada's refugee-determination process, migrants have no right of appeal on merit.
123 B. Fleury-Steiner, "Before or against the Law? Citizens' Legal Beliefs and Experiences as Death Penalty Jurors," *Studies in Law, Politics, and Society* 27 (2003): 115-37.
124 Ewick and Silbey, *Common Place of Law*, 44.
125 For example, ibid., 48.
126 I owe this suggestion to an anonymous reviewer.
127 M. Valverde et al., *Democracy in Governance: A Socio-Legal Framework* (Ottawa: Law Commission of Canada, 1999), 5.
128 Rose and Valverde, "Governed by Law?" 547-48.
129 Ewick and Silbey, *Common Place of Law*, 22.
130 Ibid., 38-41.
131 Ewick and Silbey, "Common Knowledge and Ideological Critique," 1039.

Chapter 7: Conclusion
1 Park, "The Sacrifice Theory of Value."
2 Wiltfang and McAdam, "The Costs and Risks of Social Activism."
3 Park, "The Religious Construction of Sanctuary Provisions," 418-19.
4 See Cunningham, "The Ethnology of Transnational Social Activism"; Cunningham, "Transnational Social Movements."
5 Transnational political identity may be more relevant to Canadians' border activities, not examined here, in the earlier US sanctuary effort.
6 Cunningham, "The Ethnology of Transnational Social Activism," 588.
7 Valverde, "'Despotism' and Ethical Liberal Governance"; Dean, "Liberal Government and Authoritarianism." On Michael Mann's germane distinction between the despotic and infrastructural powers of the nation-state, see Dean, *Critical and Effective Histories*, 146.
8 Dean, *Governmentality: Power and Rule in Modern Society*.
9 Hindess, "The Liberal Government of Unfreedom."
10 Others have separately argued or at least implied the need for a similar recognition of plurality; see Stenson, "Crime Control, Governmentality and Sovereignty"; Dean, "Powers of Life and Death beyond Governmentality," 124. Some might call this "sovereignty from below," but this seems inappropriate in this context, given the evident invocation of "higher" law.
11 Agamben, *Homo Sacer*. See also Dillon and Reid, "Global Governance, Liberal Peace, and Complex Emergency."
12 Agamben, *Homo Sacer*, 133-34.
13 See Fitzpatrick, "'These Mad Abandon'd Times,'" 264.
14 Cunningham, *God and Caesar*.

15 Ibid.
16 See Hunter, *Rethinking the School*; Dean, *Governmentality: Power and Rule in Modern Society*, 81.
17 On the state of emergency, see Agamben, *Homo Sacer*.
18 See Garland, "'Governmentality' and the Problem of Crime," 203; Stenson, "Crime Control, Governmentality and Sovereignty."
19 See for example, W. Larner and W. Walters, "The Political Rationality of the 'New Regionalism': Toward a Genealogy of the Region," *Theory and Society* 31 (2002): 391-432 at 420; Pratt, "Sovereign Power, Carceral Conditions and Penal Practices."
20 Stenson, "Beyond Histories of the Present." But see Lippert, "Governing Refugees"; Larner and Walters, "The Political Rationality."
21 On the difference between failure and incompleteness, see Hunt and Wickham, *Foucault and Law*, 79.
22 Kerr, "Beheading the King and Enthroning the Market," 182.
23 See Lippert, "Policing Property and Moral Risk."
24 Agamben, *Homo Sacer*, 18.
25 Rose and Miller, "Political Power."
26 Lippert, "Rationalities and Refugee Resettlement."
27 A "delegation of sovereignty" may well describe similar situations in some contexts. On this concept, see Dean, "Powers of Life and Death beyond Governmentality," 124.
28 For example, K. Hannah-Moffat, "Prisons That Empower," 510; Constable, "Sovereignty and Governmentality"; P. O'Malley, "Risk and Responsibility," in *Foucault and Political Reason: Liberalism, Neo-Liberalism, and Rationalities of Government*, ed. A. Barry, T. Osborne, and N. Rose, 189-207 (London: UCL Press, 1996), 194; Dupont and Pearce, "Foucault Contra Foucault," 151.
29 Foucault, "Governmentality," 102.
30 Rose, "Governing the Enterprise Self."
31 See R. Ericson, D. Barry, and A. Doyle, "The Moral Hazards of Neo-Liberalism: Lessons from the Private Insurance Industry," *Economy and Society* 29 (2000): 532-58; Rose, "Governing the Enterprise Self."
32 On the concept of moral regulation, see especially M. Dean, "'A Social Structure of Many Souls': Moral Regulation, Government and Self-formation," *Canadian Journal of Sociology* 19 (1994): 145-68; B. Curtis, "Reworking Moral Regulation: Metaphorical Capital and the Field of Disinterest," *Canadian Journal of Sociology* 22 (1997): 303-18; Hunt, *Governing Morals*.
33 See Hunt, *Governing Morals*.
34 O'Malley, Weir, and Shearing, "Governmentality, Criticism, Politics," 512.
35 On time in the provision of security, see M. Valverde and M. Cirak, "Governing Bodies, Creating Gay Spaces: Policing and Security Issues in 'Gay' Downtown Toronto," *British Journal of Criminology* 43 (2003): 102-21.
36 Some exceptions are Ashenden, "Reflexive Governance and Child Abuse"; Dean, *Governmentality: Power and Rule in Modern Society*; Dean, "Powers of Life and Death beyond Governmentality," 126-27.
37 On the notion of a pastoral bureaucracy in the context of education, see Hunter, *Rethinking the School*.
38 See Torfing, "Towards a Schumpeterian"; Mead, *The New Paternalism*.
39 Dean, *Governmentality: Power and Rule in Modern Society*, 96.
40 Ibid.
41 One innovative approach to this realm of discourses and practices, which draws from Bourdieu, entails deployment of the concept of moral capital; see M. Valverde, "Moral Capital," *Canadian Journal of Law and Society* 9 (1994): 213-32. But see also Curtis, "Reworking Moral Regulation."
42 On the relation between rights and needs, see R. Plant, H. Lesser, and P. Taylor-Goodby, *Political Philosophy and Social Welfare: Essays on the Normative Basis of Welfare Provision* (London: Routledge and Kegan Paul, 1980). See also I. Gough, *The Political Economy of the Welfare State* (London: Macmillan, 1979).

43 Z. Bauman, *Postmodern Ethics* (Malden, MA: Blackwell Publishers, 1993), 103.
44 Foucault, "Politics and Reason," 68.
45 Ibid., 67.
46 Ibid.
47 Ibid., 72.
48 I am grateful to Alan Hunt for this suggestion.
49 Consistent with some strands of the women's movement, addressing needs in this manner has not been without its conflict with the ideology of democratic control and self-help, which tends to prevail in shelters; see J. Clifton, "Refuges and Self-Help," *Sociological Review Monograph* 31 (1985): 40-59 at 40.
50 R.E. Dobash and R. Dobash, *Women, Violence and Social Change* (London: Routledge, 1992), 54.
51 See J. Hagan and I. Bernstein, "Conflict in Context: The Sanctioning of Draft Resisters, 1963-76," *Social Problems* 27 (1979): 109-22; M. Useem, "Ideological and Interpersonal Change in the Radical Protest Movement," *Social Problems* 19 (1972): 451-69.
52 See Bau, *This Ground Is Holy*, 161-71.
53 R. Kasinsky, *Refugees from Militarism: Draft-Age Americans in Canada* (New Brunswick, NJ: Transaction Books, 1976). Similar practices have recently come to light in relation to US military personnel migrating to Canada to avoid military service in Iraq.
54 P. Conlon, *Sanctuary: Stories from Casey House Hospice* (Scarborough: Prentice-Hall Canada, 1991), xiv.
55 See R. Moreman, "Long-Term Care and 'Managed' Aids," *Research in Sociology of Health Care* 16 (1999): 171-85.
56 C. Humphreys, "'Waiting for the Last Summons': The Establishment of the First Hospices in England, 1878-1914," *Mortality* 6 (2001): 146-66.

Postscript

1 D. Sinclair, "The Cherfi Arrest: Sanctuary Violated," *United Church Observer*, online edition, April 2004, http://www.ucobserver.org/archives/apr04_nation.htm.
2 Sara Falconer, "Where the Sun Don't Shine," *Hour*, 20 May 2004, http://www.hour.ca/news.
3 D. Dawes, "Fugitive Finds Friendship in Sanctuary," 15 July 2004, http://www.canadianchristianity.com/cgi-bin.
4 "Churches Told to Stop Being 'Backdoor' for Entry to Canada," *Ottawa Citizen*, 26 July 2004, A3.
5 E. Thompson, "Churches Refuse to Play 'Immigration Department': Deal Would Have Given Religious Groups Right to Select Failed Refugee Claimants for Reconsideration by Minister," *Ottawa Citizen*, 3 November 2004, C3.
6 "No Secret Sanctuary," *Ottawa Citizen*, 6 November 2004, B6.
7 "Grit Leader Speaks with Pecelj," *Halifax Herald*, 28 June 2004, http://www.herald.ns.ca.
8 CBC News, "Man Claiming Sanctuary Given OK to Leave Church," 13 December 2004, http://www.cbc.ca/story/Canada/national/2004/12/13bangladeshi-refugee1213.html; CBC News, "Ethiopian Family Free to Leave Montreal Church," 14 December 2004, http://www.ottawa.cbc.ca/regional.htm.
9 Interfaith Sanctuary Coalition, "Who Is Currently in Sanctuary," 28 February 2005, http://www.sanctuarycoalition.org/en/cases.htm.

Bibliography

Primary Sources
Case Files 1-12 containing unpublished documents.
Interviews 1-46.

Church Periodicals
Canadian Baptist
Canadian Unitarian
Catholic New Times
The Globe
ICCR Bulletin
United Church Observer
UUWorld
Western Catholic Reporter

Popular and News Periodicals
Canadian Welfare
Canadian Woman's Studies
HEU Guardian
Hour
Maclean's
Pic Press
Saturday Night
The Ubyssey

Refugee Periodicals
Centre for Refugee Studies Newsletter
Refuge
Refugee Update

Newspapers
Calgary Herald
Globe and Mail
Halifax Chronicle Herald
Halifax Herald
London Free Press
Montreal Gazette
Ottawa Citizen
Saint Croix Courier
St. Stephen Courier

Telegraph Journal
Times Globe
Toronto Star
Vancouver Sun
Windsor Star
Winnipeg Free Press

Secondary Sources

Adelman, H. *The Indochinese Refugee Movement: The Canadian Experience.* Toronto: Operation Lifeline, 1980.

–. *Canada and the Indochinese Refugees.* Regina: L.A. Weigl Educational Associates, 1982.

–. "Canadian Borders and Immigration Post 9/11." *International Migration Review* 36 (2002): 15-28.

Agamben, G. *Homo Sacer: Sovereign Power and Bare Life.* Stanford: Stanford University Press, 1998.

Akbari, A. "Immigrant 'Quality' in Canada: More Direct Evidence of Human Capital Content, 1956-1994." *International Migration Review* 33 (1999): 156-75.

Andrew, D. *Philanthropy and Police: London Charity in the Eighteenth Century.* Princeton: Princeton University Press, 1989.

Anglican Church. http://www.nspeidiocese.ca/netnews/2003/04_30_2003.htm.

Ashenden, S. "Reflexive Governance and Child Abuse: Liberal Welfare Rationality and the Cleveland Inquiry." *Economy and Society* 25 (1996): 64-88.

Bau, I. *This Ground Is Holy: Church Sanctuary and Central American Refugees.* New York: Paulist Press, 1985.

Bauman, Z. *Postmodern Ethics.* Malden, MA: Blackwell Publishers, 1993.

Bellamy, J. *Crime and Public Order in England in the Later Middle Ages.* Toronto: University of Toronto Press, 1973.

Bianchi, H. *Justice as Sanctuary: Toward a New System of Crime Control.* Bloomington: Indiana University Press, 1994.

Bigo, D. "Security and Immigration: Toward a Critique of the Governmentality of Unease." *Alternatives* 27 (2002): 63-92.

Blake, L. "Pastoral Power, Governmentality and Cultures of Order in Nineteenth-Century British Columbia." *Transactions of the Institute of British Geographers* 24 (1999): 79-93.

Bossin, M. "'After a Thorough and Sympathetic Review': The State of Humanitarian Applications in Canada." *Journal of Law and Social Policy* 14 (1999): 107-22.

Boucock, C. *In the Grip of Freedom: Law and Modernity in Max Weber.* Toronto: University of Toronto Press, 2000.

British Columbia Association of Social Workers (BCASW). *Guidelines for Social Work Practice with Refugees and Immigrants.* Vancouver: BCASW, 1980.

Burchell, G. "Liberal Government and Techniques of the Self." *Economy and Society* 22 (1993): 267-81.

Canada. "Canada's Refugee Programmes, 1945-1961." In *Studies and Documents on Immigration and Integration in Canada,* ed. J. Kage, 1-13. Montreal: Jewish Immigrant Aid Services of Canada, 1962.

–. *The Immigration and Population Study.* Ottawa: Information Canada, 1974.

–. *Czechoslovakian Refugee Study: A Report on the Three-Year Study of the Economic and Social Adaptation of Czechoslovakian Refugees to Life in Canada, 1968-69.* Ottawa: Department of Manpower and Immigration, 1975.

–. *Host Family Program: Summary Report.* Ottawa: Employment and Immigration Canada, 1987.

–. *Annual Report to Parliament: Immigration Plan for 1991-1995.* Ottawa: Employment and Immigration Canada, 1990.

–. *Immigration Settlement Adaptation Program: Handbook for Service Provider Organizations.* Ottawa: Ministry of Supply and Services, 1996.

–. Citizenship and Immigration Canada. *The Right of Landing Fee and Immigrant Loans Program.* Ottawa: Ministry of Supply and Services, 1995.

–. Citizenship and Immigration Canada. *Refugee and Humanitarian Immigration to Canada, 1947-1995.* Ottawa: Ministry of Supply and Services, 1995.

–. Citizenship and Immigration Canada. *Departmental Outlook on Program Expenditures and Priorities, 1996-97 to 1998-99.* Ottawa: Ministry of Supply and Services, 1996.

–. Citizenship and Immigration Canada. *Refugee and Humanitarian Resettlement Program: In Canada.* Ottawa: Ministry of Supply and Services, 1997.

–. Citizenship and Immigration Canada. *Refugee and Humanitarian Resettlement Program in Canada.* Operations memorandum. Ottawa: Ministry of Supply and Services, 1997.

–. Citizenship and Immigration Canada. *Not Just Numbers: A Canadian Framework for Future Immigration: Immigration Legislative Review.* Ottawa: Ministry of Public Works and Government Services Canada, 1998.

–. Citizenship and Immigration Canada. *Performance Report,* 2001, http://www.cic.gc.ca/english/pub/dpr2001/dpr%2D02d.html.

–. Citizenship and Immigration Canada. *Canada and U.S. Negotiators Agree to Final Draft Text of Safe Third Country Agreement,* 2002, http://www.cic.gc.ca/english/policy/safe-third.html.

–. Citizenship and Immigration Canada. *Pre-removal Risk Assessment,* 2002, http://www.cic.gc.ca/english/refugees/asylum-3.html.

–. Citizenship and Immigration Canada. *Be a Host to a Newcomer,* 2003, http://www.cic.gc.ca/english/newcomer/involve/canadian-host.html.

–. Department of Manpower and Immigration. *The Immigration Bill: Explanatory Notes of an Office of Consolidation of the Immigration Bill.* Ottawa: Ministry of Supply and Services, 1976.

–. Employment and Immigration Canada. *Final Report: Chilean Refugee Households in Canada.* Ottawa: Employment and Immigration Canada, 1976.

–. Employment and Immigration Canada. *The Refugee Status Determination Process: A Report of the Task Force on Immigration Practices and Procedures,* by W. Robinson. Ottawa: Ministry of Supply and Services, 1981.

–. Employment and Immigration Canada. *Study of the Impact of the 1979-80 Indochinese Refugee Program on Canada Immigration Centre and Canada Employment Centre Operations.* Ottawa: Ministry of Supply and Services, 1981.

–. Employment and Immigration Canada. *Indochinese Refugees: The Canadian Response, 1979 and 1980.* Ottawa: Ministry of Supply and Services, 1982.

–. Employment and Immigration Canada. *Refugee Status Determination Process for Canada,* by E. Ratushny. Ottawa: Ministry of Supply and Services, 1984.

–. Employment and Immigration Canada. "Ministers Act to Curb Refugee Claims Abuse." Press release. February 1987.

–. Employment and Immigration Canada. *Immigration Levels Planning: The First Decade.* Ottawa: Employment and Immigration Canada, 1988.

–. Employment and Immigration Canada. Refugee Affairs Branch. "Canada's Refugee Policy." *Dialogue* 1 (1992): 1-11.

–. Health Promotion and Programs Branch. *National Health Research and Development Program.* Ottawa: Ministry of Supply and Services, 1996.

–. Ministry of Employment and Immigration. *Refugee Determination in Canada: Proposals for Canada,* by W.G. Plaut. Ottawa: Ministry of Supply and Services, 1985.

–. Refugee Affairs Division Policy and Program Development Branch. *Refugee Perspectives: 1986-1987.* Ottawa: Employment and Immigration Canada, 1986.

–. Statistics Canada. *The Daily: Legal Aid 2000/01,* 2002, http://www.statcan.ca/Daily/English/020524/d020524c.htm.

Canadian Council for Refugees (CCR). *Refugee Family Reunification.* Montreal: CCR, 1995.

–. *Resettlement out of Signatory Countries,* 2000, http://www.web.net/~ccr/signatory.htm.

Canel, E. "New Social Movement Theory and Resource Mobilization: The Need for Integration." In *Organizing Dissent: Contemporary Social Movements in Theory and Practice,* ed. W.K. Carroll, 22-51. Toronto: Garamond Press, 1992.

CBC Radio. Transcript of interview with sanctuary providers. Toronto, 23 July 2003.

Centre for Research and Education in Human Services. *Refugee Resettlement in Kitchener-Waterloo: A Participatory Evaluation*. Kitchener: Kitchener Centre for Research and Education in Human Services, 1984.

Ceyhan, A., and A. Tsoukala. "The Securitization of Migration in Western Societies: Ambivalent Discourses and Policies." *Alternatives* 27 (2002): 21-39.

Clifton, J. "Refuges and Self-Help." *Sociological Review Monograph* 31 (1985): 40-59.

Cohen, S. *From the Jews to the Tamils: Britain's Mistreatment of Refugees*. Manchester: South Manchester Law Centre, 1988.

Conlon, P. *Sanctuary: Stories from Casey House Hospice*. Scarborough: Prentice-Hall Canada, 1991.

Constable, M. "Sovereignty and Governmentality in Modern American Immigration Law." *Studies in Law, Politics and Society* 13 (1993): 249-71.

Corbett, J. *Borders and Crossings*. Vol. 1: *Some Sanctuary Papers, 1981-86*. Tucson: Tucson Refugee Support Group, 1986.

Cornelius, W. "Interviewing Undocumented Immigrants: Methodological Reflections Based on Fieldwork in Mexico and the U.S." *International Migration Review* 16 (1982): 378-411.

Coutin, S. *The Culture of Protest: Religious Activism and the U.S. Sanctuary Movement*. Boulder: Westview Press, 1993.

-. "Enacting Law through Social Practice." In *Contested States: Law, Hegemony and Resistance*, ed. M. Lazarus-Black and S. Hirsch, 282-303. New York: Routledge, 1994.

-. "Smugglers or Samaritans in Tuscon, Arizona: Producing and Contesting Legal Truth." *American Ethnologist* 22 (1995): 549-71.

Cox, C. *The Sanctuaries and Sanctuary Seekers of Medieval England*. London: George Allen and Sons, 1911.

Creese, G. "The Politics of Refugees in Canada." In *Deconstructing a Nation: Immigration, Multiculturalism, and Racism in 90's Canada*, ed. V. Satzewich, 1-20. Halifax: Fernwood, 1992.

Crittenden, A. *Sanctuary: A Story of American Conscience and the Law in Collision*. New York: Weidenfeld and Nicolson, 1988.

Cruikshank, B. "Revolutions Within: Self-Government and Self-Esteem." In *Foucault and Political Reason: Liberalism, Neo-Liberalism and Rationalities of Government*, ed. A. Barry, T. Osborne, and N. Rose, 231-51. London: UCL Press, 1996.

Cunningham, H. *God and Caesar at the Rio Grande*. Minneapolis: University of Minnesota Press, 1995.

-. "The Ethnology of Transnational Social Activism: Understanding the Global as Local Practice." *American Ethnologist* 26 (2000): 583-604.

-. "Transnational Social Movements and Sovereignties in Transition: Charting New Interfaces of Power at the U.S.-Mexico Border." *Anthropologica* 44 (2002): 185-96.

Curtis, B. "Taking the State Back Out: Rose and Miller on Political Power." *British Journal of Sociology* 46 (1995): 575-89.

-. "Reworking Moral Regulation: Metaphorical Capital and the Field of Disinterest." *Canadian Journal of Sociology* 22 (1997): 303-18.

Davison, C. "Sanctuary: The Humane Response." *Law Now* 22 (1997): 1-12.

De Voretz, D. *Diminishing Returns: The Economics of Canada's Immigration Policy*. Vancouver: C.D. Howe Institute and the Laurier Institution, 1995.

Dean, M. *The Constitution of Poverty: Towards a Genealogy of Liberal Governance*. New York: Routledge, 1991.

-. *Critical and Effective Histories: Foucault's Methods and Historical Sociology*. London: Routledge, 1994.

-. "'A Social Structure of Many Souls': Moral Regulation, Government, and Self-Formation." *The Canadian Journal of Sociology* 19 (1994): 145-68.

-. *Governmentality: Power and Rule in Modern Society*. Thousand Oaks: Sage, 1999.

-. "'Demonic Societies': Liberalism, Biopolitics, and Sovereignty." In *States of Imagination: Ethnographic Explorations of the Postcolonial State*, ed. T. Hansen and T. Stepputat, 41-64. London: Duke University Press, 2001.

–. "Liberal Government and Authoritarianism." *Economy and Society* 31 (2002): 37-61.
–. "Powers of Life and Death beyond Governmentality." *Cultural Values* 6 (2002): 119-38.
Dillon, M. "Sovereignty and Governmentality: From the Problematics of the 'New World Order' to the Ethical Problematic of the World Order." *Alternatives* 20 (1995): 323-68.
–, and J. Reid. "Global Governance, Liberal Peace, and Complex Emergency." *Alternatives* 25 (2000): 117-43.
Dirks, G. *Canada's Refugee Policy: Indifference or Opportunism?* Montreal and Kingston: McGill-Queen's University Press, 1977.
–. *Controversy and Complexity: Canadian Immigration Policy during the 1980's.* Montreal and Kingston: McGill-Queen's University Press, 1995.
Dobash, R.E., and R. Dobash. *Women, Violence and Social Change.* London: Routledge, 1992.
Dreyfus, H., and P. Rabinow. *Michel Foucault: Beyond Structuralism and Hermeneutics.* Chicago: University of Chicago Press, 1983.
Dupont, D., and F. Pearce, "Foucault Contra Foucault: Rereading the 'Governmentality' Papers." *Theoretical Criminology* 5 (2001): 123-58.
Ericson, R., D. Barry, and A. Doyle. "The Moral Hazards of Neo-Liberalism: Lessons from the Private Insurance Industry." *Economy and Society* 29 (2000): 532-58.
Ewick, P., and S. Silbey. *Common Place of Law: Stories from Everyday Life.* Chicago, University of Chicago Press, 1998.
–. "Common Knowledge and Ideological Critique: The Significance of Knowing That the 'Haves' Come Out Ahead." *Law and Society Review* 33 (1999): 1025-41.
Ferris, E. "The Churches, Refugees, and Politics." In *Refugee and International Relations,* ed. G. Loescher and L. Monahan, 159-77. New York: Oxford University Press, 1989.
Fine, G., and L. Christoforides, "Dirty Birds, Filthy Immigrants, and the English Sparrow War: Metaphorical Linkage in Constructing Social Problems." *Symbolic Interaction* 14 (1991): 375-93.
Fitzpatrick, P. "Terminal Legality." *Social and Legal Studies* 7 (1998): 431-36.
–. "'These Mad Abandon'd Times.'" *Economy and Society* 30 (2001): 255-70.
Fleury-Steiner, B "Before or against the Law? Citizens' Legal Beliefs and Experiences as Death Penalty Jurors." *Studies in Law, Politics, and Society* 27 (2003): 115-37
Foucault, M. *History of Sexuality.* Vol. 1, *An Introduction.* New York: Random House, 1978.
–. *Discipline and Punish: The Birth of the Prison.* New York: Vintage, 1979.
–. "The Political Technology of Individuals." In *Technologies of the Self: A Seminar with Michel Foucault,* ed. L. Martin, H. Gutman, and P. Hutton, 145-62. Amherst: University of Massachusetts Press, 1988.
–. "Politics and Reason." In *Politics, Philosophy, Culture, Interviews and Other Writings, 1977-1984,* ed. L. Kritzman, 57-85. New York: Routledge, 1988.
–. "Governmentality." In *The Foucault Effect: Studies in Governmentality,* ed. G. Burchell, C. Gordon, and P. Miller, 84-104. Toronto: Harvester Wheatsheaf, 1991.
–. "Truth Is in the Future." In *Foucault Live (Interviews, 1961-1984),* 2nd ed., ed. S. Lotringer, trans. L. Hochroth and J. Johnston, 298-301. New York: Semiotext(e), 1996.
Frankel, B. "Confronting Neo-Liberal Regimes: The Post-Marxist Embrace of Populism and Realpolitik." *New Left Review* 226 (1997): 57-92.
Fraser, N. "Talking about Needs: Interpretive Contests as Political Conflicts in Welfare State Societies." *Ethics* 99 (1989): 150-81.
–. *Unruly Practices: Power, Discourse and Gender in Contemporary Social Theory.* Minneapolis: University of Minnesota Press, 1989.
Garland, D. "The Limits of the Sovereign State: Strategies of Crime Control in Contemporary Society." *British Journal of Criminology* 36 (1996): 455-71.
–. "'Governmentality' and the Problem of Crime: Foucault, Criminology, Sociology." *Theoretical Criminology* 1 (1997): 199-201.
Gerety, T. "Sanctuary: A Comment on the Ironic Relation between Law and Morality." In *The New Asylum Seekers: Refugee Law in the 1980's,* ed. D. Martin, 159-80. London: Martinus Nijhoff, 1988.
Gilad, L. *The Northern Route: An Ethnography of Refugee Experience.* St. John's, NF: Institute of Social and Economic Research, 1990.

Goodwyn-Gil, G. "Determining Refugee Status in Canada." *Refugees* 27 (1987): 27-8.

Gordon, C. "Afterword." In *Power/Knowledge: Selected Interviews and Other Writings, 1972-1977, by Michel Foucault,* ed. C. Gordon, 229-59. New York: Pantheon, 1980.

–. "Governmental Rationality: An Introduction." In *The Foucault Effect: Studies in Governmentality,* ed. G. Burchell, C. Gordon, and P. Miller, 1-51. Toronto: Harvester Wheatsheaf, 1991.

Gough, I. *The Political Economy of the Welfare State.* London: Macmillan, 1979.

Greenawalt, K. "Should Religious Convictions about Injustice Figure in Criminal Trials?" *Journal of Church and State* 40 (1998): 541-51.

Gregory, D. *Geographical Imaginations.* Cambridge, MA: Blackwell, 1994.

Habermas, J. *Theory of Communicative Action.* Vol. 1. Boston, MA: Beacon, 1983.

Hagan, J., and I. Bernstein. "Conflict in Context: The Sanctioning of Draft Resisters, 1963-76." *Social Problems* 27 (1979): 109-22.

Hannah-Moffat, K. "Prisons That Empower: Neo-Liberal Governance in Canadian Women's Prisons." *British Journal of Criminology* 40 (2000): 510-31.

Hathaway, J. "The Conundrum of Refugee Protection in Canada: From Control to Compliance to Collective Deterrence." *Journal of Policy History* 4 (1992): 71-92.

Hawkins, F. *Canada and Immigration: Public Policy and Public Concern.* Montreal: McGill-Queen's University Press, 1972.

Heipel, R. "Refugee Resettlement in a Canadian City: An Overview and Assessment." In *Refugee Policy: Canada and the U.S.,* ed. H. Adelman, 344-55. Toronto: York Lanes Press, 1991.

Hermer, J., and A. Hunt. "Official Graffiti of the Everyday." *Law and Society Review* 30 (1996): 455-80.

Hier, S., and J. Greenberg. "Constructing a Discursive Crisis: Risk, Problematization and Illegal Chinese in Canada." *Ethnic and Racial Studies* 25 (2002): 490-513.

Hindess, B. *Discourses of Power: From Hobbes to Foucault.* Cambridge, MA: Blackwell, 1996.

–. "The Liberal Government of Unfreedom." *Alternatives* 26 (2001): 93-111.

Howley, A., and R. Hartnett. "Pastoral Power and the Contemporary University: A Foucauldian Analysis." *Educational Theory* 42 (1992): 271-83.

Hudson, B. "Punishment and Governance." *Social and Legal Studies* 7 (1998): 553-59.

Hufker, B., and G. Cavender. "From Freedom Flotilla to America's Burden: The Social Construction of the Mariel Immigrants." *The Sociological Quarterly* 31 (1990): 321-35.

Humphreys, C. "'Waiting for the Last Summons': The Establishment of the First Hospices in England, 1878-1914." *Mortality* 6 (2001): 146-66.

Hunt, A. "Rights and Social Movements." *Journal of Law and Society* 17 (1990): 309-28.

–. *Governing Morals: A Social History of Moral Regulation.* Cambridge: Cambridge University Press, 1999.

–. "Legal Governance and Social Relations: Empowering Agents and the Limits of Law." In *Law, Regulation and Governance,* ed. M. MacNeil, N. Sargent, and P. Swan, 54-77. Don Mills, Oxford University Press, 2002.

–, and G. Wickham, *Foucault and Law: Toward a Sociology of Law as Governance.* Boulder: Pluto Press, 1994.

Hunter, A. "Post-Marxism and the New Social Movements." *Theory and Society* 17 (1988): 885-900.

Hunter, I. *Rethinking the School: Subjectivity, Bureaucracy, Criticism.* St. Leonards, NSW, Australia: Allen and Unwin, 1994.

–. "Assembling the School." In *Foucault and Political Reason: Liberalism, Neoliberalism and Rationalities of Government,* ed. A. Barry, T. Osborne, and N. Rose, 143-65. London: UCC Press, 1996.

Hussain, N., and M. Ptacek. "Thresholds: Sovereignty and the Sacred." *Law and Society Review* 34 (2000): 495-515.

Iacovetta, F. "Making 'New Canadians': Social Workers, Women, and the Reshaping of Families." In *Gender Conflicts: New Essays in Women's History,* ed. F. Iacovetta and M. Valverde, 261-303. Toronto, University of Toronto Press, 1992.

Ignatieff, M. *The Rights Revolution.* Toronto: House of Anansi Press, 2000.

Indra, D. "Bureaucratic Constraints, Middlemen and Community Organization: Aspects of the Political Incorporation of Southeast Asians in Canada." In *Uprooting, Loss, and Adaptation: The Resettlement of Refugees in Canada,* ed. K. Chan and D. Indra, 147-77. Ottawa: Canadian Public Health Association, 1987.

–. "An Analysis of the Canadian Private Sponsorship Program for Southeast Asian Refugees." *Ethnic Groups* 7 (1988): 147-77.

Inter-Church Committee for Refugees (ICCR). *Keeping Faith: A Guide for Church Group Participation in the Pilot Project.* Toronto: ICCR, 1994.

Jackman, B. "Canada's Refugee Crisis: Planned Mismanagement?" In *Human Rights and the Protection of Refugees under International Law,* ed. A. Nash, 321-26. Halifax: Institute for Research on Public Policy, 1988.

Kasinsky, R. *Refugees from Militarism: Draft-Age Americans in Canada.* New Brunswick, NJ: Transaction Books, 1976.

Kerr, D. "Beheading the King and Enthroning the Market: A Critique of Foucauldian Governmentality." *Science and Society* 63 (1999): 173-202.

Kramar, K. "Review of K. Haggerty, *Making Crime Count.*" *Canadian Journal of Law and Society* 18 (2001): 159-63.

Lanphier, M. "Host Groups: Public Meets Private." In *The International Refugee Crisis: British and Canadian Responses,* ed. V. Robinson, 255-73. London: Macmillan, 1993.

–, and O. Lukomskyj. "Settlement Policy in Australia and Canada." In *Immigration and Refugee Policy: Australia and Canada Compared,* vol. 2., ed. H. Adelman, M. Borowski, M. Burnstein, and L. Foster, 337-71. Toronto: University of Toronto Press, 1994.

Larner, W. "'A Means to an End': Neoliberalism and State Processes in New Zealand." *Studies in Political Economy* 52 (1997): 7-38.

–, and W. Walters. "The Political Rationality of the 'New Regionalism': Toward a Genealogy of the Region." *Theory and Society* 31 (2002): 391-432.

Leddy, M. *At the Border Called Hope: Where Refugees Are Neighbours.* Toronto: Harper Collins, 1997.

Lippert, R. "Canadian Refugee Determination and Advanced Liberal Government." *Canadian Journal of Law and Society* 13 (1998): 177-207.

–. "Rationalities and Refugee Resettlement." *Economy and Society* 27 (1998): 380-406.

–. "Governing Refugees: The Relevance of Governmentality to Understanding the International Refugee Regime." *Alternatives* 24 (1999): 295-328.

–. "Policing Property and Moral Risk through Promotions, Anonymization, and Rewards: Revisiting Crime Stoppers." *Social and Legal Studies* 11 (2002): 475-502.

–. "Sanctuary Practices, Rationalities and Sovereignties." *Alternatives* 29 (2004): 535-55.

–, and D. O'Connor. "Security Assemblages: Airport Security, Flexible Work and Liberal Governance." *Alternatives* 28 (2003): 331-58.

Lorentzen, R. *Women in the Sanctuary Movement.* Philadelphia: Temple University Press, 1991.

Lyon, D. "Introduction." In *Rethinking Church, State, and Modernity: Canada between Europe and America,* ed. D. Lyon and M. van Die, 3-19. Toronto: University of Toronto Press, 2000.

Macafee, M. "Canadian Churches Follow Old Testament Tradition," 2003, http://cnews.canoe.ca/CNEWS/Canada/2003/08/10/pf-157964.html.

Macklin, A. "Refugee Women and the Imperative of Categories." *Human Rights Quarterly* 17 (1995): 213-77.

Macrides, R.J. "Killing, Asylum, and the Law in Byzantium." *Speculum* 63 (1988): 509-38.

Mandel, M. *The Charter of Rights and the Legalization of Politics in Canada.* Rev. ed. Toronto: Thompson Educational Funding, 1994.

Matas, D. *The Sanctuary Trial.* Winnipeg: Legal Research Institute of the University of Manitoba, 1989.

Mead, L. *The New Paternalism.* Washington: Brookings, 1997.

Merry, S. *Getting Justice and Getting Even: Legal Consciousness among Working-Class Americans.* Chicago: University of Chicago Press, 1990.

Miller, P., and N. Rose. "Governing Economic Life." *Economy and Society* 19 (1990): 1-31.

–. "Political Rationalities and Technologies of Government." In *Texts, Contexts, Concepts: Studies on Politics and Power in Language*, ed. S. Hanninen and K. Palonen, 166-83. Helsinki: Finnish Political Science Association, 1990.

Moreman, R. "Long-Term Care and 'Managed' Aids." *Research in Sociology of Health Care* 16 (1999): 171-85.

Nash, A. *International Refugee Pressures and the Canadian Public Policy Response*. Ottawa: Institute on Research on Public Policy, 1989.

O'Malley, P. "Risk, Power and Crime Prevention." *Economy and Society* 21 (1992): 252-75.

–. "Indigenous Governance." *Economy and Society* 25 (1996): 310-26.

–. "Risk and Responsibility." In *Foucault and Political Reason: Liberalism, Neo-Liberalism, and Rationalities of Government*, ed. A. Barry, T. Osborne, and N. Rose, 189-207. London: UCL Press, 1996.

–. "Genealogy, Systematisation and Resistance in 'Advanced Liberalism.'" In *Rethinking Law, Society and Governance: Foucault's Bequest*, ed. G. Wickham and G. Pavlich, 13-25. Portland, OR: Hart Publishing, 2001.

–, and D. Palmer. "Post-Keynesian Policing." *Economy and Society* 25 (1996): 137-55.

–, L. Weir, and C. Shearing. "Governmentality, Criticism, Politics." *Economy and Society* 26 (1997): 501-17.

Park, K. "The Sacrifice Theory of Value: Explaining Activism in Two Sanctuary Congregations." *Sociological Viewpoints* 12 (1996): 35-50.

–. "The Religious Construction of Sanctuary Provisions in Two Congregations." *Sociological Spectrum* 18 (1998): 393-421.

Pavlich, G. "Mediating Community Disputes: The Regulatory Logic of Government through Pastoral Power." PhD dissertation, University of British Columbia, 1992.

Phillips, J., and R. Gartner, *Murdering Holiness: The Trials of Franz Creffield and George Mitchell*. Vancouver: UBC Press, 2003.

Plant, R., H. Lesser, and P. Taylor-Goodby. *Political Philosophy and Social Welfare: Essays on the Normative Basis of Welfare Provision*. London: Routledge and Kegan Paul, 1980.

Plaut, W.G. *Asylum: A Moral Dilemma*. Wesport, CT: Praeger, 1995.

Pratt, A. "Dunking the Doughnut: Discretionary Power, Law and the Administration of the Canadian Immigration Act." *Social and Legal Studies* 8 (1999): 199-225.

–. "Sovereign Power, Carceral Conditions and Penal Practices." *Studies in Law, Politics, and Society* 23 (2001): 45-78.

–, and M. Valverde. "From Deserving Victims to Masters of Confusion: Redefining Refugees in the 1980s." *Canadian Journal of Sociology* 27 (2002): 135-61.

Reynolds, P. *Faith Subdues Kingdoms: A Pastor's Challenge to Immigration*. New Westminster, BC: Conexions Publishing, 1992.

Rose, N. "Governing the Enterprise Self." In *The Values of the Enterprise Culture: The Moral Debate*, ed. P. Heelas and P. Morris, 141-64. London: Routledge, 1992.

–. "Government, Authority and Expertise in Advanced Liberalism." *Economy and Society* 22 (1993): 263-300.

–. "The Death of the Social? Re-figuring the Territory of Government." *Economy and Society* 25 (1996): 327-56.

–. "Governing 'Advanced Liberal' Democracies." In *Foucault and Political Reason: Liberalism, Neo-Liberalism, and Rationalities of Government*, ed. A. Barry, T. Osborne, and N. Rose, 37-64. London: UCL Press, 1996.

–. "Contesting Power: Some Thoughts on Governmentality." In *New Forms of Governance: Theory, Practice, Research*, ed. M. Valverde, 6-9. Toronto: Centre of Criminology, University of Toronto, 1997.

–. *Powers of Freedom: Reframing Political Thought*. Cambridge: Cambridge University Press, 1999.

–, and P. Miller, "Political Power beyond the State: Problematics of Government." *British Journal of Sociology* 43 (1992): 173-205.

–, and M. Valverde, "Governed by Law?" *Social and Legal Studies* 7 (1998): 541-51.

Sanctuary Network, *Support the East Timorese Refugees*, 2002, http://www.uq.net.au/~zzdkeena/NvT/55/1.html.

Schmitt, C. *Political Theology: Four Chapters on the Concept of Sovereignty.* Cambridge, MA: MIT Press, 1985.

Sharma, Y. *Religion-Germany: Church, State Clash over Sanctuary for Refugees,* 1998, http://www.oneworld.org/ips2/jul98/03_34_002.html.

Simmons, A., and K. Keohane. "Canadian Immigration Policy: State Strategies and the Quest for Legitimacy." *Canadian Review of Sociology and Anthropology* 29 (1992): 421-52.

Simon, J. "In the Place of the Parent: Risk Management and the Government of Campus Life." *Social and Legal Studies* 3 (1994): 15-45.

–. "Refugees in a Carceral Age: The Rebirth of Immigration Prisons in the United States." *Public Culture* 10 (1998): 577-607.

Soper, K. *On Human Needs: Open and Closed Theories in a Marxist Perspective.* Brighton: Harvester, 1981.

Southern Ontario Sanctuary Coalition. "A Promise of Civil Initiative to Protect Refugees." Press release, Toronto, 31 May 1993.

–. "Mission Statement of the Ontario Sanctuary Coalition." Press release, Toronto, November 1998.

–. "A Declaration: A Civil Initiative to Protect Refugees." Press release, Toronto, 7 October 2002.

Springborg, P. *The Problem of Human Needs and the Critique of Civilization.* London: George Allen and Unwin, 1981.

Stastny, C. "The Roots of Sanctuary." *Refugee Issues: BRC/QEH Working Papers on Refugees* 2 (1985): 19-39.

–. "Sanctuary and the State." *Contemporary Crises* 11 (1987): 279-301.

–, and G. Tyrnauer, "Sanctuary in Canada." In *The International Refugee Crisis: British and Canadian Responses,* ed. V. Robinson, 175-95. London: Macmillan, 1993.

Stenson, K. "Community Policing as a Governmental Technology." *Economy and Society* 22 (1993): 373-89.

–. "Social Work Discourse and the Social Work Interview." *Economy and Society* 22 (1993): 42-76.

–. "Beyond Histories of the Present." *Economy and Society* 27 (1998). 333-52.

–. "Crime Control, Governmentality and Sovereignty." In *Governable Places: Readings on Governmentality and Crime Control,* ed. R. Smandych, 45-73. Aldershot: Ashgate, 1999.

Stoffman, D. *Pounding at the Gates.* Toronto: Atkinson Charitable Foundation, 1992.

Torfing, J. "Towards a Schumpeterian Workfare Post-National Regime: Path-Shaping and Path-Dependency in Danish Welfare State Reform." *Economy and Society* 28 (1999): 369-402.

Unitarian Church of Calgary. "A Checklist of Practical Considerations When Offering Sanctuary." Unpublished information sheet, May 1996.

United Church of Canada. *Sanctuary for Refugees? A Guide for Congregations.* Etobicoke, ON: Division of Mission in Canada, United Church of Canada, 1997.

–. *History,* 2003, http://www.united-church.ca/ucc/history/home.shtm.

Useem, M. "Ideological and Interpersonal Change in the Radical Protest Movement." *Social Problems* 19 (1972): 451-69.

Valverde, M. *The Age of Light, Soap, and Water: Moral Reform in English Canada, 1885-1925.* Toronto: McClelland and Stewart, 1991.

–. "Moral Capital." *Canadian Journal of Law and Society* 9 (1994): 213-32.

–. "'Despotism' and Ethical Liberal Governance." *Economy and Society* 25 (1996): 357-72.

–. *Disease of the Will: Alcohol and the Dilemmas of Freedom.* Cambridge: Cambridge University Press, 1998.

–. *Law's Dream of a Common Knowledge.* Princeton: Princeton University Press, 2003.

–, and M. Cirak. "Governing Bodies, Creating Gay Spaces, Policing and Security Issues in 'Gay' Downtown Toronto." *British Journal of Criminology* 43 (2003): 102-21.

–, and R. Levi, C. Shearing, M. Condon, and P. O'Malley, *Democracy in Governance: A Socio-Legal Framework.* Ottawa: Law Commission of Canada, 1999.

Vernant, J. *The Refugee in the Post-War World.* New Haven, CT: Yale University Press, 1953.

Walters, W. "Mapping Schengenland: Denaturalizing the Border." *Environment and Planning D: Society and Space* 20 (2002): 561-80.

Weiss, R. "Charitable Choice as Neo-Liberal Social Welfare Strategy." *Social Justice* 28 (2001): 35-53.

Weller, P. "Sanctuary and the British Churches." *Modern Churchman* 30 (1989): 12-17.

–. "Sanctuary as Concealment and Exposure: The Practices of Sanctuary in Britain as Part of the Struggle for Refugee Rights." Paper presented at the conference "The Refugee Crisis: British and Canadian Responses," Keble College and Rhodes House, Oxford, England, 4-7 January 1989.

Wiltfang, G., and D. McAdam. "The Costs and Risks of Social Activism: A Study of Sanctuary Movement Activism." *Social Forces* 69 (1991): 987-1010.

Winland, D. "Christianity and Community: Conversion and Adaptation among Hmong Refugee Women." *Canadian Journal of Sociology* 119 (1994): 21-45.

Woon, Y. "The Mode of Refugee Sponsorship and the Socio-Economic Adaptation of Vietnamese in Victoria: A Three-Year Perspective." In *Uprooting, Loss, and Adaptation: The Resettlement of Refugees in Canada,* ed. K. Chan and D. Indra, 132-46. Ottawa: Canadian Public Health Association, 1987.

Yarnold, B. "The Role of Religious Organizations in the U.S. Sanctuary Movement." In *The Role of Religious Organizations in Social Movements,* ed. B. Yarnold, 16-46. New York: Praeger, 1991.

Index

Ikechi Mgbeoji, *Global Biopiracy: Patents, Plants, and Indigenous Knowledge* (2006)

James B. Kelly, *Governing with the Charter: Legislative and Judicial Activism and Framers' Intent* (2006)

Dianne Pothier and Richard Devlin (eds.), *Critical Disability Theory: Essays in Philosophy, Politics, Policy, and Law* (2006)

Susan G. Drummond, *Mapping Marriage Law in Spanish Gitano Communities* (2006)

Louis A. Knafla and Jonathan Swainger (eds.), *Laws and Societies in the Canadian Prairie West, 1670-1940* (2006)

Randy K. Lippert, *Sanctuary, Sovereignty, Sacrifice: Canadian Sanctuary Incidents, Power, and Law* (2005)

Florian Sauvageau, David Schneiderman, and David Taras, with Ruth Klinkhammer and Pierre Trudel, *The Last Word: Media Coverage of the Supreme Court of Canada* (2005)

Gerald Kernerman, *Multicultural Nationalism: Civilizing Difference, Constituting Community* (2005)

Pamela A. Jordan, *Defending Rights in Russia: Lawyers, the State, and Legal Reform in the Post-Soviet Era* (2005)

Anna Pratt, *Securing Borders: Detention and Deportation in Canada* (2005)

Kirsten Johnson Kramar, *Unwilling Mothers, Unwanted Babies: Infanticide in Canada* (2005)

W.A. Bogart, *Good Government? Good Citizens? Courts, Politics, and Markets in a Changing Canada* (2005)

Catherine Dauvergne, *Humanitarianism, Identity, and Nation: Migration Laws of Australia and Canada* (2005)

Michael Lee Ross, *First Nations Sacred Sites in Canada's Courts* (2005)

Andrew Woolford, *Between Justice and Certainty: Treaty Making in British Columbia* (2005)

John McLaren, Andrew Buck, and Nancy Wright (eds.), *Despotic Dominion: Property Rights in British Settler Societies* (2004)

Georges Campeau, *From UI to EI: Waging War on the Welfare State* (2004)

Alvin J. Esau, *The Courts and the Colonies: The Litigation of Hutterite Church Disputes* (2004)

Christopher N. Kendall, *Gay Male Pornography: An Issue of Sex Discrimination* (2004)

Roy B. Flemming, *Tournament of Appeals: Granting Judicial Review in Canada* (2004)

Constance Backhouse and Nancy L. Backhouse, *The Heiress vs the Establishment: Mrs. Campbell's Campaign for Legal Justice* (2004)

Christopher P. Manfredi, *Feminist Activism in the Supreme Court: Legal Mobilization and the Women's Legal Education and Action Fund* (2004)

Annalise Acorn, *Compulsory Compassion: A Critique of Restorative Justice* (2004)

Jonathan Swainger and Constance Backhouse (eds.), *People and Place: Historical Influences on Legal Culture* (2003)

Jim Phillips and Rosemary Gartner, *Murdering Holiness: The Trials of Franz Creffield and George Mitchell* (2003)

David R. Boyd, *Unnatural Law: Rethinking Canadian Environmental Law and Policy* (2003)

Ikechi Mgbeoji, *Collective Insecurity: The Liberian Crisis, Unilateralism, and Global Order* (2003)

Rebecca Johnson, *Taxing Choices: The Intersection of Class, Gender, Parenthood, and the Law* (2002)

John McLaren, Robert Menzies, and Dorothy E. Chunn (eds.), *Regulating Lives: Historical Essays on the State, Society, the Individual, and the Law* (2002)

Joan Brockman, *Gender in the Legal Profession: Fitting or Breaking the Mould* (2001)